FINANCE FOR

An introdu

Cathy Davis

First published in Great Britain in 2013 by

Policy Press
University of Bristol
6th Floor
Howard House
Queen's Avenue
Clifton
Bristol BS8 1SD
UK
Tel +44 (0)117 331 4054
Fax +44 (0)117 331 4093
e-mail tpp-info@bristol.ac.uk
www.policypress.co.uk

North American office:
Policy Press
c/o The University of Chicago Press
1427 East 60th Street
Chicago, IL 60637, USA
t: +1 773 702 7700
f: +1 773-702-9756
e:sales@press.uchicago.edu
www.press.uchicago.edu

British Library Cataloguing in Publication Data
A catalogue record for this book is available from the British Library

Library of Congress Cataloging-in-Publication Data
A catalog record for this book has been requested

ISBN 978 1 44730 648 1 paperback
ISBN 978 1 44730 649 8 hardcover

Cover design by www.thecoverfactory.co.uk
Front cover: image kindly supplied by istock
Printed and bound in Great Britain by Hobbs, Southampton
Policy Press uses environmentally responsible print partners.

FSC
www.fsc.org
MIX
Paper from
responsible sources
FSC® C020438

For Alan Wigfield

Contents

List of boxes, tables and reflections

Boxes

Tables

Reflections

Preface

It was the best of times, it was the worst of times ... (Charles
Dickens, *A Tale of Two Cities*)

The 21st century has demonstrated exactly this. Up until 2007, many
owner-occupiers enjoyed steadily increasing property values and
could use their home as security for additional borrowing for holidays,
healthcare or private education. At the same time, the numbers of
homeless people being helped by local authorities in England, Scotland
and Wales were still unacceptably high, having peaked at 188,000 in
2003. Many thousands more were 'non-priority homeless', living
temporarily with family or friends, 'sofa surfing', squatting or literally
living on the streets.

This picture of well-being for owner-occupiers in the early part
of the century was shattered by what became known as the 'credit
crunch'. Television pictures of Northern Rock savers queuing round
the block in Newcastle-upon-Tyne to withdraw their cash were simply
one stark image now forever associated with the global financial crash
of 2007–08. International Monetary Fund and government-instigated
deficit-reduction programmes have followed across the 'developed'
world. Poverty, if measured by income and access to housing, has
grown in the UK. Extremes of wealth and poverty in this country
now mirror aspects of life as it was in Victorian England, 150 years
ago, when Dickens wrote *A Tale of Two Cities*.

Where people live and how much housing costs in rent or mortgage
have become serious political and financial issues. It is predicted
that by 2020 the average home is likely to cost £300,000 (Oxford
Economics, 2011). For many private tenants, rents are too high and
housing management is often poor. Millions are hoping for a council
or housing association home, but relatively few council and housing
association homes for rent are likely to be built until after the next
general election, in 2015 (and perhaps not even then). At the same
time, rents for these will increase dramatically.

In Part One, two chapters provide an overview of themes which
run throughout the book. Chapter One focuses on political choices
and how these have affected the financial arrangements underpinning
the development of the different housing tenures. The global financial
crisis is dealt with in Chapter Two: the astonishing story of how sub-
prime mortgages sold to poor Americans led in the space of two years
to the nationalisation of key banks in the UK. The impact of the UK's

subsequent financial deficit, built up to protect the country from the potentially catastrophic collapse of the banking system provides the background for the rest of the book.

Part Two looks at issues specific to tenures, including owner-occupation, housing associations and the private rented sector. Two of the chapters in this part deal with the role of the local authority: Chapter Three focuses on general housing services and building work (or the capital programme), while Chapter Five looks at the changing council housing management service.

Part Three looks at housing costs from different perspectives. Chapter Eight concentrates on problems associated with marginal owner-occupation. This includes the difficulties of obtaining a mortgage, problems with keeping up with repairs and improvements, and then the trauma of having to sell the home to pay for care costs later in life. All of these engender insecurity and signal problems in a supposedly secure sector. The various ways in which landlords have fixed rents in private, housing association and council housing are discussed in Chapter Nine. The perspectives of both tenants and landlords are covered, including instances where decisions on rent levels have been challenged. The final chapter in this part, Chapter Ten, outlines the nature of the housing benefit cutbacks which have been imposed by the Coalition government as part of its austerity measures. These will see some tenants returning to a situation last seen before the Second World War – of expensive rents and little or no help available for those on the lowest incomes.

Chapter Eleven, in Part Four, is deliberately provocative. It is a summation of some of the themes that have been addressed in different parts of the book. It argues that a different balance between state and market is required. For that, we need a transformation, a paradigm shift, not just in practice but, most importantly of all, in values.

The detail of housing finance changes rapidly. The balance in this book has been to provide some selected historical background against which to consider current issues. Historical monetary values have not usually been updated to give current equivalent prices or levels of public expenditure, but it is possible to make these comparisons by consulting measuringworth.com. The 'Reflection' boxes help with thinking more widely about a topic. The resources indicated at the end of each chapter are intended to focus on important texts or to enable themes to be easily updated by using current literature.

This book would not have been started or written without the continued encouragement, advice and support of Alan Wigfield. He is now heartily glad to see it published! Thanks are also due to Tony

Simpson, who published our first two critiques of New Labour and Coalition housing policy, to Jenny Brierley for advice on current housing association issues, to the staff at Policy Press and to the anonymous reviewers. Thanks also to Professor Hal Pawson of the University of South Wales, Professor Steve Wilcox of the University of York, and the Chartered Institute of Housing as publisher for permission to reproduce various tables from *UK Housing Review* throughout the book. More generally, housing staff and students at Salford University, London South Bank University, Sheffield Hallam University and the University of York have helped me to develop some of the themes and issues to be found in this book. I hope that they and anyone else who uses it will find it an accessible, and thought-provoking, resource.

Dr Cathy Davis
Sheffield

List of abbreviations

ALMO	arm's-length management organisation
BSA	Building Societies Association
CIEH	Chartered Institute of Environmental Health
CIH	Chartered Institute of Housing
CIPFA	Chartered Institute of Public Finance and Accountancy
CLG	Communities and Local Government
CML	Council of Mortgage Lenders
CPI	Consumer Prices Index
CSR	Comprehensive Spending Review
DCLG	Department for Communities and Local Government
DETR	Department of the Environment, Transport and the Regions
DHS	Decent Homes Standard
DSS	Department of Social Security
DWP	Department for Work and Pensions
FSA	Financial Services Authority
GDP	Gross Domestic Product
GLA	Greater London Authority
HAG	Housing Association Grant
HB	housing benefit
HCA	Homes and Communities Agency
HMO	house in multiple occupation
HRA	Housing Revenue Account
IFS	Institute for Fiscal Studies
JRF	Joseph Rowntree Foundation
LB	London Borough
LHA	local housing allowance
LSVT	large-scale voluntary stock transfer association
MIRAS	mortgage interest relief at source
MITR	mortgage interest tax relief
MRA	Major Repairs Allowance
NHF	National Housing Federation
NIHE	Northern Ireland Housing Executive
PFI	Private Finance Initiative
PWLB	Public Works Loan Board
RPI	Retail Prices Index
RSG	Revenue Support Grant
RTB	right-to-buy
SCE(R)	Supported Capital Expenditure (Revenue)

SHG   Social Housing Grant
SLHA   standard local housing allowance
SMI   Support for Mortgage Interest
TSA   Tenant Services Authority

Part One

Overview

ONE

Political choices and housing finance

Introduction

Although some form of housing is needed by everyone in the UK, the ways in which it is provided and paid for often remain a mystery. People complain about rent increases or worry about rising mortgage costs, but what thought is there about how these are calculated and whether they should be challenged? The numbers of properties built each year, whether they are available to rent or buy and the costs of maintenance and longer-term improvement are also rarely considered. Instead, newspapers laud recent signs of increasing house prices as if these were a positive sign for the future. In reality, they signify fewer first-time buyers and increased mortgage debt.

Having been thoroughly distracted by New Labour consumerist 'choices' up to the 2010 general election, UK citizens are now facing Coalition austerity measures. These stigmatise and penalise the poor for being poor and 'squeeze' the apparently more deserving 'middle'. The wealthiest have been left to continue creating wealth that will 'trickle down' for everyone's benefit at some point in the distant future. Politicians have done better than this in the past. They can do better than this in the future, but only if pressure for progressive change is exerted by the electorate.

This chapter focuses on the influence that politicians may exercise on the financing of housing, tenure changes and housing costs. It looks at:

- the influence of formal politics on the funding of different housing tenures, showing the changing balance between state and 'market' housing solutions;

- the way in which the balance between different housing tenures has shifted over time, considering whether the growth of owner-occupation represents 'modernisation' and what the prospects might be for a resurgent council housing sector;

- the impact of devolution on housing in the different countries which make up the UK: England, Northern Ireland, Scotland and Wales. Are the priorities of the devolved governments 'converging' or 'diverging' with England's? Can they provide better alternatives?

- the growth in income inequality and increased housing costs under the New Labour and Coalition governments. Are these acceptable?

These ideas are important for the rest of the book and thread through many of the chapters that follow.

The impact of party politics on housing finance

Up until the 1980s, the Labour Party and the Conservatives had distinct approaches to private renting, owner-occupation, council housing and housing associations, due in part to differing views about the extent to which 'the state' or 'the market' should be involved in the building or improvement of property. Nevertheless, the state's considerable involvement and government subsidy for building council homes were political vote-winners for Labour and Conservative governments alike, especially in the 1940s and 1950s. That said, there were key areas of disagreement between the parties: the relative balance between private owner-occupied and public sector council housing and the importance or otherwise of building to high standards in the public sector. This changed in the 1980s, and much became shared between the two, supposedly opposing, political parties.

Four different periods are considered: the Labour (1945–51) and Conservative governments (1951–64) are used to illustrate contrasting approaches; the Conservative (1979–97) and New Labour governments (1997–2010) show the similarities that developed. To avoid over-complication, the main focus in this section will be on the extent to which governments of different political persuasions have provided subsidy to enable local authorities to build council housing

The Labour government 1945–51

Most of the framework of the welfare state was established by this government, under Clement Attlee as Prime Minister. Council housing as 'general needs' housing was seen as an important aspect of this, and built to high standards, to be available for anyone who wanted to rent. The overarching idea was to establish flourishing mixed communities.

Box 1.1: Building council housing after the Second World War

Local authorities as 'plannable instruments' and the importance of housing standards

After the Second World War, in 1945 the Labour government of Clement Attlee (1945–51) undertook an enormous council house building programme with a target of building 240,000 new council homes a year. Building on this scale was needed to respond to pent-up demand and the devastation of war-time bombing. Local authorities did most of the work. The private sector was restricted by the government to 20% of the output, through a system of licensing. Local authorities were 'plannable instruments', according to Aneurin Bevan (the minister responsible up to 1955), while the private sector was not. At the time, private sector builders could not undertake house building on the scale needed: they were not large enough to coordinate the building work or to recruit the skilled construction workers needed. Bevan famously remarked that the aim of council housing was to create 'the living tapestry of a mixed community' with the doctor, grocer and farm labourer living on the same street (quoted in Foot, 1997, p 273).

The subsidy available to local authorities for 'general needs' housing, combined with considerable Ministry pressure, ensured that, in Bevan's time in office, homes were built to high standards. Legislation in 1946 provided for a Treasury subsidy for the building costs of each home of £16 10s 0d for 60 years, provided that a local authority contributed £5 10s 0d over the same period. These amounts were used to generate a loan for the building costs, which was usually obtained from the Public Works Loan Board. In 1946 and 1947, 120,000 council homes were built. This rose to 190,000 in 1948. Labour had built 900,000 homes by 1951, but this astonishing achievement, given the conditions at the time, was not enough. It lost the election in that year to the Conservatives, partly because of this housing record.

The Conservative government 1951–64

The Conservative government, with Winston Churchill as Prime Minister, was elected in 1951. Council house building for 'general needs' for any family that wanted it continued as an important feature of government activity, though scaled down in the second half of the 1950s. Less expensive slum clearance then became the priority for local authorities.

Box 1.2: Building council housing in the 1950s and 1960s

Local authorities versus the private sector: housing standards versus volume

The Conservative government under Winston Churchill as Prime Minister (1951–55) determined to build more than the previous Labour government had done – 300,000 a year – to make a political point. Churchill had always argued in the 1940s (unrealistically) that the private sector should be building most of these houses. The private sector was now given the predominant role, with councils filling the shortfall between the target and the production totals of private house builders. In 1952 the subsidy for 'general needs' council housing was increased to £26 14s 0d. Although the government reached its target in 1953 and 1954 (in both years exceeding 200,000 new council homes within totals of over 300,000), space and other standards fell significantly. These properties became known as 'Macmillan homes' (after the minister concerned with overseeing this programme).

In hindsight, Peter Hennessy has remarked that to build 300,000 new homes a year was 'economically and industrially disastrous' (Hennessy, 2000, p 183). Sure enough, the 'general needs' building subsidy was reduced in 1954 and abolished two years later. The Treasury then increased the rate of interest charged to local authorities borrowing through the Public Works Loan Board. The Conservative government argued (wrongly) that the housing shortage had been tackled. It argued that 'general needs' housing could be provided by the private sector, building for owner-occupation. This was the form of ownership 'most satisfying to the individual and most beneficial to the nation'. Limited slum clearance now became the government's priority for local authorities, with a lower subsidy.

Conservative and Labour governments alike established a level of subsidy for each house to be built and specified a local authority contribution from the local rates (a predecessor of council tax). These amounts were fixed for particular developments, but changed over the years (as can be seen in Boxes 1.2 and 1.3). The subsidy enabled local authorities to borrow money for a 60-year period to build new housing. Loans were usually taken out from the Public Works Loan Board, which was part of the Treasury. It charged local authorities lower interest rates than did the banks.

In those times, government subsidies for building were not politically problematic, but were seen as essential, as can be seen from these two contrasting examples of government intervention. Nowadays, subsidies for house building are barely acceptable to the Coalition government (see Chapter Six), even though they are still needed. The word 'subsidy' also has recently become a weasel word. It can mean different things in different contexts and has also become a term of abuse. For example, when some politicians talk about 'subsidised housing for rent' they are deliberately referring to council housing in what they regard as a derogatory way, designed to stigmatise the sector. The terms 'subsidy' and 'investment' will be used interchangeably in this book to present a more progressive picture of what is possible with government intervention in the 'market'.

Box 1.3: What is a subsidy?

In strictly financial terms, a 'subsidy' is simply an amount of money that is given, allocated or awarded to an organisation or a person towards the costs of producing something (for example, building housing) or to provide a service (for example, providing a support service for clients) or to supplement individual incomes (for example, housing benefit helps with paying the rent).

'Positive' economic theory (and the financial assumptions that derive from it) would class a subsidy as an amount representing the deficit between the market price and the actual price of goods (like new council housing) and services (like a housing support service). The main problem with this is that housing expenditure undertaken by governments is often provided in the absence of any privately provided equivalent. Nor have such goods and services used 'the market' as the sole arbiter of what they are or should be (until recently). They are more important than that. The effects of this public investment stretch much more widely than simply filling funding gaps. For example, council housing is a 'public good' and housing benefit is a 'welfare benefit', in a beneficial sense. Their aim is to enable all people living in the UK to live in reasonable housing that they can afford. This is not the same as the aims of the market. Market pricing is designed to make a profit. 'The market' is indifferent to wider moral, social or political imperatives.

Garnett and Perry (2005, p 57) suggested that it would be more appropriate to think about subsidies as 'cash-flows' or transfers of money. Most are paid in cash (grants, allowances or contract income), but not all: mortgage interest tax relief was tax foregone (that is, not claimed by government), but financially valuable to homeowners nonetheless (see Chapter Four).

The 'New Right' Conservative government 1979–97

During the Conservative governments of Margaret Thatcher and John Major (1979–97) the state's role in housing was seen as minimal. These governments invested in some house building by housing associations, but council housing was anathema. Owner-occupation was strongly preferred, with the 'right to buy' council homes being introduced in 1980.

'One nation' Conservatives and the New Right

In the 1950s the Conservative Party had been dominated by traditional Conservatives, sometimes called 'one nation' Tories. Conservative governments of that time often had a patrician view of society. They believed themselves to be the *natural* party of government. They were socially conservative too: everyone should know their place and keep to it. They preferred to support a world of privately provided goods and services but accepted the idea of the welfare state for those less fortunate than themselves (usually known as 'the deserving poor').

The approach of the 1979 Conservative government could not be more different: the 'New Right' was in the ascendant among ministers, if not in the party. The New Right was a distinct, more ideological and more divisive version of Conservatism, placing far more emphasis on the need for free market, economic liberalism than had previously been the case. In a period of recession and high inflation, the 'New Right' Conservative government of Margaret Thatcher believed that public expenditure should be reduced and that the role of the state should be minimised.

Monetarism and a neoliberal approach

Thatcher was a follower of Milton Friedman, an economist who advocated minimal state intervention in 'the market', and 'monetarism'. This now discredited economic theory entailed a strategy for dealing with the high levels of inflation in the British economy at that time. With inflation at 22% in 1980, this involved a strict control of the money supply: in practice, reductions in public expenditure and the privatisation of nationalised industries. Unemployment increased dramatically to 3 million in the early 1980s. This was essentially a neoliberal economic approach which was based on the belief that 'the market' would automatically establish a competitive economy if state involvement in economic affairs was kept to a minimum.

–

Unsurprisingly, the period marked a profound change in attitude to housing policy, the role of local authorities and council housing.

> Housing policy in the 1980s ... was quite clear and significantly different from earlier years ... housing was to be treated as a commodity and policy was to be framed accordingly ... the position adopted by the Conservatives after 1979 represented a particularly aggressive intensification of this view and an explicit rejection of the idea of housing as a social service for a wide spectrum of the population ... Government ministers were scornful of arguments for planned levels of output based on need, and dismissive of the pleas of lobbying organisations and academics who pointed to rising numbers of homeless people and other indicators of a system under stress. Above all, perhaps, the Thatcher governments were hostile to local government as such, depicting it as bureaucratic, inefficient and self-serving. (Malpass, 2005, p 110)

Under successive Conservative governments led by Margaret Thatcher (1979–90) and John Major (1990–97), government investment in new council housing fell substantially. About three-quarters of public expenditure 'savings' during this time were inflicted on the government's housing investment programme. Council house building fell in absolute terms too, as can be seen in Table 1.1.

The Conservatives preferred to fund housing associations, as they were smaller, were more easily influenced than local authorities and were seen as being part of the 'voluntary' sector. Their house building for rent gradually increased to 31,000 new homes in 1994–95, but this was the high point. Housing associations built only 21,000 new homes for rent in 1997.

Table 1.1: Council houses built in England 1980–97

	1980	1985	1990	1991	1992	1993	1994	1995	1996	1997
Local authorities	67,337	22,483	13,873	8,051	3,274	1,402	1,094	782	511	290

Source: Drawn from Davis and Wigfield (2010, p 9) using data drawn from Wilcox (2008), Table 19b.

The New Labour government 1997–2010

Finally, the New Labour governments led by Tony Blair and Gordon Brown (1997–2010) are considered here in detail. They provide the context against which to consider many of the chapters in this book and the current Coalition government's housing policy. New Labour actively encouraged the privatisation of council housing through stock transfer to housing associations. Ostensibly, this was because associations could use private finance to repair and improve the housing. Up until 2007, there was little government investment to build new housing association rented housing. Virtually no new council housing was built either, but the 'right to buy' council housing continued. Why was this?

The political perspective of New Labour

The Labour Party won the general election in 1997, with a landslide victory. Despite expectations that many Conservative policies would be reversed, New Labour, with Tony Blair as Prime Minister (1997–2007) and Gordon Brown, the Chancellor of the Exchequer (and Prime Minister from 2007–10), did the opposite. Although the Labour Party, with its working-class socialist roots, still claimed to be 'democratic socialist', most of the housing policy directions that had first been established by the Conservatives were maintained or strengthened by Tony Blair's government (1997–2007).

Social democracy and neoliberalism

Part of the explanation for this lies in the Labour Party's abandonment in 1995 of Clause IV of its original constitution. This had committed the party to secure 'the common ownership of the means of production' – essentially, the public ownership of many services and industries. Following the unexpected death of party leader John Smith in 1994, Tony Blair was elected to this position. The prospect of election success beckoned, but on Tony Blair's terms, which included dropping Clause IV.

Tony Blair saw himself more as a social democrat than as a 'democratic socialist', so using state power to bring private services into public ownership was not something he would countenance. The Labour Party Manifesto of 1997, *New Labour because Britain deserves better*, indicated the increasingly clear 'blue water' between New Labour and the socialist ideals of the past. A different approach to policy and politics was promised.

In each area of policy a new and distinctive approach has been mapped out, one that differs from the old left and the Conservative right. This is why new Labour is new. New Labour is a party of ideas and ideals but not of outdated ideology. What counts is what works. The objectives are radical. The means will be modern. (Labour Party, 1997)

Yet what often stood out was the *continuity* between New Labour's approach and the Conservative governments of Thatcher and Major – not the differences (Davis and Wigfield, 2010). Although the claim was made that New Labour was beyond 'outdated ideology', its approach drew on two distinct political strands. These were neoliberalism (shared with some Conservatives) and social democracy. Stuart Hall identified that the New Labour government:

has adapted the fundamental neoliberal programme to suit its conditions of governance – that of a social democratic government trying to govern in a neoliberal direction while maintaining its traditional working-class and public-sector middle-class support, with all the compromises and confusions that entails. (Hall, 2003)

This was reflected in the political choices made by New Labour. 'Modernising' the welfare state did not mean investing in and improving public services. New Labour supported privatisation, public-private partnerships and the incorporation of so-called 'entrepreneurial values' into public services. In this way, public services came to mimic the market, arguably becoming simply too focused on being 'efficient' in market terms (see Whitfield, 2012, chapter 6 for a detailed alternative).

Surprisingly for a Labour Party politician, Tony Blair had a low opinion of local government, and certainly little time for local authorities as landlords. Despite evidence to the contrary, he believed they were a 'flawed model' and claimed that 'the council was – and often still is – an unresponsive and incompetent landlord' (quoted in Malpass, 2005, p 194). During New Labour's time, council housing as a tenure shrank due to right-to-buy sales, no replacement council housing building programme and, most importantly, council house stock transfer to housing associations and housing companies.

The right to buy and new council housing

Senior New Labour politicians thought the 'right to buy' was politically popular, and so this Conservative policy was retained. Individual council house sales continued (and the right was 'preserved' for any council tenant living in a home that was transferred to a housing association). Discounts were reduced later in some areas, but New Labour presided over an average of 50,000 individual sales a year during its 13 years in office. The council homes that were sold were never replaced with like-for-like funding for new council housing (see Chapter Five).

Council house building declined even further than it had done under the Conservatives. In 1997, 290 council houses were built in England and Wales. This fell to 54 in 1999. The numbers increased after 2005, but remained miniscule compared to the numbers registered on council waiting lists and projections of what was required.

Stock transfer

The introduction of stock transfer for council housing under the Conservatives had been designed to break up what Margaret Thatcher believed to be monopolies of council ownership and estates full of Labour Party voters. New Labour inherited a different problem with the sector: an estimated £19 billion of outstanding repairs and maintenance, built up over years of severely reduced funding for maintenance under the Conservatives. The Decent Homes Standard (DHS) was introduced for local authorities and housing associations. Local authorities had to undertake an 'option appraisal' by 2005 at the latest in order to decide the best route to achieving the DHS by 2010, the target date. Pawson and Mullins (2010, p 48) report that ministers described stock transfer as a 'pragmatic' policy, but this is not credible. It proved to be very expensive and controversial.

Senior New Labour politicians preferred stock transfer. A housing association could raise private finance to do the work needed, without this counting as public expenditure. The policy was set out in New Labour's Green Paper *Quality and Choice: a decent home for all*. The government would:

> From 2001–2002 ... support the transfer of up to 200,000 dwellings each year. If local authorities submit transfer proposals at that level, and if tenants support them, registered social landlords will become the majority providers of social housing from 2004 onwards. (DETR/DSS, 2000, p 61)

Stock transfer was implemented mainly through offering extra funding to any local authority that was accepted onto an annual government programme. Tenants voted on transfer proposals: a simple majority of those voting being sufficient to determine the future of all the housing stock. The government programme ensured that there were never too many new organisations trying to borrow heavily from banks at any one time in order to buy council housing stock (see Chapter Five).

By 2010, about 180 local authorities had transferred all of their council housing to a new housing organisation set up specifically to own and manage it. About 40 partial transfers had also been completed, some to new, some to already-established associations (Pawson and Mullins, 2010, p 54). Transfers continue, but at a much reduced scale. It was notable that there was no additional financial assistance from government for those councils that wished to continue directly as local authority landlords or where tenants had voted against transfer. Instead, 'arm's-length' management was offered as a way of obtaining funding for DHS work (see Chapter Three).

Arm's length management

Arm's-length management organisations (ALMOs) first appeared in 2002. An ALMO could be set up by a local authority to repair, improve and manage its council housing. It acted as a managing agent, doing this work on behalf of the local authority. The local authority retained ownership but paid a fee to the ALMO for doing this work. There was a government programme, and additional funding available for ALMOs accepted onto it each year. A local authority had to convince the Audit Commission that its ALMO was worthy of additional funding before being accepted but, once it had been accepted, the local authority could bid for additional Housing Revenue Account subsidy based on the extra borrowing that it needed in order to complete DHS work (see Chapter Three). Nearly 70 ALMOs had been established by 2007–08, covering about one half of local authority housing. Up to then, an additional £3.7 billion had been made available for ALMOs. This provided an extra £1,700 per house per year for repairs and improvements (Waite, 2009, p 6). Most but not all ALMOs were time-limited to complete work by 2010.

Some commentators regarded ALMOs as 'hybrid' organisations. Others thought that they were 'Trojan horses', an ALMO simply being the first apparently innocuous step on a journey that would end in privatisation. In the event, once DHS work was completed some transferred to the private sector, setting up as housing associations or joining already established housing association groups. A small number of ALMOs continue, but diversifying the work that they undertake. For example, Barnet Homes is managing social care as well as housing services for the Conservative-controlled Barnet Council and has joined forces with Capita to bid for more local authority contracts. However, not all ALMOs have done this. By 2010, more ALMO tenants were voting to return to direct council management at the end of their programme of improvements (see Chapters Three and Five).

The Private Finance Initiative

Finally, the Private Finance Initiative (PFI) was also adopted from the Conservatives by New Labour and used for housing refurbishment and new house building for housing associations. This 'new pathway to privatisation' (Whitfield, 2012) has proved complicated to set up and very expensive for local authorities and the taxpayer. Housing PFIs have been described as:

> long-term contracts between local authorities and private consortia to deliver and maintain housing to a specified standard. The costs are paid by the local authorities to the private consortia though annual payments. Central government allocates funds to cover capital and finance costs whilst local authorities pay ongoing service costs from their own revenues (National Audit Office, 2010, p 4)

Critics have pointed to the steady transfer of public assets to the private sector, the on-going costs for the public sector and general 'value for money' issues, with contract delays being commonplace. The National Audit Office confirmed concerns about costs in its recent investigation (National Audit Office, 2010). It has been estimated that the use of PFI more generally has created a public debt of £210 billion to be paid back over 30 years (see Chapters Three and Five).

The changing tenure balance within the UK – is this 'modernisation?'

'Modernisation' can mean different things

Tony Blair's 'modernising agenda' for public services involved a pro-market stance in relation to council housing. Academics too have written about the 'modernisation' of the housing system, but they have had a wider time-span and broader field of view for their ideas. They have tried to explain long-term tenure change: essentially why owner-occupation grew and private renting declined and why council housing expanded dramatically and then, just as dramatically, diminished over the 20th century.

These two versions of modernisation are important to separate, as they are distinctly different. Politicians have had an important role to play in relation to developments in housing over the last 150 years, but their story is not the only one. The housing system needs to be considered from different and broader perspectives if any sense is to be made of the sometimes quite unexpected changes that have occurred.

Different forms of ownership, investment opportunities and occupation rights have developed over the last century, responding to a developing capitalist system (as well as the intentions of politicians in power). Governments have intervened in the market, with varying degrees of enthusiasm, to ensure that council housing (or its housing association equivalent) has been built to provide homes for people who cannot afford a mortgage or private rents; but in a capitalist economy 'housing' as a built form is usually traded for a profit or loss by owners (as owner-occupiers or landlords, with a degree of risk accepted as part of the transaction). In economic language, this is treating housing as a 'commodity'. More recently, mortgage debt could be traded too, through 'securitisation' (see Chapter Two). These different possibilities play out over time and are reflected in changes between the tenures.

Tenure change over time

Broad changes between the tenures – especially in relation to private renting and owner-occupation, can be seen in Table 1.2, which focuses on England and Wales (Table 1.4 provides additional detail for England, Wales, Scotland and Northern Ireland). In 1914, approximately 10% of the population were owner-occupiers, while 90% rented their home from a private landlord. By 1951, approximately 30% were owner-occupiers, 50% rented privately and 20% were council tenants

Table 1.2: Changing housing tenure in England and Wales 1986–2011

	Owner occupied (%)	Local authority or new town (%)	Private landlord (%)	Housing association (%)
1986	65	23	9.5	2
1997	71	16.5	8.5	4.4
2011	67.2	7.1	15.8	9.9

Source: Pawson and Wilcox (2013, p 123, Table 17b).

(Malpass and Murie, 1999, p 11). These trends continued through the 1970s and into the 1980s.

Looking at just one aspect of these changes, consider how private renting changed from a tenure in which 90% of the population lived in 1914 to a tenure that had been written off by the 1970s. Malpass and Murie claimed that 'the decline of this system reflects its economic obsolescence in the twentieth century' (Malpass and Murie, 1990, p 14). Private landlordism had been one facet of the 'local capitalism' of the burgeoning and chaotic towns and cities of Victorian England, which was based mainly on small-scale individual ownership of a handful of properties; but what role did politicians play in the decline of private landlords? Politicians imposed rent control on the sector during the First World War so as to prevent profiteering. Was this the death knell of private landlordism for most of the rest of the 20th century (see Chapter Seven)? Has abandoning control over rent levels led to its resurgence in the 21st century?

The private ownership represented by private landlordism gradually gave way to another form of private ownership, owner-occupation. Nearly three-quarters of the population of the UK are now buying or have bought their home. The growth of owner-occupation over the 20th century became possible because politicians strongly supported the tenure, sources of long-term finance became available to householders with increasingly smaller and insecure incomes and the financial institutions that were involved in lending devised ways of dealing with the financial risks involved. The problems that have ensued will be discussed in Chapter Two (the global financial crisis) and Chapter Eight (marginal owner-occupation).

More widely, the sustained growth of owner-occupation at the expense of private renting has been seen by academics as the main characteristic of a modernised housing system. They presume that political and financial arrangements have evolved such that, despite all the difficulties, it would be very difficult to return to the arrangements of an earlier historical period when (for example) council housing or private renting was more prevalent. Is this the case?

International comparisons

Michael Harloe and associates investigated housing provision in the UK, France, the former West Germany, the Netherlands, Denmark and the US to see how housing systems in these countries had developed over time (Harloe, 1995, pp 5–6). Three stages of housing change were identified for these countries (with the exception of the US, where publicly owned and managed housing has largely disappeared). The three stages were:

- private landlordism – in the 18th and 19th centuries, accompanying rapid urban growth following the beginning of industrialisation. Housing in this form (owned or rented) was seen as a small-scale commodity to be bought or sold in the market;
- public or council housing – especially after the Second World War, when this form of housing took an intermediate place between private renting (which was in decline) and owner-occupation (which was still too expensive for many working-class households). This housing was regarded as partly 'decommodified'. It operated outside of market relations, financially supported by state funding;
- owner-occupation – gradually replacing private rented housing as a mass form of private housing. This housing was 'commodified' – purchase with mortgages becoming common and extending down the income range in the later 20th century.

Harloe's view was that most housing in an advanced capitalist society such as Britain is 'commodified'. It will be owned privately and be bought and sold in 'the market' for profit (or loss). He argued that council housing stood outside of these market relationships. It is 'decommodified'. Because of this, council housing as a tenure will never be welcomed or promoted by those institutions that work to make a profit out of housing (banks, building societies, estate agents and the like). This antagonism (or indifference) acts as a brake on council housing ever becoming a 'mass' or large-scale sector. Only certain circumstances enable it to grow to a 'mass' tenure.

Harloe argued that only the two periods immediately after the First and Second World Wars presented such circumstances. This was because a 'mass' model

> gains major significance and state support only in 'abnormal' times, that is, when varying combinations of social, economic and political circumstances limit the scope for private provision and when this limitation is of strategic significance for certain aspects of the maintenance and development of the capitalist social and economic system. (Harloe, 1995, p 7)

He believed that the 'residual' role was the 'default' model for council housing. It would stay in that position relative to other tenures unless or until the private sector was unable or unwilling to provide housing.

The 'modernisation process' in council housing?

But this is only one view of 'modernisation'. Peter Malpass and Ceri Victory (2010) have tried to move beyond Harloe's typology of 'mass' and 'residual' forms of council housing. They have argued that Harloe focuses too much on 'consumption', rather than looking at housing in the round. Their view is that Harloe's analysis cannot explain the recent restructuring and remodelling of council housing (stock transfer, ALMOs and housing PFIs). A more up-to-date model is needed to understand 'modernisation'.

The 'modernisation' of the housing market described by Harloe implied what has been called the 'residualisation' of council housing. This term is used sometimes to refer to a smaller 'residual' council sector with more tenants reliant on low wages or benefits income than in the past. Malpass and Victory (2010) argue that this process of 'residualisation' may have ended. The 'social rented' sector (significantly, including housing associations as well as council rented homes) may be growing again. More people in paid work are becoming tenants as these landlords have altered waiting-list (housing register) priorities. Consequently, they argue, it is more appropriate to use the term 'modern' or to describe current processes of 'change and transition' as 'modernisation'. They simply view the substantial stock transfer from local authorities to housing associations as

> one key indicator of the way that social housing has been undergoing its own modernisation process... (Malpass and Victory, 2010, p 8)

It is clear that these writers are using the term 'modernisation' differently from Harloe as a way of making sense of recent changes to council housing. Interestingly, they prefer to write about 'a process of migration of social housing towards the private sector', where 'a variety of opportunities have been created for private companies to seek profits directly from social housing' (Malpass and Victory, 2010, p 10). This seems closer to Tony Blair's view of modernisation, involving substantial privatisation. But has this New Labour mix of public and private strategies in relation to council housing led to its renewal and

---

growth as a sector, or has this been creeping privatisation? (See Chapters Three and Five.)

The impact of devolution on housing in the UK

Politicians can affect the way that specific housing tenures grow or contract, but 'the market' is also a powerful force for change. Despite owner-occupation being seen by theorists as the 'modern' form of housing, it is clear that it has reached its limit (see Chapters Two, Four and Eight). The Coalition government is now keen to support a resurgence of the private rented sector in England. With no 'rent control' in sight, the strong recent growth of this sector may continue, but rents are expensive. Many landlords also prefer tenants in paid employment. This limits the sector's accessibility. Are the devolved administrations of Scotland, Wales and Northern Ireland likely to demonstrate a renewed interest in building council housing again as an alternative?

The organisational arrangements

Devolution involves the decentralisation of the central power of the British state away from Westminster and towards the different countries that make up the UK. Scotland, Wales and Northern Ireland are now responsible, in slightly different ways, for their own housing and housing policy. For example, there are different arrangements for financing council housing and for setting rents in the council and housing association sectors of each country. The government in London continues to exert direct influence in relation to 'reserved' areas, including welfare benefits and the financial regulation of banks and building societies. Most importantly, although each country can decide many of its own priorities for spending, the main source of funding for these devolved administrations is a block grant decided through the government's Comprehensive Spending Review (CSR).

The organisational arrangements indicated in Table 1.3 reflect the particular histories of each country. Before devolution, Scotland already had a separate legal and education system and a mainly separate administration: there was far more enthusiasm for devolution in Scotland than in Wales. Northern Ireland has a more complicated set of arrangements, which reflect the impact of British colonialism in Ireland and the problems that Catholic families encountered in the administration of local authority housing – hence the establishment of the Northern Ireland Housing Executive (NIHE).

Table 1.3: Devolution in the UK – the impact on housing

Wales	Scotland	Northern Ireland
http://wales.gov.uk	http://www.scottish.parliament.uk	http://www.nihe.gov.uk/
• The National Assembly for Wales • Established with elections in 1999	• The Scottish Parliament • Established with elections in 1999	• The Northern Ireland Assembly • Established by elections in 1998, suspended from 2002 and restored in May 2007
• Has executive control over housing • The Government of Wales Act 2006 gives the Assembly 'legislative competence' to make its own laws in relation to housing • Funded by block grant from Westminster	• Has executive control over housing • Has primary legislative powers • Funded by block grant from Westminster, and the Scottish Parliament can vary the rate at which income tax is levied	• Has executive and strategic responsibility for urban regeneration and housing, exercised through the Department for Social Development • Has primary legislative powers • Funded by block grant from Westminster • Works closely with the NIHE (an executive non-departmental public body) and registered housing associations in implementing social housing policy.

The budget for the Scottish Parliament and its work is initially based on the outcome of the UK government's CSR, followed by its own Scottish Spending Review which sets detailed spending priorities for Scotland. The UK government can increase or reduce this resource between CSRs if necessary. The Scottish Parliament may levy additional funds through increased income tax (up to 3p in the pound).

The Welsh Assembly budget is established in the same way, but the Assembly cannot vary the rate of taxation. It also has more limited powers in relation to making laws. As in England, these two administrations work with local authorities and housing associations in implementing housing plans.

The Northern Ireland Assembly is also reliant on a block grant from Westminster. It has strategic control over housing, working mainly through the NIHE. The NIHE is a government quango with a 10-person Board appointed by the Assembly's Executive. It, and not the local authorities, operates as the strategic authority and primary social rented landlord in Northern Ireland. (The Northern Ireland Housing Council, a body made up of elected representatives from the 26 local authorities, influences its work to some degree.) It also provides services to owner–occupiers and the private rented sector. These arrangements may change in the future, with the NIHE retaining its strategic role but the landlord function being transferred to associations. Currently, associations are a very small but expensive sector.

Were housing policies 'converging' before devolution?

Mullins and Murie (2006, pp 7–8) provided historical data from the Second World War onwards that indicated that, despite differences due to history (and, in the case of Scotland, a different legal system) and markedly different starting-points in terms of tenure arrangements, 'convergence' between these different countries had become more evident than might have been expected. To demonstrate this, they referred to the growth of owner–occupation (with the right to buy having a significant effect until about 2004) and, with the exception of Northern Ireland, the extent to which local authorities transferred their housing stock to housing associations and other housing bodies.

Table 1.4 shows the impact of these two changes over time in England, Wales, Scotland and Northern Ireland. The trends evident from 1971 both within and between the different tenures seem similar in all four countries, although the *sharpness* of decline or growth of particular tenures has varied between them.

Table 1.4: Tenure differences by country, 1971–2011

	1971	1981	1991	1997	2001	2011
England (percentages of total housing stock)						
Owner-occupied	52.5	59.8	68.1	68.4	70	64.4
Private landlord	19.3*	11.3	9.0	10.3	10.1	18.1
Housing association	included in above	2.3	3.1	4.8	6.7	9.9
Local authority	28.3	26.6	19.8	16.5	13.3	7.6
Wales (percentages of total housing stock)						
Owner occupied	55.8	61.9	70.7	73.1	72.4	70.0
Private landlord	15.6*	9.6	8.2	6.6	8.5	13.5
Housing association	included in above	2.2	2.4	3.9	4.3	9.9
Local authority	28.5	26.4	18.8	16.4	14.7	6.6
Scotland (percentages of total housing stock)						
Owner occupied	31.2	36.4	52.4	59.0	62.7	63.9
Private landlord	16.7*	9.7	7.1	6.9	7.3	12.2
Housing association	included in above	1.8	2.6	4.4	6.0	11.0
Local authority	52.0	52.1	37.8	29.7	24.0	12.8
Northern Ireland (percentages of total housing stock)						
Owner occupied	–	54.1	65.6	69.4	72.4	67.5
Private landlord	–	7.6	3.5	3.8	5.5	16.0
Housing association	–	0.6	1.7	2.5	2.8	4.0
NIHE	–	37.9	29.1	24.3	19.1	12.5

Source: Pawson and Wilcox (2013, pp 123, 125, Tables 17b and 17d).

Note: *Housing associations and private rented housing recorded together.

Mullins and Murie thought that these similarities had come about because government policy-making became more centralised from the 1970s onwards, accompanied by diminishing local authority discretion (see Chapter Five). Successive governments (especially Conservative governments) exerted considerable control over the fate of council housing and provided continuing and expensive support for owner-occupation (see Box 4.4). In each country of the UK:

- it was difficult to build council housing to a great extent because of the subsidy systems in place over this time;
- the right-to-buy discounts encouraged many tenants to buy their council homes;
- stock transfer also reduced council housing and expanded associations' portfolios, in all but Northern Ireland.

The growth (and more recent decline) of owner-occupation requires a different explanation. In each country this was due in part to central government policy, and also to changes in the private sector. For example:

- Mortgage interest tax relief continued as an unacknowledged subsidy for owner-occupation up to the end of the 20th century (see Chapter Four).
- The private rented sector contracted in the 1960s and 1970s as alternative investments became more attractive to landlords and sitting tenants often bought their homes (see Chapter Seven).
- The liberalisation of bank mortgage lending from the late 1990s onwards enabled the extension of marginal or sub-prime homeownership (see Chapters Two and Eight).

Over time has devolution led to 'divergence' of housing policy?

Steve Wilcox and colleagues (2009) found that there were broad similarities in terms of housing policy in the different countries of the UK when they researched this in 2008. They noted, however, that there were differences in each country in relation to how enthusiastic politicians might be in relation to different policies (for example, the right to buy). Two years later, differences had begun to emerge (Wilcox, 2012d). For example, in relation to councils or housing associations building new rented housing:

- house building was and is more important in terms of spending priorities for the Scottish Government and Northern Ireland Assembly than it is in England or Wales;
- the number of new social rented homes being built each year had fallen in each country, with the right to buy exceeding the provision of new homes. This was most acute in Scotland and Northern Ireland. By 2012, however, the right-to-buy losses had declined substantially (see Chapter Five). The council sector remains a larger part of the housing system as a whole in Scotland than in England and Wales. Scottish local authorities are becoming important again in terms of house building;
- housing association stock increased up to 2009, partly because of new building, but especially because of council stock transfers. In England 24% of council stock was transferred during this decade. The equivalent in Scotland was 19%. In Wales it was 14%, although more transfers are planned. The Northern Ireland situation is different because of the NIHE;
- England is the only country in which associations and local authorities are trying to build new council and housing association rented housing, using minimal or no subsidy (using the Coalition government's 'affordable rents' model – see Chapter Six; and Pawson and Wilcox, 2013, pp 72-83).

New Labour never prioritised funding for the devolved administrations, but block grants increased steadily up to 2009. The Coalition government has had a different approach. Its 2010 CSR translated into significant block grant reductions for all the devolved governments, presenting them all, for the first time, with budget cuts. Working within constrained budgets, with aspects of economic management and cutbacks to welfare spending with which many politicians outside of England disagree (but have no control over) creates a very different political environment to that which had gone before (see Social Policy Association, 2011). The impact of cuts to housing benefit (and welfare cutbacks generally) imposed by the Coalition are particularly contentious.

Apart from divisions within devolved government over priorities, there will now be added strains between the Coalition government in Westminster and those elected to govern in Scotland (the Scottish National Party), Wales (the Labour Party) and Northern Ireland (the Democratic Unionist Party and Sinn Fein). The extent to which politicians can pursue a different set of priorities from those laid down by the Coalition will be severely tested, especially in relation to subsidy for council or housing association rented housing and restrictions on the right to buy. The Scottish electorate's recognition of the extent to which a different political path within the Union is possible (and whether those limits are acceptable) will inform the vote on independence that is due to be taken in Scotland before 2015.

Nevertheless, there are additional external pressures that will tend to encourage 'convergence' in relation to the different housing sectors and government policy in these different countries. Reliance on owner-occupation (and private renting) has increased in all of them. This is the case in many European countries too, and is likely to continue because of the nature of austerity programmes being pursued in different countries (see Lowe, 2011, pp 135–66).

Over time, alternatives to owner-occupation and private renting will have to be found as these private 'solutions' become unaffordable to increasing numbers of people. Given the Coalition government's policies, it seems likely that these will be found first outside of England. This needs to be held in mind when considering the issues discussed in the rest of this book.

Widening income inequality – what are the implications?

Charles Dickens, writing in Victorian England, was recalled in the Preface to this book. In this last section the increasing inequalities of wealth and income that are evident in Britain today will be considered – a topic with which Dickens was very familiar.

Margaret Thatcher's Conservative governments left a legacy of increasing inequality which was not paralleled in the rest of Europe at the time and which New Labour inherited in 1997. Thatcher also left an old idea, the 'trickle-down' effect, to justify the increasing wealth of the richest. Much research has been undertaken since the early 1990s into issues associated with poverty, but the trickle-down effect has never been found. Instead, the period of Conservative government under Margaret Thatcher and John Major (1979–97) was notable for:

> a marked shift towards greater inequality. While average incomes grew rapidly during the 1980s, the benefits were spread very unevenly. Between 1979 and 1996/97, the median income of the richest 10% increased by over 60% in real terms, but that of the poorest 10% rose by just 11% (or fell by 13% if incomes are measured after housing costs)…
> (Sefton and Sutherland, 2005, p 231)

Britain had not experienced such disparities in income for many years. John Hills (2004) identified other changes: widening differences between sectors of the workforce; increasing differences between those in or out of paid work; the growing importance of private income provision such as private pensions. A summary of these findings from John Major's time in office is contained in Box 1.4.

Box 1.4: The Conservative government's legacy in 1997

During the period of the last Conservative governments (1989–1997), Britain saw:

- 'a dramatic rise in the dispersion of earnings between low- and high-skilled workers, which is widely attributed to technological changes favouring those with greater skills';
- 'a large increase in the proportion of workless households, even after individual employment rates returned to the levels they were at in the late 1970s';
- 'the increasing importance of other sources of income, such as occupational pensions and income from savings and self-employment, which are even more unequally distributed than earnings';
- 'tax and benefits policies that did not dampen the rising inequality in market incomes: uprating benefits in line with prices, rather than earnings, meant that a growing minority fell gradually further behind the rest of the population, while discretionary changes in taxes during the 1980s favoured the rich.'

Source: Hills (2004, chapter 4).

Surprisingly for some, when New Labour took office in 1997 it became clear that the approach to the wealthiest and income inequality would not differ much from that of the Conservatives: for example New Labour made an electoral commitment not to raise the basic or higher rate of income tax. Tony Blair encapsulated his government's approach in a BBC *Newsnight* interview:

> The issue isn't in fact whether the very richest person ends up becoming richer. The issue is whether the poorest person is given the chance that they don't otherwise have ... the justice for me is concentrated on lifting incomes of those that don't have a decent income. It's not a burning ambition of mine to make sure that David Beckham earns less money. (quoted in Bromley, 2003, p 74)

New Labour did not concentrate on reducing income inequality and inequalities of wealth (as might have been expected). Instead, the government focused on poverty, inequality of opportunity and the possibilities of increasing social mobility (see Hills and Stewart, 2005, chapter 1 for a detailed account of New Labour's position). In evaluating New Labour's achievements up to 2005, John Hills and Kitty Stewart referred to an analysis prepared by the Institute for Fiscal Studies that looked at the way in which net incomes changed over the period covered by three different prime ministers: Margaret Thatcher, John Major and Tony Blair (Hills and Stewart, 2005, pp 340–3). The results were displayed as graphs in their book, but the commentary was succinct and is contained in Box 1.5.

Box 1.5: Real income growth

'New Labour's record in perspective (up to 2002/03)
- While [Margaret] Thatcher was prime minister, incomes at the top grew rapidly. Lower down the distribution they grew much less fast and at the bottom by very little. Average living standards grew, but income inequality widened rapidly, and the poor fell behind.
- During the Major years, the growth in inequality was partly reversed, but there was only slow growth in living standards for any of the groups.
- After 1997, all income groups enjoyed quite rapid growth in living standards. This did not mean much fall in *inequality*, and only a slow decline in relative poverty, but it did involve a much faster growth in living standards for the poor than either of the earlier periods, and so resulted in rapid falls in absolute poverty.

For many concerned with disadvantage, the latest period is clearly preferable to the other two. Whether this makes it a 'success' depends on expectations.'

(Hills and Stewart, 2005, pp 341–2)

The analysis behind the summary in Box 1.5 was based on looking at and comparing the net incomes of households (adjusted for family size and before housing costs) across the income spectrum from the poorest fifth through to the wealthiest fifth of the population. New Labour went on to target some of the poorest households and devised strategies to try to improve their incomes, access to childcare, employment or entry into further and higher education.

Box 1.6: The New Labour government's achievement by 2005

- 'Efforts to bring down the rate of child poverty have had a positive impact on the UK's ranking in Europe, and the UK has also made the most progress of EU countries in bringing down the overall poverty rate ...
- Unemployment is at historically low levels and is resisting the downturn in other parts of Europe and the US; there is also evidence that "make work pay" policies have been more successful (and less punitive) than elsewhere.
- The package of tax credits and benefits for lower-income households with children appears now to be among the most generous in the industrialised world.
- Recent increases in health and education expenditure have shifted the UK from among the very lowest spenders in the OECD to the middle rank.

However:

- Inequality remains very high and no progress has been made. Indeed, the UK's inequality ranking has got worse ...
- Despite improvements, the level of worklessness among households with children remains the highest in Europe.
- The rate of in-work poverty among lone parent households also remains among the highest, in part due to shorter working hours (which may reflect parental preference) but in part [due] to relative low wages.
- Almost all households dependent on income support are likely to remain well below the poverty line ...
- Comparisons of overall social expenditure show that the UK remains alongside the Southern European countries and Ireland as a low-spending economy.'

(Hills and Stewart, 2005, pp 319–20)

Absolute poverty declined and the position of the poorest improved but New Labour's approach was essentially social-democratic rather than socialist. Despite achievements (see Box 1.6), the continuing poverty of existence on income support, the growth of the low-wage economy and hardening of income inequality were all unacceptable. Many recognised that income differences between the wealthiest and poorest citizens were now on a par with those last seen in Victorian England (High Pay Commission, 2011).

The cost of housing increased dramatically from 1997, both absolutely and as a proportion of household incomes. In England, local authority and housing association rents were subject to a New Labour policy of rent convergence from 2002 and council rents increased substantially in some areas (see Chapter Nine). Council rents also increased in Northern Ireland, Scotland and Wales, but more slowly, as there was no policy of rent restructuring. During the same period housing association rents in England, Scotland and Wales all increased, though more slowly, matching increases in average earnings (Wilcox, 2012d). The exception was Northern Ireland, where housing association rents increased very quickly and by 2009 were more than £20 a week more than NIHE equivalents.

Private sector rents soared, as supply could not meet demand: relatively cheaper council and housing association vacancies were in very short supply in many areas. The sector grew because there appeared to be no likelihood of rent regulation of any sort being imposed (see Chapters Three and Seven).

Unsurprisingly, the housing benefit bill increased to protect those on the lowest incomes. New Labour took measures to curb increases, but this was mainly through introducing the standard local housing allowance scheme for private tenants, which restricted their benefit entitlement to standard amounts, whether the landlord charged more or not (see Chapters Three and Ten).

Up until 2007, owner-occupation too was becoming increasingly unaffordable, especially for first-time buyers. Household incomes had not increased to keep pace with house-price inflation. Many first-time buyers found it impossible to save for a deposit or to repay a mortgage that might be secured on many times the household income (see Chapter Four).

When New Labour left office in 2010, issues related to the global financial crisis dominated debate (see Chapter Two), but there were also serious concerns about the kind of society the UK had become. New Labour's tenure had been scarred by the growth of extreme wealth for a few and deadening poverty for many. These extremes matter, not least because they seriously affect life chances and certainly affect housing prospects. The top 0.1% of the population in Britain earned £33 billion or about 4% of all personal earnings in the UK in 2007 (Peston, 2008, p 8). The wealthiest continue to do very well. By 2011, executive pay in FTSE 100 companies rose by 49%, while the average employee saw a salary increase of just 2.7%.

> There is now a strong sense of injustice at the fact that those at the top of our companies continue to reap significant rewards, while the wages of many ordinary workers are cut in real terms and their jobs become more uncertain. (High Pay Commission, 2011, p 9)

These vast differences in income had grown under New Labour, due to the government's unwillingness to countenance the high general taxation (found in other European countries) to fund comprehensive, high-quality public services and welfare benefits.

REFLECTION 1.1

'Grotesque payouts send wrong signals'

The chief executives of the biggest housing associations (up to 70,000 homes) earned £250,000–£300,000 a year in 2012. Their salaries increased by nearly 5% over the previous year.

A housing support worker or housing assistant was paid £14,000–£20,000, depending on their location. Their salary declined by 1% over the previous year.

A housing association tenant was living on £12,000–£14,000 if in paid full-time work but about £5,000 if single and living on Jobseeker's Allowance (benefits were increased in line with the Consumer Price Index [CPI] but will be limited to 1% in 2014 and 2015).

What signals do these differences send out to politicians, housing staff, tenants and the general public about housing associations?

Source of box headline: Letter from Davis and Wigfield in *Inside Housing*, 12 October 2012, protesting about a compensation package (the severance award in question was £209,163, taking total pay for the year to £412,897). See *Inside Housing* (2012) 'Record payout for ex-housing association boss', http://www.insidehousing. co.uk/regulation/record-payout-for-ex-housing-association-boss/6523949.article, 28 September.

The Coalition government has different aims in relation to income inequality. It is becoming evident that it is interested in the UK becoming more like the US in terms of social policy objectives (a country where income inequality is even more extreme). It has instituted draconian cutbacks in welfare benefits for the poorest, and through a number of other measures (not least, job reductions in the public sector) has created a 'squeezed middle' of working households that are experiencing serious reductions in living standards. The implications of the Coalition's preferred direction of travel for housing will become clearer in later chapters, but Chapter Two will focus on the global financial crisis of 2007–08. This provides some explanation as to why these radically changed priorities are now politically possible.

Further reading

For critical analysis of the way in which housing and related policy has developed, see:

Cathy Davis and Alan Wigfield (2010) *Did it have to be like this? A socialist critique of New Labour's performance,* Nottingham: Spokesman Books.

Peter Malpass (2005) *Housing and the welfare state: The development of housing policy in Britain,* Basingstoke: Palgrave Macmillan.

John Hills and Kitty Stewart (2005) *A more equal society? New Labour, poverty, inequality and exclusion,* Bristol: The Policy Press.

Lindsay Judge (2012) *Ending child poverty by 2020 - progress made and lessons learned,* London: Child Poverty Action Group. Available at: www.cpag.org.uk/sites/default/files/CPAG-ECPby2020-1212.pdf.

Steve Wilcox (2012d) 'The quickening pace of devolution', in Hal Pawson and Steve Wilcox, *UK Housing Review 2011–2012,* Coventry: CIH, Heriot-Watt University and University of York, pp 33–42.

TWO

The global financial crisis and the UK government's role

Introduction

Following the 2010 general election, a coalition of Conservative and Liberal Democrat politicians came to power. They have a markedly different approach from New Labour to handling the long-term effects of the 2007–08 global financial crisis and subsequent recession. The circumstances that led to the global crisis and how the turmoil in financial markets was handled by the New Labour government will be considered first. This is important, as senior Coalition politicians claim that the country's financial deficit is simply due to New Labour's financial mismanagement, when clearly it is not. The first part of the chapter will consider:

- New Labour's approach to the economy and financial management;
- the effects of deregulation of the banking system on UK mortgage lending and the role of the financial regulator;
- sub-prime mortgages in the US and the effects of mixing these with tradeable bonds;
- poor financial management in UK banks, leading to nationalisation and recapitalisation.

The chapter will then move on to look at the impact of the global financial crisis on New Labour's spending plans laid out in the 2007 Comprehensive Spending Review (CSR). It will consider how additional government investment in rented housing and tax foregone were used as strategies to encourage economic growth in the face of the recession that followed the upheaval in the international banking system and money markets.

The way this issue was dealt with in the 2010 general election is then considered. The Coalition government continues to downplay the global financial crisis and chooses to blame New Labour for the financial deficit that it inherited. This is a long-term political strategy, rather than a financial or economic one. Its financial strategy for dealing with the deficit became clear in the 2010 emergency budget, the 2010 CSR and subsequent budgets. The different economic and fiscal approaches of New Labour and the Coalition have now been thrown into sharp relief. The final theme of this chapter will focus on the Coalition government's fiscal approach, the 2010 CSR and the way in which cutbacks are intended to restructure the welfare state.

Although this chapter focuses on aspects of government financial management and their impact on housing programmes, there are wider issues at stake too. The Coalition government's views about the role of the state (and government) are different from New Labour's and underpin its approach to the economy and to public spending. This issue will be introduced at this stage; the detailed implication of these views will be explored in the chapters that follow.

New Labour's approach to the economy and financial management

In 1997, the legacy of 18 years of Conservative government included the substantial privatisation of formerly publicly provided services; the decimation of heavy industry and manufacturing (steel, heavy engineering, coal, the docks) and, with them, the organisational strength of the trade unions; the growth in power and influence of the City of London and the financial services sector; and an emerging 'flexible' labour market with low-paid, short-term employment in many sectors. Considering these changes, Tony Blair and Gordon Brown were both of the view that the Labour Party needed to demonstrate its economic competence if it were to win a general election and have a measure of success in terms of running the country (Brown, 2010; Heffernan, 2011, pp 165–6). Senior Labour politicians spent time before the general election in 1997 convincing business leaders that New Labour's election would not mark a sharp reversal away from some of the features of economic management that had been established under the Conservatives. Blair and Brown believed that showing New Labour to be more competent than the Conservatives in running the economy was the key to electoral success. Consequently, their message in the general election of 1997 was that, if elected, a New Labour government would keep within Conservative spending plans for the first two years of office and not raise income tax for five years.

These election pledges were kept, despite their unpopularity with many Labour Party members. Gordon Brown went on to achieve a reputation for being a 'prudent' Chancellor, building on the tentative economic growth that he had inherited from the Conservatives.

During his time as Chancellor, there was low inflation, low interest rates and steady economic growth. There was tight control over public expenditure until the global financial crisis of 2007–08.

The CSR system was started in 1997. This was a three-yearly system of financial planning that enabled departmental expenditure to be established in advance and monitored more effectively than before. Gordon Brown designed a set of fiscal rules that were used to determine the extent to which the government could borrow to fund public expenditure, and the proportion of national debt (compared to gross domestic product) that the government might sustain over a given period. According to Alistair Darling (Chancellor from 2007), New Labour's fiscal rules were designed to achieve 'long-term stability in public finances and economic growth' (Darling, 2011, p 43). These fiscal rules came to be known as the 'Golden Rule' and the 'Sustainable Investment Rule'.

Box 2.1: Definitions: The Golden Rule and the Sustainable Investment Rule

- The Golden Rule: The government will only borrow to finance capital investment, not to finance current expenditure over the period of an economic cycle.
- The Sustainable Investment Rule: The government will not allow public sector net debt to exceed 40% of the Gross Domestic Product.

Source: HM Treasury (2007, p 20).

Successive budgets saw increases in spending for education and health (see Box 1.6). Public expenditure on housing was focused on stock transfers, ALMOs and large-scale regeneration projects designed to restructure failing markets (see Chapter Three), and not on directly managed council housing or on building local authority or housing association homes for rent, despite evidence of growing shortages. This preference for privatisation strategies (for example, council stock transfer) or the use of the private sector in public projects (for example, PFIs) was expensive and controversial. There were additional concerns that the government was relying too heavily on economic growth generated by the City's successful financial trading and increased consumer spending (fuelled by easily available credit). By 2007, a million people were employed in the financial services sector and 25% of the government's corporate taxes came from that sector (Darling, 2011, p 7).

By 2007, Britain had become a very 'open' economy, perhaps more reliant on the global economy for economic success than any other country. For example, one fifth of British manufacturing industry was foreign owned (as were many utilities). Many British firms had moved parts of their company overseas to cheaper areas and regularly traded across Europe and the Far East. Combined with the role of the City in financial trading, this meant that Britain was – and remains – reliant on international flows of capital and credit to a much greater degree than do other European countries. This meant that it was particularly vulnerable during the worst of the global financial crisis.

The effects of the 'Big Bang' and 'light touch' financial regulation

Deregulation

Up until October 1986, the City of London's financial trading was conducted on the floor of the Stock Exchange. Business was dependent on personal contacts and intimate knowledge of companies. Stockbrokers acted independently and advised clients on possible investments. The Financial Services Act 1986, which deregulated the financial sector, was introduced by Margaret Thatcher's Conservative government. The day on which the legislation became operational became known as the 'Big Bang', as it transformed the City and the way it conducted business.

Deregulation helped to create a financial environment that encouraged greater risk taking and the potential for conflicts of interest. Instead of acting in the best long-term interests of clients, traders and bankers came to view business more as a short-term transaction in which the objective was to maximise profit as quickly as possible. The profit might not be their clients' or their company's, but their own (see Peston, 2008, pp 181–216).

Deregulation and the mortgage market

The mortgage market was affected by deregulation too. Intense competition between banks and some building societies led to a wide range of mortgages being available (see Chapter Four). Some banks and specialist lenders granted mortgages to people at levels many times their household income in order to maintain or increase their institution's market share (and profitability). As mortgages became easier to obtain, the demand for property increased and led to vastly inflated house prices in many parts of the UK. The government benefited too, as stamp duty was paid on most property sales.

In the UK, more than 1,000 different mortgage products with low interest rates were available by 2006–07, due to the intense competition between banks and building societies. At the extreme, a mortgage could be calculated on 125% of the property price and the length of repayment might extend to 40 years, well beyond the usual retirement age of the purchaser.

Box 2.2: Some characteristics of mortgage lending in the UK, 2006–07

- The multiples of household income (based on two people) used to calculate the amount of mortgage that mortgagors could secure varied between lending institutions.

  78% of mortgages were based on four times annual earnings, but higher multiples could be obtained; 18% were four to five times the household's earnings; 1% were based on six times a household's annual earnings!

- A mortgage might cover the whole purchase price – or very close to it.

  50% of mortgagors were given 90–99% of the asking price; 10% of first-time buyers were given 100% mortgages.

- Minimal or no income checks were commonplace.

  45% of all mortgages were 'non-income-verified' by the bank or 'self-certificated' by applicants.

  Source: Wilcox and Williams (2009, p 44).

Self-certificated mortgages, with few or no financial checks, enabled people with low, erratic incomes or a poor credit history to obtain a mortgage. Granting mortgages without financial checks also tempted mortgagors to overreach themselves. In the UK, people in this situation were referred to as marginal (rather than 'sub-prime') mortgagors. They were high risk in terms of possible mortgage default, but that was not the end of the story. There were more significant complications, especially in the US where sub-prime mortgage lending had become extensive.

Growing financial risks and 'light touch' regulation

The UK's Financial Services Authority (FSA), set up in 2001, had as two of its aims identifying financial risks in the regulated banking and building society sector and dealing with risk in a way that would maintain market confidence. In hindsight, the FSA was ill-prepared for its task. Former Prime Minister Gordon Brown explained that his and others' understanding was that:

> risk had ... been dispersed across the system. The very new, very diverse range of institutions and instruments implied that the failure of one institution did not necessarily lead to the failure of some or all ... if there was a diversification of risk across the financial system, then the leveraging of financial institutions [the ratio of borrowing compared to capital held] was less a system-wide threat than a matter for risk management in the individual institutions ... (Brown, 2010, pp 19–20)

The problem was that this understanding was wrong. No financial regulator in the US, the UK, Canada or Europe in the period up to 2006 realised or understood the extent to which investment bankers were using financial instruments based in large part on high-risk sub-prime mortgages in international financial exchange. These were not fully understood by those trading them, but they appeared to be profitable and sound investments.

Sub-prime US mortgages and mixing these debts with bonds: 'a man-made economic assault'?

In August 2007, when financial companies in the US started to report problems with their profitability, many in the financial world believed that the disruption to financial markets would be short-lived and that housing markets and the wider economy would barely be touched. However, the effects have been far more profound. It is now thought that it will take many years for housing markets and the wider economy to recover.

The origin of this crisis was greed. In the US, banks had been lending to people who should not have been given mortgages because they had a poor credit rating and were unlikely to be able to sustain mortgage repayments over the long term. In the mid-1990s, only about 5% of new mortgages in the US had been 'sub-prime'. Over a period of 10 years that increased to 15–20% of all mortgages in the US, with a value of $1.3 trillion (that is, $1,300 billion). Nearly one half of all sub-prime mortgages in the US were issued in 2006, when house prices were at an all-time high and interest rates were increasing (Peston, 2008, pp 164). Why was this?

- Mortgagors obtain mortgages from brokers in the US, not direct from banks. Brokers are paid by banks simply by volume, that is, by the number of mortgages that they arrange. There is an inbuilt incentive to encourage sub-prime borrowing with minimal or no income checks.
- Banks charge higher interest rates on mortgage lending to anyone regarded as sub-prime. If a mortgagor is regarded as a high risk, they pay more because of this (increasing the banks' returns).

In banks where day-to-day high-street banking was mixed with investment banking, the investment bankers saw an opportunity to make more money. Mortgage debt was pooled (and often mixed with other debts) to create bonds out of the combined debt. In creating the bonds, the risk of default was assessed. The bonds were given a rating by a credit agency (like Standard and Poor's) and then priced. Each bond could then be sold (at a profit) as an 'asset-backed security' to different banks and other institutions (the 'asset' being the mortgaged property).

Many banks preferred to do this. They secured immediate financial returns rather than holding on to the mortgage debts of individual mortgagors that would be paid off over a much longer term. With the sale of the bond, risk (of non-payment) transferred to the purchaser.

The packaging and selling of debt like this (known as securitisation) did not stop there. Asset-backed securities themselves were redesigned with other asset-backed securities with a view to being resold – again for profit – this time as 'collateralised debt obligations'. These were then subject to the same process *again*, but this time they were called 'structured credit vehicles'.

Box 2.3: Definition: Structured credit vehicles

A structured credit vehicle is simply a mechanism through which bonds may be assembled and packaged, given a credit rating and sold on.

There are different kinds of structured credit vehicle: collateralized debt obligations, collateralised loan obligations, structured investment vehicles or conduits. They are financed in different ways.

> The aim of these was to use bonds packaged in different ways to trade and make more profit. It was believed that they were low-risk transactions: sub-prime loan debt was mixed with other kinds of debt that was probably less risky.
>
> The existence of these financial instruments was not well known: their construction and use was limited to financial experts in commercial and investment banks and hedge funds [privately owned investment companies].
>
> (See Peston, 2008, pp 160–8.)

As Robert Peston pointed out:

> some of the new securities [bonds] were priced as if they were the best quality assets in the world – thanks to the willingness of specialized insurance companies to insure them against default. [This] created the illusion that the risk of losses had vanished on what had started life as high-risk loans to US homeowners, many of whom were in low-paying, insecure jobs. In fact the risk still existed ...
> (Peston, 2008, p 166)

Commercial banks, including European banks, made matters worse by putting these bonds into conduits.

Box 2.4: Definition: Conduits

These are off-balance sheet entities for borrowing *cheaper* short-term funds from the money market in the form of securities known as asset-backed commercial paper.

Banks bought commercial paper using structured investment vehicles (SIVs) and collateralised debt obligations (CDOs) as security.

'Citigroup claimed that "European conduits held $500 billion of assets as collateral for commercial paper at the end of March 2007."

'When the scale of defaults on sub-prime mortgages became known in 2007-08, funds acquired via commercial paper, borrowed through conduits on a short-term basis, became increasingly difficult to repay. These should have been repaid by selling the bonds or debt obligations that had been used as security but no-one wanted to buy them because of their possible link with sub-prime mortgages.

This left banks with enormous debts, which they had to repay using their own money instead of the money locked into SIVs and CDOs.'

(Peston, 2008, p 167)

US mortgage interest rates rose in 2007. Many sub-prime mortgagors fell into substantial arrears and foreclosures followed. House prices in the US peaked in 2006, and then fell sharply. Even if the mortgagor sold up, the reduced sale price meant that the original loan might not be repaid.

A major housing problem was quickly transformed into a major banking problem. No one in the US banking sector could know with certainty whether the bonds in structured credit vehicles or conduits were still worth their original price. If the risk had not been evaluated correctly, they might be worthless, due to the now *very risky* sub-prime mortgages mixed into them.

HSBC was the first bank to signal possible problems with sub-prime debt when it announced a profits warning (the first in its 142-year history) in February 2007, following the acquisition in 2003 of Household International, a US firm lending mainly to sub-prime households. Most major problems emerged in the US, and spread to the UK, Europe and the Far East and Australia due to the connections between banks. Most banks had operations across the world and sub-prime bond trading had become an integral part of the business transactions of the banking system.

The impact of credit-rating agencies is worth noting. Initially they had given these bonds a triple A rating (indicating a good investment). By 2007, they were downgrading their ratings and creating major problems in doing so. In December 2007, Standard and Poor's downgraded its investment rating for a number of monoline insurers that specialised in insuring bonds (that is, these insurers would repay the value of the bond if the issuer could not).

Table 2.1 shows the impact the following year (see entries for MBIA and AIG) and it also demonstrates the inter-connections between US banks, government-sponsored organisations and insurers. This meant that once problems emerged, they quickly spread. It also gives some idea of the amounts of money involved in the US alone. Apart from the calamitous impact that sub-prime activity has had on the world's banks, many thousands of people unconnected with high-powered investment banking lost their jobs and homes.

Table 2.1: Some US casualties of the sub-prime scandal

2007 – April **New Century** **Financial** **Corporation**	One of the largest sub-prime mortgage lenders in the US, it filed for bankruptcy protection. Creditors, including Goldman Sachs and Barclays Bank, demanded repayment of billions of dollars as many people defaulted on their sub-prime loans.
2007 – July **Bear Stearns**	One of Wall Street's largest banks, it warned investors that they would get little return from two of its hedge funds as they could not sell their investments (linked to sub-prime bonds) to realise profits.
2007 – October **Citigroup**	Announced a loss of $3.1 billion related to sub-prime investment and then a further write-down of $5.9 billion. By March 2008, these losses grew to $40 billion.
2007 – October **Merrill Lynch**	One of the first banks to repackage mortgage debt into tradeable bonds, it reported that it had lost $7.9 billion, due to 'exposure to bad debt.'
2008 – January **MBIA**	MBIA, a major bond insurer or monoline, announced a loss of $2.3 billion for the three months ending December 2007, blaming the fall in value of mortgage-backed debt.
2008 – March **Bear Stearns**	In 2007 Bear Stearns was valued at $18 billion. In 2008, its value fell to $236 million. Its shares lost 98% of their value in one year. Its problems were due to sub-prime investments. Other banks stopped lending to it. It was bought by JP Morgan Chase with the financial backing of the US Federal Reserve.
2008 – September **Fannie Mae and** **Freddie Mac**	These are two government-sponsored enterprises set up in the Great Depression as part of the New Deal. They have no equivalent in the UK. They do not lend directly to borrowers, but buy mortgages from approved lenders at low cost, repackage them and sell them on as bonds. They own or are guarantors for about half of all mortgages in the US. This amounts to $5 trillion of mortgage debt. By September 2008, they reported losses of $14 billion. At this time 9% of mortgage holders in the US were either behind with payments or facing foreclosure, so worse was expected. There was a fear in the US government that if these two companies became insolvent, the effects would be devastating both for the US mortgage market and internationally (as bonds had been sold around the world.) In an unprecedented step, the government agreed to their take-over by federal administrators, the Federal Housing Finance Agency, with an injection of $25 billion in the short term. The senior management and Board were sacked. By December 2011, it emerged that sacked senior officers would face fraud charges. In 2008, Fannie May was thought to have $4.8 billion of sub-prime loans on its books, but this turned out to be more like $43 billion. Similarly, Freddie Mac's portfolio was not made up of 11% sub-prime loans. The figure was nearer 18%.
2008 – September **Lehman Brothers**	This was the fourth-largest US investment bank until September 2008. It announced losses of $3.9 billion for the three months to August. It could not find a buyer and so was forced to file for bankruptcy. Lehman Brothers was the first major bank to fail. It had 25,000 staff, of whom 5,000 worked in the UK.

(continued)

Table 2.1: Some US casualties of the sub-prime scandal (continued)

2008 – September Merrill Lynch	Merril Lynch revealed that it had $7.9 billion exposure to sub-prime debt and posted losses of $2.3 billion in the third quarter of the year. At the point of collapse, it was taken over by Bank of America for $50 billion. This created the world's largest financial services company. By December 2008, 36,000 job losses were announced across both companies. Bank of America received $46 billion in total from the federal government to help it absorb Merrill Lynch's business. It also had a government guarantee to protect it against potential losses of $118 billion.
2008 – September AIG	The largest insurance company in the US was loaned $85 billion by the US Federal Reserve to save it from bankruptcy, in exchange for an 80% stake in the firm. It had $1 trillion in assets but posted significant losses throughout the year. It insures bank loans around the world. The loan was designed to protect the financial system, as AIG had far greater geographical reach than Lehman Brothers, employing 116,000 people in 100 countries (2,000 in the UK).
2008 – September Washington Mutual (WaMu)	WaMu was closed by Federal regulators in the largest bank failure in US history. It was valued as having assets of $307 billion and was a big sub-prime mortgage lender. Its $188 billion of deposits were sold to JP Morgan Chase. The Senate sub-committee investigating WaMu in 2010 found that it had knowingly created a 'mortgage time bomb' by including fraudulently acquired loans in with others, packaging them up as bonds and selling them on. The organisation is also under investigation by the Justice Department.
2008 – November Citigroup	By November the bank (which has offices in 140 countries and employed over 350,000 staff), had suffered enormous losses due to toxic assets and poor performance. To prevent complete collapse, the federal government bought a 36% equity share, guaranteed the bank against losses on toxic assets of $300 billion and injected $20 billion. Over 100,000 staff have lost their jobs in recurrent restructuring.

Source: Updated and extended from BBC News (2009).

The US Justice Department is investigating particular organisations associated with sub-prime lending and the US Senate has undertaken a number of formal inquiries. In the case of Washington Mutual, the chairman of the Senate subcommittee investigating this bank's sub-prime mortgage business did not mince his words:

> Washington Mutual built a conveyor belt that dumped toxic mortgage assets into the financial system like a polluter dumping poison into a river. Using a toxic mix of high-risk lending, lax controls and destructive compensation [salary] policies, Washington Mutual flooded the market with shoddy loans and securities that went bad ... It is critical

to acknowledge that the financial crisis was not a natural disaster, it was a man-made economic assault. (Puzzanghera and Scott Reckard, 2010)

Others regard the global financial crisis as one engendered by the capitalist system itself, driven by its constant search for profit.

Poor financial management in UK banks

The sub-prime crisis originated in the US and its most serious effects have been felt there. Individual home foreclosures have increased and the market prices for property have fallen dramatically. As far as banks are concerned, it has been estimated that sub-prime-affected bonds, structured credit vehicles and conduits amount to $1.4 trillion of lending, half of which was originated by US companies.

There has been no equivalent to the US sub-prime phenomenon in terms of the extent of mortgage repossession in the UK. Marginal home-ownership (the UK equivalent of 'sub-prime') has been growing since the early 1990s supported by Conservative and New Labour governments alike. Lending practices became increasingly risky in the period up to 2007 but action was taken to avoid large-scale repossessions through a New Labour pre-action protocol imposed on mortgage lenders (see Chapter Four).

Banks in the UK were not caught up in this financial crisis because of the extent of 'marginal' or 'sub-prime' mortgage default in the UK (as was the case in the US, where this acted as a trigger). Instead, UK banks were affected by the global financial crisis because of:

- overly risky bond trading (originated in banks here or acquired through UK banks buying overseas banks);
- poor financial investments (especially in property);
- having insufficient capital to weather the effects of inter-bank lending becoming increasingly difficult from 2007 onwards.

Northern Rock – not enough capital

Northern Rock was the first mortgage lender in the UK to adopt securitisation and had an aggressive mortgage sales policy. In 2007, it held 18.9% of the UK mortgage market but relied heavily on short-term lending between banks to fund its mortgages. The FSA commented:

> Comparison would have shown Northern Rock, relative to its peers, as having a high public target for asset growth (15–25% year-on-year) and for profit growth; a low net interest margin; a low cost:income ratio; and relatively high reliance on wholesale funding and securitization. (Brown, 2010, p 24)

The wholesale finance markets available to banks in the UK (through which they could borrow money from each other relatively cheaply) had to all intents and purposes dried up in September 2007. This put Northern Rock in a perilous situation. It had been discussing its financial options with the Bank of England for several months and finally approached the Bank of England for financial assistance as lender of last resort in September.

The BBC led with the news, creating public panic: £1 billion was withdrawn in one day by nervous savers. This was disastrous for a bank that held only £24 billion of deposits and mortgage payments as capital cover, against £113 billion of outgoings. The government stopped the panic by intervening to guarantee all savers' deposits in Northern Rock and other UK banks.

Northern Rock's growth had been built on sand, with insufficient capital compared to its lending. It relied too heavily on short-term finance from other banks to meet its financial obligations. In an aggressive corporate growth culture, senior staff had regularly disguised the extent of mortgage arrears. These were 300% greater than had been publicly acknowledged inside the company (Brown, 2010, p 24).

By February 2008, 10 private companies had expressed an interest in buying Northern Rock. All were offering less than its share price and Virgin wanted three additional years of financial support from the government. Nationalisation was the only realistic option, although it was a political approach that jarred with New Labour, as can be seen from Gordon Brown's comments in Box 2.5.

Box 2.5: Nationalising Northern Rock – the Prime Minister's view

'All options [for Northern Rock] would require a degree of effective public subsidy in the short term; in the case of public ownership, to offset this subsidy the government would secure the full value released by any future sale compared to only a very small share of any upside with a private-sector solution. Given the current market conditions, it seemed extremely unlikely that significantly better terms could be secured from one of the private-sector bidders through

> negotiation. I accepted with an incredibly heavy heart the reality of the choice the Treasury presented me with. I had no idea that six months later I would be the one initiating the government's buying into the biggest banks in the country.'
>
> (Brown, 2010, p 29)

It was not the only bank heading in that direction.

Bradford & Bingley – poor results and losses

Bradford & Bingley bank was established in 2000 following the demutualisation of the building society of the same name. In March 2006, this bank had been valued at £3.2 billion. It had sold other providers' mortgages as well as its own, but from 2006 decided to become a specialist mortgage provider. It continued to sell its own mortgage products but it now also provided a Mortgage Express service, selling buy-to-let mortgages and self-certificated mortgages (see Chapters Four and Eight).

By 2008 it had run into serious financial difficulties. Business in the buy-to-let market had slowed. Even worse, the bank lost £18 million through organised buy-to-let fraud. Sub-prime-backed investments had faltered. It had been downgraded by ratings agencies. A share issue in the summer 2008 had not been well taken up.

Bradford & Bingley later announced losses of £26.7 million for the first half of 2008. However, its most serious difficulty was reliance on the wholesale market to fund its activities. By the late summer, it was in talks with the government and the FSA about its future.

It was nationalised by the government in September 2008 when the only other alternative was its collapse (Brown, 2010, p 47). The government decided to split it up, and took control of Bradford & Bingley's £41.3 million mortgage and loan portfolio, some of which was potentially 'toxic' (a journalistic term to describe worthless bonds). The savings side of Bradford & Bingley (with customer deposits of £22.2 million) and its chain of branches was sold to Abbey (part of Santander) for £612 million.

The crisis continues – recapitalising banks in the UK

During 2008 it became clear to the Prime Minister and Chancellor that the UK's banking sector was facing an unprecedented collapse. In the US, Lehman Brothers had filed for bankruptcy (see Table 2.1) and 5,000 Lehman Brothers' staff lost their jobs in the UK. Others looked as if they would follow. The wholesale market had effectively stopped working, making the position of the larger banks that relied on it completely untenable. In addition, several of the major banks had made very expensive investment mistakes that were coming to light because of 'toxic' mortgages. They could not raise additional funds through share issues, either.

The Prime Minister, Gordon Brown, working with the Chancellor, Alistair Darling, and a team of economic and financial advisors, decided that an announcement would be made that government funding was available to help with any bank's liquidity (cash flow) problems, to offer guarantees in relation to their assets and to provide capital. But a bank would get none of this help unless it agreed to be recapitalised (see Box 2.6).

Box 2.6: Recapitalising the banks in the UK – the Prime Minister's view

'September 26–27, 2008

For too long banks had argued that they had a liquidity problem and denied that their real problem was deeper. Now they were so undercapitalised and overleveraged with unimaginable losses from toxic assets that many could not, in our view, survive in their current form. This was reflected in the collapse in their share prices and the stress in the interbank market ...

We knew that the banks were not sufficiently well capitalised to deal with these impaired assets and their other problems ... Instead of the government buying assets from the banks, why didn't we recapitalise the banks that needed capital, and, with them now for the first time in years properly financed, make sure that they cleaned out their bad assets immediately? ... If the banks were to be able not just to deleverage, but to lend again, we had no alternative but to recapitalise the banking system.'

(Brown, 2010, pp 47–8)

Alistair Darling announced the plan in October 2008. The FSA would assess the situation in each bank and make a proposal for the bank's board and shareholders to consider. There were three elements to the package on offer from the government:

• Firstly, the government publically made a total of £50 billion of public funding available to recapitalise any bank that needed this (in fact more had to be provided).

- Secondly, £250 billion was offered to provide guarantees for bank assets. The government protection was 'designed to draw a line under problems arising from impaired assets' (Budget, 2009, p 53).
- Thirdly, an additional £100 billion was added to the £100 billion Bank of England Special Liquidity Scheme. This scheme had been set up to help UK banks that had liquidity (cash flow) problems. Assets could be swapped for Treasury bills that could be more easily converted into cash by the recipient bank. The Bank of England had issued £185 billion in Treasury bills by February 2009 in exchange for assets with a nominal worth of £287 billion. (This scheme eventually closed in January 2012.)

Two very large banks looked particularly financially precarious, though neither cooperated with the government.

Halifax Bank of Scotland (HBOS) – seriously declining investments

The Prime Minister Gordon Brown thought that the main reason why HBOS failed was that it 'staked everything on rising prices in the property market' (Brown, 2010, p 98), but there was more to it than that. In 2004 Paul Moore, HBOS's former head of group regulatory risk, had warned that the company was too concerned with sales and growth and had inadequate internal controls to deal with the risks that it was taking on. He was ignored, and later sacked (*Daily Telegraph*, 2009).

A share issue over the summer of 2008 was not well subscribed to. Potential investors were now increasingly cautious. For example, HBOS's corporate lending was valued at £116 billion, but £40 billion of that was in property or construction companies at a time when this sector was quickly declining in value.

Eventually, HBOS was taken over by Lloyds in September 2008 for £12 billion, a take-over engineered by the government to avoid HBOS's collapse. By then, there was a £120 billion gap between its deposits and its agreed lending. It had to agree to recapitalisation. With wholesale markets effectively frozen, it could no longer trade independently. At that time it held £255 billion in mortgage lending and other loans and £61 billion in international lending.

Royal Bank of Scotland – 'capitalism without capital'

The Royal Bank of Scotland (RBS) became an example of 'capitalism without capital' (Brown, 2010, pp 95–8). Although it was one of the world's largest banks, by 2007 it had begun to make serious errors. In that year it had bought a large Netherlands-based bank, ABN Amro, for £60 billion in a consortium including two other banks, Santander and Fortis. This was a lot to pay for one bank, but RBS failed to check Amro's portfolio of lending before buying. It later found Amro riddled with 'toxic' debts. This major mistake was then compounded with expensive mistakes in the German property market, in America and Eastern Europe.

By 2008, RBS had doubled its debt and inter-bank borrowing to £500 billion in just over a year. Its capital base of 6% made it absolutely reliant on inter-bank lending to continue trading – lending which had effectively dried up. By October 2008, RBS was very near collapse. This was a bank which had been valued at very nearly the same as the British economy. Its collapse was prevented only by government action.

Recapitalisation might save the banking system from collapse, but it had its political ambiguities for New Labour, and political risks for the Prime Minister and the Chancellor. Alistair Darling, then Chancellor of the Exchequer, reflected on the effective nationalisation of RBS to stop its collapse. His comments show how far New Labour had moved away from the ideas embodied by the Labour Party's Clause IV.

> I was in the Treasury before 6am on the Monday morning … I sat down to sign the documentation that effectively transferred the world's largest bank into public ownership. There was page after page of it, which Gordon [the Prime Minister] and I signed, as Her Majesty's Lords of the Treasury. This was a dramatic moment.
>
> Sitting there, in the silence of my room, looking out over St James's Park before dawn broke, I reflected on how much some of my Labour predecessors would have loved to have done this. The last thing I wanted was to nationalise this bank, bringing with it all the problems that threatened to bring down the world's banking system … The economy was in jeopardy. I knew it. And the rest of the world was about to wake up to how bad things were. (Darling, 2011, pp 173–4)

The costs

RBS and HBOS/Lloyds finally agreed that they needed to be recapitalised in order to survive. Literally on the point of financial collapse, they were recapitalised by the government (HM Treasury, 2009, p 53), but only after considerable protest and apparently failing to recognise the seriousness of their financial predicament. In return for a 57% public stake in the company £20 billion was transferred to RBS; £17 billion went to HBOS in return for a 58% public stake in that company and a 32% public stake in Lloyds Banking Group (once HBOS had been absorbed into it). These figures released to the public at the time masked the 'covert' emergency support that had to be provided in October/November 2008. The Bank of England actually had to provide £25.4 billion to HBOS and £36.6 billion to RBS (see National Audit Office, 2009, p 20). The Chair and Chief Executive of RBS resigned and the Chief Executive of HBOS left, following the merger with Lloyds. Some salaries were reduced and dividends were cancelled, although arguably not enough. Both Brown and Darling independently remarked on the attitudes displayed by some senior staff in the banks in dealing with the crisis (Brown, 2010, chapter 1; Darling, 2011, chapter 7). The chief executives of both banks at the time of their recapitalisation subsequently publicly apologised to the House of Commons Treasury Select Committee for the financial crises engendered by their mishandling of investments – but, of course, by then it was far too late.

The UK's recapitalisation strategy was the first in any country affected by the financial crisis, but others quickly followed: Germany, France, Spain, Denmark, Portugal, the Netherlands, Austria, Switzerland and, eventually, the US (Brown, 2010, p 66). This approach helped to avoid a systemic collapse, which had looked likely after the bankruptcy of Lehman Brothers in September 2008. The enormous amount of money that had to be made available by governments is indicated in Table 2.2.

Table 2.2: Global capital injections

Capital injections	Private US$ billion	Public US$ billion	Public sector as a percentage of the total
Total capital	505.3	567.7*	52.9
America	253.6	392.5	60.8
Europe	219.3	111.8	43.8
Asia	32.3	3.4	9.5

Source: Bloomberg, 8 April 2009.

Note: Figures relate to the period Q3 2007 to 8 April 2009 and have been rounded to one decimal place. This forms part of Box 3.3 in HM Treasury (2009, p 56). The total public capital figure asterisked here should have been recorded as $507 billion, not $567.7 billion as in the original.

<table>
<tr><td></td></tr>
</table>

REFLECTION 2.1

What would have happened if Northern Rock, Bradford and Bingley, HBOS and RBS had not received financial assistance from the government?

Consider the fate of some of the US institutions listed in Table 2.1.

Would New Labour have won the 2010 general election if these UK banks had been left to collapse?

The 2007 Comprehensive Spending Review

In the autumn of 2007 the Chancellor, Alistair Darling, felt that it was by no means clear that the financial crisis in the banking system would have such a profound effect on the country's finances, so the 2007 CSR went ahead as usual. Spending for government programmes was laid out for the next three years. Given how the financial crisis was unfolding in the US, Chancellor Darling decided to halve the rate of growth of public expenditure to 2% over the period covered by the 2007 CSR (Darling, 2011, p 41). Public expenditure was planned to increase from £345 billion to £397 billion. Expenditure in the Department of Communities and Local Government (DCLG) was predicted to be £112.2 billion over this period, an increase of 1.4% as compared to the previous period. At this point, Darling worked within the fiscal rules established in 1997, as can be seen by considering the data in Table 2.3.

Table 2.3: 2007 CSR: The golden rule and the sustainable investment rule

	Percentage of Gross Domestic Product						
	Out-turn	Estimate	Projections				
	2006–07	2007–08	2008–09	2009–10	2010–11	2011–12	2012–13
Golden rule							
Surplus on current budget	–0.4	–0.6	–0.3	0.2	0.6	0.8	1.1
Average surplus since 1997/98	0.1	0.1	0	0.1	0.1	0.1	0.2
Cyclically adjusted surplus on current budget	–0.2	–0.7	–0.2	0.3	0.6	0.8	1.1
Sustainable investment rule							
Public sector net debt	36.7	37.6	38.4	38.8	38.9	38.8	38.6

Source: HM Treasury (2007, p 3).

The government Green Paper of July 2007, *Homes for the future – more affordable, more sustainable* (CLG, 2007), had provided the details of the government's new enthusiasm for rented housing. Public expenditure relating to housing was planned to increase from £10.3 billion in 2007–08 to £12.1 billion in 2010–11. There was £8 billion for new affordable housing up to 2010 (£3 billion more than had been allocated in the 2004 CSR).

- £6.5 billion was allocated to build new social rented housing. Housing associations were expected to build 45,000 new homes annually by 2010 (see Chapter Six).
- £1.5 billion was allocated for low-cost home-ownership schemes (see Chapter Eight).
- There was also £4 billion for the ALMO programme and for gap funding and other costs for more stock transfers to associations from local authorities (see Chapters Three and Five).

The impact of the recession, less than a year later, meant that economic circumstances became quite different from the assumptions that had been used in creating the 2007 CSR plans. Fuel and food prices were increasing (because of difficult market conditions) and house prices had fallen dramatically. Banks virtually ceased lending to each other, to businesses and to people who wanted to buy a home. Subsequent pre-Budget reports and Budgets in 2009 and 2010 dealt with the changes needed.

New Labour's approach to the financial crisis and recession was to invest in public services and projects to encourage economic growth, create jobs and reduce unemployment. This approach owed much to Keynesianism (Stratton and Seager, 2008 and see Box 2.7). In this view, doing nothing (or a laissez-faire approach) and waiting until markets recovered without any government intervention would not restore growth.

Box 2.7: John Maynard Keynes 1883–1946

John Maynard Keynes was the author of *The General Theory of Employment, Interest and Money* (1936) and was the most influential economic thinker of the 20th century. His ideas have proved particularly useful to governments dealing with recessionary periods, in their attempts to avoid economic depression.

He showed that when growth in an economy is limited or negative (that is, the economy is contracting, with firms going out of business) a 'counter-cyclical' approach to public expenditure and economic management is required. It cannot be assumed that an economy will bounce back without this intervention. A government needs to actively invest at this time, rather than reduce public expenditure.

Following a Keynesian economic approach, a government should:

* increase government borrowing to pay for investment in targeted areas/industries;
* intervene in the economy (in firms or regions) by providing funding, tax breaks, partnerships and new projects designed to maintain and create jobs and encourage others to invest as well.

Over time, when the economy improves and growth returns:

* public expenditure can be scaled back;
* taxes can be raised to reduce borrowing and the government can plan to reduce further government investment, letting the private sector take on this role.

Most countries affected by the 2007 financial crisis and subsequent recession adopted a Keynesian approach to public expenditure and growth. In Britain, the fiscal rules that had been devised for normal times had to be set aside. A temporary set were devised, linked to the original 1997 'Golden Rule' and 'Sustainable Investment Rule', but flexible enough to allow for the government to provide the financial support needed by the banks and to invest in economic recovery (see Darling, 2008).

Box 2.8: Fiscal rules for a financial crisis

The Chancellor of the Exchequer's view

'The argument was whether we should impose new ceilings on spending and borrowing, or whether they should instead reflect a more general aspiration. I did not want to be placed in a straightjacket ... If we set rules, especially in a time of crisis, and then broke them, the markets would turn against us, which would mean that the cost of our borrowing would rocket. Rules would require us to do things such as cut public spending or increase taxes, so they do have a direct impact on people.'

(Darling, 2011, p 180)

Britain's economy had contracted by 4.7% in 2009 (compared to Japan at 7.7%, Germany at 5.6% and the US at 3%). This performance was in no small part due to the action taken by the government at the time. New Labour invested in the economy from 2007 in different ways.

- House building and jobs: The affordable housing budget was used to give a boost to housing supply by bringing forward £925 million which had been due to be spent in 2009–10. This was designed to help builders bring mothballed sites back into production (through the Kickstart programme) and to enable housing associations and, latterly, local authorities to build more homes (increased public expenditure). Apprenticeship schemes and other training were established for young people (public expenditure).
- Home sales: Stamp duty was suspended for one year for properties under £175,000 to encourage sales (tax revenue foregone). A 'homebuy' scheme enabled first-time buyers with less than £60,000 combined income to get an interest-free loan to use as a deposit. This encouraged sales at the lower end of the market [(increased public expenditure).

The cost of financial intervention to deal with the banking crisis in Britain was estimated by 2011 at £120 billion or 8% of GDP (Wilcox and Pawson, 2010, p 5).

The general election 2010 and the new Coalition government

By 2010, it was becoming clear that New Labour's pro-growth approach was working, growth having reappeared at 0.5% at the end of 2009 (Darling, 2011, p 265 quoting Office of National Statistics data). However, in May 2010 New Labour lost the general election, in part because the Prime Minister, Chancellor and cabinet members could not agree on a coherent way of presenting their approach to the electorate.

New Labour's success in managing the immediate financial crisis brought about by sub-prime lending and the recklessness of international bankers was either misunderstood or forgotten by the electorate. The Conservatives were able to play on voters' concerns about increasing job insecurity and unemployment, rising inflation and increasing food prices. Voters were also having considerable difficulties raising mortgage finance or personal loans, and this did not increase New Labour's popularity. Ironically, the effects of the global financial crisis were transformed by the Conservatives into questions about New Labour's economic competence.

The general election of 2010 was notable for the lack of detail about how *any* of the main parties would deal with the deficit (see the discussion in Wilcox, 2012b).

The Institute for Fiscal Studies (IFS) calculated from Alistair Darling's last Budget in 2010 that New Labour's public spending cuts were planned to increase gradually to 4.8% of national income or £71 billion a year (in 2010/11 values). It thought that the Liberal Democrats 'informally endorsed this tightening profile'. The Conservatives planned to cut expenditure more severely than this, starting with £6 billion of cuts in 2010. They wanted to reduce the deficit more quickly. In the long term, the IFS estimated, this would not make much difference.

Box 2.9: Filling the hole

How do the three main UK parties plan to repair the public finances?

'The Conservatives' greater ambition would make a relatively modest difference to the long-term outlook for government borrowing and debt. The Conservative plans imply total borrowing of £604 billion over the next seven years [2010–17], compared with £643 billion under Labour or the Liberal Democrats.

Assuming no further change in borrowing beyond 2017–18, we project that the Conservative plans would return government debt below 40% of national income in 2031–32, the same year as it would under Labour or the Liberal Democrats.'

(Chote et al, 2010)

In 2010, the general election produced a situation in which no political party had an absolute majority. New Labour lost 91 seats, while the Conservatives gained 97, both mirroring the pattern from the 2005 general election. The Liberal Democrats actually lost five seats. In the event, a coalition of Conservatives (with 306 seats) and Liberal Democrats (with 57 seats) was formed. The Labour Party (with 258 seats) became the official Opposition.

A Coalition government is a completely new phenomenon in postwar modern Britain. The Conservatives dominate, as the largest party, with David Cameron as Prime Minister and George Osborne as the Chancellor of the Exchequer. The strategy for dealing with the financial deficit built up from 2008 onwards is predominantly a Conservative one. In 2008 the Liberal Democrats had publicly supported New Labour's Keynesian approach. In 2010 they changed their view and opted to support the Conservatives' approach. The Liberal Democrats achieved some concessions from the Conservatives in joining the Coalition, but avoiding substantial cuts to welfare spending was not one of them.

The Conservatives achieved agreement from the start that welfare cuts (so-called 'reforms') would be implemented almost without change from their general manifesto and more detailed pre-election reports.

Unsurprisingly, by mid-term, the political opportunism of 2010 has given way to very public argument and bargaining before each Budget, relating to Liberal Democrat manifesto promises (for example, in relation to personal tax allowances and the so-called 'mansion tax'). It is clear that, as far as senior ministers are concerned, political self-interest as much as policy agreement is keeping the Coalition together.

The 2010 Comprehensive Spending Review

The Coalition government claimed that the CSR in 2010 would set 'the country on a new path towards long term prosperity and fairness' (HM Treasury, 2010, p 5). Instead of the fiscal rules of its New Labour predecessor, the Coalition prefers a 'fiscal mandate'. This simply describes an approach rather than a framework with specific targets, as had been devised by New Labour (see Box 2.1, Table 2.3 and Box 2.8).

Box 2.10: The fiscal mandate

'The fiscal mandate ... is to eliminate the structural current budget deficit over a five year rolling horizon.'

(HM Treasury, 2010, p 5)

As far as economic growth is concerned, the Coalition wants to create 'a broad-based economy supporting private sector jobs, exports, investment and enterprise'. This is significant, as it does not mention the public sector. The CSR was used to 'align the allocation of public resources with the Coalition's overall objectives as set out in the Coalition Agreement'. These included 'spending that promotes long term economic growth, introducing structural reforms to enable a private sector led recovery and building a low carbon economy' and 'fairness and social mobility, providing sustained routes out of poverty for the poorest'. The Chancellor, George Osborne, also wanted:

> radical reform of public services to build the Big Society where everyone plays their part, shifting power away from central government to the local level as well as getting the best possible value for taxpayers' money. (HM Treasury, 2010, p 6)

The CSR set out the government's plans to restructure and reduce welfare state provision for the poorest, claiming that this was going to be done to 'promote a new vision for a fairer Britain [which] at its heart is social mobility'. At the same time it would make the welfare system 'affordable'.

On average, the Coalition expects to see a reduction of 19% in most departmental expenditure, but the DCLG's Communities budget will be reduced by an extraordinary 51% by 2014–15 and local government will be expected to reduce expenditure by 27%. Table 2.4 shows this decline in funding. The size and influence of the department nationally has been reduced and regional offices have closed.

Table 2.4: 2010 CSR departmental and administration budgets up to 2014–15

	2010–11 baseline £billion	2011–12 plans £billion	2012–13 plans £billion	2013–14 plans £billion	2014–15 plans £billion	Variation
DCLG: Local government	28.5	26.1	24.4	24.2	22.9	−27%
DCLG: Communities	2.2	2.0	1.7	1.6	1.2	−51%

Source: Pawson and Wilcox (2011, p 52), Table 2.1.2.

Some funding was partly protected. For example, Supporting People funding at £6.5 billion was cut by 11% up to 2014–15, but it is not ring fenced, and changes to the programme will make it more difficult to obtain. Performance-related grants and restricting the definition of 'support' are two ways of cutting the programme further. The DCLG's capital budget has been reduced even more as can be seen in Table 2.5.

Table 2.5: 2010 CSR departmental capital budgets up to 2014–15

	2010–11 baseline £billion	2011–12 plans £billion	2012–13 plans £billion	2013–14 plans £billion	2014–15 plans £billion	Cumulative real growth
DCLG: Local government	0.0	0.0	0.0	0.0	0.0	0.0
DCLG: Communities	6.8	3.3	2.3	1.8	2.0	−74%

Source: Pawson and Wilcox (2011, p 52), Table 2.1.2.

As far as housing capital programmes are concerned, a number of activities will be very severely affected.

- The grant programme for new association house building for rent and for shared ownership was reduced to £1.8 billion. Associations have been urged to build without grant, where possible (see Chapter Six).
- £200 million was allocated to tackle empty homes. If brought back into use, whatever their quality, these properties will be counted as contributing towards achieving the Coalition's aim to build 150,000 affordable homes by 2015 (see Chapter Three).
- The New Homes Bonus initially was set up with £900 million for local authorities that encourage new house building in their area. However, this amount is largely top-sliced from formula grant (see Chapter Three)
- £2 billion was available to finish outstanding DHS work, but only ALMOs or local authorities with more than 10% 'non decent' housing stock could apply for funding. In 2009, New Labour estimated that £9 billion would be needed (see Chapter Three).

Although these reductions will make 'savings', it is difficult to see how this approach will lead to economic growth in the short or longer term. The Coalition government's simple reliance on private sector growth has weakened prospects for recovery. It does not appear to be aware of (or interested in) the substantial links between the public sector and the private sector. Much of the private sector relies on public sector investment/work to survive. Many notable economists and academics have warned about 'deficit hysteria' and many have suspicions that the approach that the Coalition has adopted has more to do with Conservative antagonism towards the public sector rather than a viable approach to economic growth. These reductions put Britain below the US in terms of spending for public services and welfare benefits. This has never been the case before.

> Advocates of the US solution should remember that, in liberal competitive capitalism with a weak labour movement and limited social protection, it's the rich that gets the gravy. (Taylor-Gooby, 2011, p 15)

In other words, this change of direction will be implemented at enormous cost to those who are the least well-off.

Further reading

Gordon Brown (2010) *Beyond the crash: Overcoming the first crisis of globalisation*, London: Simon & Schuster, chapters 1–4, pp 1–134.

Alistair Darling (2011) *Back from the brink: 1000 days at number 11*, London: Atlantic Books.

National Audit Office (2009) *Maintaining financial stability across the United Kingdom's banking system*, London: The Stationery Office. Available at: http://media.nao.org.uk/uploads/2009/12/091091.pdf.

National Audit Office (2011) *Maintaining the financial stability of UK banks*, London:The Stationery Office.Available at: http://media.nao. org.uk/uploads/2010/12/1011676.pdf.

Christine Whitehead and Peter Williams (2011) 'Causes and consequences? Exploring the shape and direction of the housing system in the UK post the financial crisis' in *Housing Studies*, vol 26, no 7-8, pp 1157-69.

Steve Wilcox (2011c) 'Housing expenditure trends and plans' in *UK Housing Review 2010/11*, Coventry: CIH, University of York and Heriot Watt University, pp 67-71.

For more analysis of what is meant by 'globalisation' and its implications, see David Harvey (2000) *Spaces of hope*, Edinburgh: Edinburgh University Press, chapter 4, pp 53–72.

A number of websites will prove useful for current updated analysis:

Department of Communities and Local Government housing documents: www.communities.gov.uk/housing/.

HM Treasury documents: www.hm-treasury.gov.uk/.

David G. Blanchflower (for informed commentary on the economic situation): www.dartmouth.edu/~blnchflr/.

Institute for Fiscal Studies: www.ifs.org.uk/.

Centre for Labour and Social Studies: http://classonline.org.uk/.

Part Two

Tenure

THREE

Local authority general housing services and building work

Introduction

Housing advice, homelessness services including temporary housing, housing support services, strategic work across the area and the maintenance of housing standards in the private sector are all important, locally provided local authority services. The local authority also can undertake or support a range of building and improvement work associated with these housing services.

Local authorities in England are more reliant on central government for funding than their European counterparts, so the impact of austerity measures is particularly severe. The Labour leader of Birmingham City Council remarked in 2012 that the £600 million that has to be cut from that authority's budget up to 2017 marked 'the end of local government as we have known it'. This chapter will explore this view from the perspective of housing services and will discuss:

- the range of housing services provided through the General Fund and their main sources of revenue funding;
- funding issues connected to three important services: the homelessness service, the Supporting People programme and the housing benefit service;
- possible sources of capital funding for new building and improvement work, including funding to achieve the DHS in any retained council housing.

The management of any council housing will be discussed in Chapter Five. The limitations of space are such that this chapter is focused mainly on England.

The relationship between central and local government

Central government has exercised considerable influence at local government level in recent times. Practically, this has been to maintain a firm control over public expenditure. Overall, local authority General Fund expenditure (of which general housing services form a part) accounts for 25% of total public expenditure in England and Wales. Successive governments have also been concerned to try to ensure that favoured policies are implemented at a local level, whether or not their party is in control locally.

Both these objectives can be successfully pursued by central government because local authorities in the UK have had relatively few means of raising money independently to pay for services: namely, through local council tax, fees and charges. Most larger local authorities and London boroughs have relied on central government for about two-thirds of their annual income to provide services. Central government funding for these has been available through grants (especially the Revenue Support Grant and, up to 2013, Area Based Grant). From April 2013, this has changed, as will become clearer in this chapter. The government influences local council tax charges too. In the past, this was by capping increases. Currently, the Coalition government offers a council tax freeze grant. Capital funding for new building or improvement work is also carefully controlled by central government through the changing availability of grants, 'supported' capital expenditure and spending caps.

'Hollowing out' or the minimal local authority?

From the late 1980s, the Conservative government of the day started to promote the idea that local authorities should be 'enablers' rather than direct providers of housing and housing services. This idea was followed through by New Labour and has had a particular impact on housing services. For many people, the most obvious demonstration of the changing local authority role has been the transfer of council housing to housing associations. The administration of Supporting People funding is another example of 'enabling' where the local authority has a strong commissioning role but is far less likely to be the direct provider of services.

These developments have led to discussions about whether the state has become 'hollowed out' (see Rhodes, 1994 and Holliday, 2000 for opposing perspectives; Hudson and Lowe, 2004, pp 127–44, for a wider discussion). At the level of central government some commentators thought this idea was not credible, considering the way in which policy implementation was controlled from the centre to a great degree by the New Labour government. At the level of local government, however, there might be some justification for this view if considered in terms of the reduction in local authorities' democratic independence and the reduction in the number and range of services that the local authority now provides directly. The Coalition's austerity programme will reinforce that trend, as will become evident in this chapter.

Local democracy

Local authorities are democratically elected institutions, although the balance of power between elected councillors and senior staff has changed in recent years. The committee structure through which councillors made decisions about services was 'modernised' under New Labour. Cabinets of senior councillors or directly elected mayors have replaced specialist committees. The 'public service ethos' common in local authorities has given way to managerialism. 'New public management' was one collection of management practices popular in the 1990s and early 2000s that boosted the power of senior managers. In the process, the democratic political authority of elected members was undermined.

Ironically, despite introducing cabinets and a mayoral system closely modelled on the private sector and American politics, New Labour felt that this fragmented system needed to be closely regulated so as to ensure that public money was being well spent and that services met centrally determined standards. The overwhelming managerialism inculcated by intense regulation by the Audit Commission led to a simple focus on the 'value for money' of services. This too diminished the practice of local democratic control and ideas of public service.

Localism

This determination to control and change directed by the centre has now given way to 'localism' and the 'Big Society', the Coalition government's alternative vision of the future in which local authorities and other providers decide for themselves what their priorities are locally, and make full use of volunteers rather than paid staff where possible (see Kisby, 2010 for a critical discussion). The government is no longer interested in monitoring how local authorities provide services or whether they are achieving good standards of service. The

Audit Commission and the Tenant Services Authority, New Labour's regulators of choice in the housing field, have both been abolished in the Coalition's 'bonfire of the quangos'.

This does not mean political indifference on the part of the Coalition. The 'marketisation' of public services will continue even more strongly, setting in train ways of working that are intended to mimic the market. This is often a forerunner to restructuring and reducing public services or transferring them (sometimes via ALMOs) to the private sector or the individual citizen (who can then make 'choices' about what they require). Unless challenged, local authorities are being pushed in the direction of the American idea of minimal government.

The organisation of local government

In England, some local authorities are 'first tier' authorities, providing all services at a local level (and linking with fire and police services). For example, in England 'first tier' authorities are the large metropolitan authorities and unitary authorities (like city councils). In more rural areas, services are likely to be provided in 'two tier' arrangements: county councils provide social services and some housing functions (as the 'first tier'), while district councils work beneath them (as the 'second tier') and may provide council housing and other housing services, including the housing benefit service. The commissioning of Supporting People funding is a 'first tier' responsibility, there being 152 authorities (including county councils) that administer it.

In London there is a different arrangement. The Mayor and London Assembly are elected and provide the strategic and scrutiny roles, respectively, for the Greater London Authority ('first tier'). The Greater London Authority (GLA) works closely with the 33 London boroughs (as the 'second tier') to implement cross-London policies. The London boroughs themselves work independently in the provision of local services but have to work within the strategic framework for housing emanating from the Mayor (see GLA, 2012a and 2012b).

Housing services within local authorities have always had to vie with other, larger departments for funding (like education and adult social care), but more recently there are external competitors too. Conservative and New Labour governments in succession have used financial mechanisms of various kinds to bring about 'quasi-markets' in housing services, changing the balance between local authorities and other organisations that operate within and across their boundaries.

Some services have been 'outsourced' or contracted out to the voluntary sector or housing associations that then provide the service on behalf of the local authority for a price, with varying success. For example, some authorities have contracted out the homeless service or the housing benefit service. Part of a local authority's 'enabling' role has also included the encouragement of partnership working. For example, the Supporting People commissioning process has led to a wide range of organisations being funded. The Coalition is encouraging 'community' budgets whereby different organisations' resources are pooled, with savings being made. As a consequence, working relationships between a local authority and other service providers, both public and private, are likely to be complicated. They may not necessarily provide a seamless service for the people who rely on them. It also cannot be assumed that important services will survive austerity budget cuts. Birmingham Council plans to cut over 1,100 jobs by 2016, at a minimum, and will have to decommission services (BBC News, 2012). Decommissioning or closing down services is a decision not taken lightly. A range of other possibilities might be explored first. But this is the organisational context against which to consider the range of housing services currently provided by local authorities.

Housing services paid for through the General Fund

One characteristic of General Fund services is that they are potentially available for all residents within a local authority's boundaries. This distinguishes these services from the management of council housing. The costs of services which are provided include:

- local authority strategic housing work – designed to 'to influence markets and funding flows' as well as to attempt to coordinate services in their area (Audit Commission, 2009, p 4; also see Leng and Davies, 2011);
- staffing to maintain private sector standards – for example, to establish and maintain a registration scheme for houses in multiple occupation (HMOs), enforcement work to make sure that private properties are safe or work to bring empty properties back into use;
- housing advice and homelessness services – for example, 'housing options' staff, homelessness staff and the provision of temporary accommodation for homeless people;
- housing support work for a range of vulnerable people who need help in the short term to maintain independence at home;
- allocations and lettings work – for example, maintaining the housing register and advising potential or actual applicants;

- housing benefit – providing a service to all residents who are or may
  be eligible for housing benefits (local authority, housing association
  and private sector tenants).

Most of these services are provided as a long-term commitment to local
residents and are staff intensive. In organisational terms, they will be
situated in different local authority departments, but in financial terms,
wherever they are located, staff salaries and office costs are considered
to be revenue expenditure and they have to be paid for out of revenue
income. Oddly, there is no simple definition of 'revenue' income and
expenditure: it is easiest to consider that it covers everything that cannot
be defined as 'capital' income and expenditure (that is, finance related
to time-specific building or improvement work). Most local authority
income for these services comes from central government grants (part
funded by business rates), business rates and council tax income retained
locally and local authority fees and charges for local services.

In the 2010 CSR, as part of the deficit reduction programme, the
Coalition decided to substantially reduce local government funding
for a wide ranges of services (see Chapter Two, Tables 2.4 and 2.5 for
the impact on CLG-funded programmes). The 2010 CSR revealed
that council revenue spending supported by the government was to
be cut by 27% in cash terms by 2014/15. Additional grant cuts have
been announced by the Chancellor since then for future years with
the need for austerity measures stretching to 2018.

Many council leaders are concerned about the effects of severely
reduced budgets on services in their area and the impact on people who
rely on them. The most severe budget reductions are being faced in cities
across the country, especially in the North and Midlands. The majority
of the worst 30 affected authorities are known to have significant poorer
local populations and happen to be Labour-controlled. The leaders of
Birmingham, Bristol, Leeds, Liverpool, Manchester, Newcastle and
Sheffield have warned publically of a 'looming financial crisis' (Helm,
2012; Hetherington, 2013). Authorities in the North tend to have a
weaker council tax and business rate tax base than those in the South
East and have lost out as specific Area Based Grant funding has been
ended by the Coalition.

The government remains unconvinced despite growing opposition
to the scale and speed of budget reductions it wants. Instead, it has
changed the way in which local government services are funded. From
2010, most government grants became un-ring fenced. The Coalition
argues that this enables politicians (and residents) to make 'choices'
locally. From April 2013, half of the income from a local authority's

business rates can be retained locally, ostensibly to give authorities greater incentives to encourage private sector economic growth. But whichever political party is in control locally, the opportunities for local discretion are limited because of the extent of reductions in expenditure that the Coalition expects. In the current financial climate, some services will disappear. Others will survive because they are popular or politically sensitive (for example, some services for older people) but they will be much reduced. Statutory services that the local authority is legally obliged to provide may remain but retreating to these absolute 'core' services is surely not what local authorities are supposed to do?

Officially, the government now refers to local authority 'revenue spending power' when presenting expenditure cutbacks. They argue that this gives a fuller picture, but this is not the case. The Local Government Association has calculated that local government spending cuts will be an average 12% in 2014/15 compared to 4% in 2013/14 because the government has assumed business rate growth and reduced the RSG by an equivalent amount for 2014/15. The Secretary of State for Communities and Local Government, Eric Pickles, has announced that the average reduction in spending power for local authorities in 2013/14 is 1.7% and for 2014/15 it will be 3.8%. The definition of 'revenue spending power' includes NHS spending on social care (which increases the apparent amount available to local authorities) but omits local authority income from fees and charges (which is likely to decline in a recession). Using 'revenue spending power' as a way of describing local authority spending also makes comparisons over time very difficult to make.

Box 3.1: Definition: Revenue spending power

From 2013/14, a local authority's revenue spending power is made up from the combined total of:

- Council tax requirement;
- Top-up grant;
- Assumed business rate income;
- Revenue Support Grant;
- NHS funding for social care;
- New Homes Bonus;
- Any other core grants transferred into the funding allocation.

It is worth noting that from April 2013 local authorities become responsible for providing their own, local council tax support schemes to replace the national council tax benefit scheme (Local Government Finance Act 2012). About £3.7 billion has been transferred from the DWP to local authorities within their funding settlements for 2013/14. A provisional figure for these schemes has not been ring-fenced for 2014/15. Different authorities will develop local regulations in ways that they think are fair and affordable, leading to inevitable reductions in benefit entitlement (although ignoring its localist preferences, the government insists that pensioners must not be adversely affected).

The housing benefit service provided by local authorities on behalf of central government is slightly different. Expenditure on housing benefit is not considered within the CSR plans but is dealt with annually as 'annually managed expenditure' or AME. This is because expenditure on welfare benefits fluctuates more than other government spending. Large reductions in housing benefit expenditure were announced by the Coalition to be implemented in stages from 2011. Local authorities are simply expected to follow the law and regulations, using a cash-limited, small discretionary fund if tenants' actual benefit entitlements become insufficient to enable them to remain in their home because they cannot pay the rent.

The different sources of revenue funding

From April 2013, a new set of financial arrangements have been introduced for local government. The Revenue Support Grant (RSG) to help pay for local government services is retained but the way in which business rates income is treated has changed (Local Government Finance Act 2012). Local authorities are now able to retain 50% of their business rates income raised locally.

The amounts concerned vary between local authorities depending on their local needs and council tax profile. For example, Sheffield has just over half a million residents and has a budget of about £1.5 billion a year. 13% is contributed by council tax and 15% by fees and charges, leaving most to be funded by Revenue Support Grant, the 'local share' of business rates and any other grants it may be eligible for. Sheffield Council has seen funding reduce by £130 million in the two-year period 2011–13, £50 million in 2013/14 and expects similar reductions in 2014/15. A smaller authority in the South would have a different profile, less reliance on the Revenue Support Grant and other grants and will not have lost so much income so quickly.

Formula grant, including the Revenue Support Grant

Formula grant from central government provides a significant proportion of the funding used by local authorities to provide services. It is made up of distinct elements, including funding for the police and fire services. This contribution from central government (funded by taxation and business rates) was intended to ensure that similar services could be provided across the country, whether a local authority was situated in a de-industrialised area with a relatively poor population with few economic prospects or was in an economically strong area with relatively better-off residents. That principle has been set aside by the Coalition. It seems more concerned with localism and economic growth in relation to the changes that have been made to the way in which funding is distributed to local government (certainly the way the business rates are now treated indicate this). However, the speed and depth of cutbacks to the funding available for local authorities (with the reduction in Revenue Support Grant income and termination of many grants) suggests that it is primarily interested in permanently reducing the role of the local state.

The Revenue Support Grant, or RSG (mainly funded by business rate income), is one key element of financial assistance to many local authorities and the most important for local authority housing and housing-related services. The RSG element of the local government settlement in 2013/14 was worth £15.2 billion in England..

Box 3.2: The Revenue Support Grant

There are four parts to the RSG:

- an amount for each local authority's relative needs;
- an amount to compensate for the differences in income due from council tax in different areas;
- a common allocation per head for local authorities that provide the same services;
- adjustments ('damping') to make sure that different local authorities have specific limits to the reductions in funding they will experience as a result of the Coalition's deficit reduction programme.

The business rates

The business rates are collected by local authorities from shops, offices and factories. The government sets the rate in the pound each year for business rates – which is then multiplied by the rateable value of the business premises. Before 2013, all business rate income was pooled by the government and then redistributed to local authorities on the basis of a complicated formula (hence 'formula grant'). But from April 2013 a new way of treating business rate income has been introduced. The income generated by business rates has now been divided by the government into a 'local share' (which will be under the control of the local authority directly) and the 'central share' (which central government uses to pay for Revenue Support Grant).

In 2013/14, the 'local share' as it is known, was calculated by the government as worth £10.9 billion. Individual local authorities will be notified of the exact amounts of business rates income that they can retain. The other 50% of the income generated by the business rates levied across the country is available to the government as the 'central share'. It uses this revenue income to pay for the varying amounts of Revenue Support Grant, police funding and other core grants allocated each year to individual local authorities.

This is a new system and there were concerns that this way of treating the business rates would mean that local authorities' income became subject to serious and unpredictable fluctuations (as major employers might close or individual businesses might appeal against their rating). The government has recognised this in the calculation of the 'central' and 'local' shares. To avoid the difficulties associated with a significant loss of income (for example, if a major employer closes), the government has devised a system of 'tariff' and 'top–up' authorities. Box 3.3 provides more detail. These specific arrangements will stay in place until 2020 when they will be reviewed and reset.

Box 3.3: Business rates: some detail

'Top-up' and 'tariff' authorities

- Local authorities have been designated as 'top-up' and 'tariff' authorities.
- Some business rate income will be transferred from the 'tariff' authorities to the government. They may be economically stronger and have a high yield from business rates. The government will then redistribute this to 'top-up' authorities (which have a low yield from business rates in their area).
- The levels of 'tariff' and 'top-up' payments will remain the same until 2020 apart from annual increases for inflation.

Safety net thresholds

- These are in place to protect any authority that has a shortfall in business rates income of 7.5% or more compared to their business rates funding baseline.

A levy

- 'Tariff' authorities are levied to provide funding for these safety net arrangements.
- The need for payments due to the operation of a safety net and the levy payments that will be needed to pay for them, will be worked out at the end of each financial year (although the government is willing to consider payments on account if, for example, a major employer closes in the middle of the financial year).

Local council tax

Local authorities set a rate for local council tax charges each year after considering what funding will be available from central government and other sources to provide the range of local services that the electorate expects. The amount that each householder has to pay is calculated by multiplying the local rate that councillors agree each year with the rateable value of the property in which the household lives.

There have always been pressures on local councillors to minimise council tax increases, as they are politically unpopular. The New Labour government made it clear that in 2009/10 it would regard any council tax increase of more than 5% as potentially excessive. It warned local authorities that it would consider using its capping powers to prevent any authority from raising council tax higher than this. The Coalition government has made a council tax freeze grant available for each year since 2011. Not all local authorities take up the offer. For example, in 2012/13 a significant minority of Conservative-, Labour- and Green-controlled local authorities decided to increase council tax because of rising costs and the impact of the Coalition's reductions in funding. Nevertheless, the Localism Act 2011 now gives the government different powers to deal with local authorities that set what it regards as 'excessive' council tax rises. In the future, any local authority that sets a rate above the Secretary of State's recommended level will have to run a full local referendum in order to obtain the specific approval of the local electorate for its preferred higher rate.

The New Homes Bonus

The government has also linked council tax with new house building, providing an apparent incentive to local authorities to support plans for new house building in their areas. The New Homes Bonus was introduced by the Coalition as a grant to encourage and reward communities that support house building, although most funding for this will be top-sliced off formula grant. Nearly £1 billion has been earmarked from 2011–15 for the scheme. For a period of six years the government will match the additional council tax generated by:

- new homes built in any local authority area;
- empty properties brought back into use as homes in that area.

The amount calculated for each local authority is based on the new homes' council tax band. The Bonus will be paid to the local authority as un-ring fenced grant (that is, the local authority can decide how it wants to spend it). There is an extra premium if any of these new homes are 'affordable' homes.

It is not yet clear how many homes – affordable or unaffordable – will be built in the next few years. Private house building generally is at a very low level. Housing associations and some local authorities may be participating in the Coalition's building programme for 'affordable rent' homes, but there are doubts as to how many will be built from that programme too (see Chapters Six and Eleven). That aside, the Bonus scheme has proved controversial from the start. It rewards local authorities on the basis of council tax banding, so poorer local authorities will usually receive proportionately less than wealthier ones even if new building takes place at the same rate. Labour's then Shadow Housing Minister, Alison Seabeck, used data from the Bonus allocated in 2010/11 to demonstrate this (Box 3.4).

Box 3.4: The New Homes Bonus

In Yorkshire, differences in poorer and wealthier local authorities can be seen.

- Richmondshire is 261st in the indices of deprivation and received £6,272.16 per home;
- Scarborough is ranked 83rd and received £1,600.

There is also a problem associated with the amount of money paid when it is averaged over the local authority's population.

- The City of London receives £28 per person;
- Scarborough receives 7p per person.

Source: Hardman (2011)

Unsurprisingly, many local authorities have used the New Homes Bonus to help reduce funding gaps in other programmes, rather than use the money to 'reward' local communities as the government anticipated, but there is an equity issue here too. Far more Bonus will be available to authorities in the South-East and London, where building programmes are more extensive. Consequently, their income will be higher, providing more protection from austerity cuts than is available to local authorities in other parts of the country.

Fees and charges for services

As income from other sources has become more restricted, local authorities have reviewed and increased their fees and charges. Housing-related fees and charges include rents for council garages and shops; fees for planning permission for individual home improvements; charges for planning permission for developers via Section 106 agreements (see Chapter Six for the way in which this funding source is used by local authorities working with local housing associations); charges in council-owned residential care homes; and charges to private landlords to join local authority-run private landlord accreditation schemes.

Fees and charges may grow as a proportion of overall General Fund revenue as local authorities search for ways to fill funding shortfalls for vital services. The Audit Commission's report *Positively charged* (Audit Commission, 2008) indicated that the public may prefer individual charges for a variety of services, rather than increases in council tax to provide a service available to all residents without necessarily charging for it. The argument is made that if there is an individual charge, residents can then choose whether or not to pay for services, but there is more to this issue. The prospect of individual charging raises the prospect of fluctuating income for the local authority, and difficulties in ensuring that a particular service is available for those who really need it (as opposed to those who can pay for it).

This is an issue that has dogged local authority (and housing association) housing managers when they have had to set service charges for housing schemes. Council house rental and service charge income are both 'charges', but are a source of income that is ring fenced to pay for the council's housing management service (see Chapter Five).

Service example: the service for homeless people

The number of homeless applicants being accepted as statutory homeless by local authorities rose to 50,290 in 2011/12, a 14% increase over the previous year. These numbers are expected to rise even more dramatically by 2015. Most local authority costs to provide a homelessness service are funded through the RSG. This includes staffing and office costs for the service and the costs of temporary accommodation like hostels and rooms in bed-and-breakfast hotels (where some of the costs are met by the Department for Work and Pensions – DWP). It is worth noting that bed-and-breakfast hotels increasingly are coming back into use in some areas as emergency housing, in the absence of alternatives (DCLG, 2012e).

The homelessness service provided by local authorities is vulnerable to cutbacks along with all other local authority services funded via the RSG, but the government is also currently investigating the costs to various government departments of responding to homelessness, as well as the costs of dealing with homelessness at a local authority level (DCLG, 2012c). The most recent data, for 2010/11, revealed that local authorities in England spend in the region of £345 million annually in providing the service to homeless or potentially homeless families and single people. This includes providing temporary accommodation (£100 million), and more specialist homeless prevention work (£70 million).

Governments in the recent past have used additional grant funding to introduce changes or to reward 'good performance' in homelessness services. New Labour introduced the local authority 'Housing Options' initiative in this way. The Coalition government is doing the same. It has kept the 'homelessness prevention grant', first introduced by New Labour in 2002, and slightly increased it. For the two years 2012–14, the grant has been increased, from £71 million in 2011/12 to £90 million in each of the following two years; but is planned to decline to £88 million in 2014/15. This grant pays for the staff and running costs of schemes to prevent rough sleeping, to reduce the number of families in temporary bed-and-breakfast accommodation, to pay for rent deposit guarantee projects and for private landlord liaison work. The focus of the grant is consistent with the government's preference for local authorities to use the private rented sector to resolve homelessness, but these figures are small compared to the size of the problem facing many local authorities.

The Coalition has also retained (but renamed) New Labour's Places for Change programme, which ran for three years up to 2011. The programme provided £80 million for 111 different projects across England. The projects that successfully bid for the programme included hostel and day centre refurbishment programmes as well as other services such as specialist training programmes. The Coalition's replacement, the Homelessness Change programme, funded 39 projects with the £37.5 million available to it for 2011–15 (with an additional £5 million allocated in 2012). The focus was on projects for rough sleepers, to get them off the streets. Only four of the successful bidders for a grant from this programme were local authorities. Most were housing associations and voluntary organisations.

Local authorities have a statutory responsibility to provide housing for people who are homeless in specific circumstances. They have an obligation to provide advice and assistance to all others who approach them for help. Homelessness is set to increase dramatically: there will be more mortgage repossessions as increasing numbers of people become unemployed or reliant on low-waged work (see Chapter Eight), and evictions as more people find that they cannot afford the rent (see Chapter Ten).

REFLECTION 3.1

Breaching statutory responsibilities because of funding cuts

With funding cuts planned, it is likely that some local authorities will not be able to meet their statutory responsibilities for homeless people. If this is the case, what should local councillors be doing?

Service example: the Supporting People programme

The Supporting People programme was first established in 2003 for the provision of housing-related support to a wide range of vulnerable people who might otherwise find it difficult or impossible to manage a home independently. It replaced a wide range of different sources of funding for hostels, shared homes, refuges and home-based services for vulnerable people. In 2003, 1.2 million people were being helped by staff providing time-limited support that was paid for by this funding.

Some of the people who rely on this programme of support include frail older people, people with learning difficulties, women leaving situations of domestic violence, people who are mentally ill and young people who are homeless. The numbers of people being helped increased steadily over the five years from 2003, although recent cutbacks have forced sharp reductions in services in many areas.

> **Box 3.5: Definition: Housing-related support**
>
> • Develops or supports a person's abilities to live independently in the community.
> • Helps people who might otherwise become homeless or have difficulties keeping their tenancy or have to live in an institution because they cannot manage to live completely independently.

The Supporting People programme was initially very well funded, the grant originally being ring fenced and paid within Area Based Grant. Supporting People commissioning staff administered the grant within 152 first-tier local authorities and awarded contracts to a wide range of organisations that provided these services. Services receiving Supporting People funding were subject to service inspection and audit. The security of the funding stream outweighed the sometimes burdensome bureaucracy and was seen as an improvement on the somewhat haphazard funding arrangements that had existed before 2003.

Over more recent times, the programme has been subject to financial cutbacks. This can be traced back to the time before its launch. Service providers (local authorities, housing associations and a wide range of voluntary organisations) had been encouraged by the Office of the Deputy Prime Minister (ODPM, the DCLG's predecessor) to submit funding claims designed to 'size the pot'. The New Labour government hoped in this way to establish a reasonable baseline for the programme, but by 2004 it became clear that the resultant level of required funding could not be sustained. The original estimate for Supporting People had been too low at £700 million, but the final figure of £1.8 billion a year was not sustainable. It was never clear whether this dramatic increase was as a result of organisations taking the opportunity to establish new support services (as they were encouraged to do) or whether it was a problem with accounting systems being discrepant. Whatever the reason, the size of the programme could not be justified politically.

The ODPM, and latterly the DCLG, tried to equalise the funding across the country. Some areas were subject to reductions. Local authorities that had a large number of 'legacy' schemes (which might not be completely eligible, such as residential care homes) or housing projects with very high charges found their funding reduced following a formal service review. Alternatively, they might lose out to a cheaper provider when re-tendering for the service.

Those receiving funding had to tender for the continuation of the service with other local competitors and there was an increased emphasis on 'value for money', which was new to many. This tended to squeeze smaller, specialist providers out of the field. Unsurprisingly, the Supporting People budget for 2008–11 was £4.9 billion, a planned New Labour reduction of 11% compared to previous years. By 2009, the programme was worth about £1.6 billion a year. New Labour felt that this was good value for money. Alternatives, involving institutional care for some, would have cost far more (Ashton and Hempenstall, 2009; CLG, 2009b). The New Labour government un-ring fenced the programme in 2009, despite protests from many who feared for the future. From 2011/12 Supporting People funding has been paid to local authorities within the RSG. Organisations that are successful in bids for this grant funding now regard Supporting People funding as insecure (CIH/Local Government Group, 2010) and 'contract income' (see Leafy Glades HA in Chapter Six).

The programme was partly protected in the Coalition's 2010 CSR, with reductions in funding of 11% by 2015. However, this £6 billion programme is no longer ring fenced and local authorities are looking for ways in which they can find funding to protect statutory services and continue to provide services deemed more urgent or to those deemed more 'deserving' than some of Supporting People's client groups. Different approaches to the Supporting People programme have emerged across the country, depending on the financial position of the local authority and political priorities. In an early survey conducted in 2012 (Bury, 2012), the emerging picture was that some local authorities were either:

- keeping existing priorities but making cuts to services across the board: across England and Wales in 2011/12, 685 services had funding reduced, affecting nearly 40,000 people;
- using this funding to pay for other General Fund services (for example, adult social care): in 2011/12, Cornwall reduced its Supporting People funding by 44%; Hull by 42% and Peterborough by 39%. These 'savings' have been diverted into other services;
- ending the funding of services that were likely to have less popular support locally and retaining those with 'mainstream' support':

305 Supporting People services helping nearly 7,000 people were decommissioned in 2011/12.

Successful service providers – housing associations, voluntary organisations and the local authority itself – now have less to spend. This affects organisations in different ways, as some are more reliant on Supporting People funding than others. For example, refuges in the formal voluntary sector, established to provide safe temporary housing for women and children escaping violence and abuse, have no funding alternatives (Towers and Walby, 2012).

REFLECTION 3.2

Cutting costs

A refuge wins a three-year Supporting People contract but the amount of funding is reduced in subsequent years. What might be the implications of measures that it could take to reduce costs:

*   employing cheaper agency staff;
*   reducing staffing levels where possible;
*   reducing the support service;
*   increasing charges for some services provided?

Service example: the housing benefit service

Paying for the service

Local authorities administer the £21 billion housing benefit scheme on behalf of central government. About £6 billion of these payments are for people who have retired. £15 billion is paid to 'working age' households. These payments are due because tenants are living on a very low income and need financial help to pay the rent. The costs of paying the local housing allowance (to eligible private tenants), rent allowances (to eligible housing association tenants) and rent rebates (to eligible council tenants) are reimbursed by the DWP. Within the reimbursement of benefit costs the DWP includes a small amount for providing the service locally. This is matched by a small amount in the RSG.

In the 2010 Budget the Chancellor of the Exchequer, George Osborne, announced his intention of cutting back expenditure on housing benefit. The Coalition government has estimated that these reductions will save £1,710 million in the DWP's budget by 2014/15, although the Office for Budget Responsibility has cast doubt on this because of the anticipated growth in unemployment and low-waged work in the next few years (Brown and Lloyd, 2011).

Some benefit changes have required primary legislation but others have been introduced by regulation. The cuts in housing benefit have been staggered, with varying reductions coming into force each year up to 2013 and beyond. The Chancellor announced in the 2012 Budget that further cuts would be implemented after 2015. This deliberate strategy of cutting year by year is intended to minimise the potential political damage to the Coalition. The London Mayor, Boris Johnson, a handful of Liberal Democrat MPs and Parliament's Social Security Advisory Committee all expressed their opposition in 2010 (Box 3.6), but the Coalition has not changed its course. Private tenants were affected first, with changes to the way in which the standard local housing allowance (SLHA) was calculated. This provides help with housing costs for those with the lowest incomes. The government dropped 'standard' from the name of this allowance recently so subsequent references to SLHA after 2010 have been changed to LHA to avoid confusion. The impact of these reductions in help will be considered here. Chapter Ten contains more information about the housing benefit scheme that is applicable to council and housing association tenants.

Box 3.6: The Social Security Advisory Committee's protest

'4.12 The scope and scale of individual losses are striking and, set against an increased allocation for Discretionary Housing Payments that represents around 4% of the Department's estimate for total cash losses, we find it hard to accept that LAs [local authorities] will have sufficient funds to support even the most vulnerable customers who find themselves unable to meet their rent and/or unable to access cheaper alternative accommodation. At the same time much of the burden and additional costs associated with housing stress – homelessness applications, and the disruption of schooling and social care support, will fall on LA budgets that are already under pressure from other cuts measures ...'

'4.15 Whether considered separately or as a package, these measures constitute a high risk approach to managing down the costs of the LHA [local housing allowance] arrangements. The proposed timetable offers little time for tenants, landlords and other key stakeholders, such as LAs and housing support and advice services, to prepare for the changes.'

(Social Security Advisory Committee, 2010)

Private tenants and housing benefit reductions

The LHA was introduced into the housing benefit scheme specifically for eligible private tenants. It is based on standard amounts of rent that are calculated across broad areas. Some private tenants may find accommodation within the standard amounts, but many do not and have to make up the shortfall from their other income (from which they are supposed to buy food and clothes and pay fuel bills). It is estimated that 25% of all private tenants are reliant on LHA and receive an average payment of £107 each week, with an average actual rent of £160. The LHA represents 43% of their gross weekly income (DCLG, 2012a, p 23). The DWP has estimated that 48% of private tenants who rely on LHA are *already* making up a shortfall in LHA in order to pay their rent (Fenton, 2011, p 15). More details about the scheme and the reductions that the Coalition government has made are to be found in Chapter Ten.

Some LHA restrictions announced by the Coalition apply to all eligible private tenants. Some of them apply only to those in specific circumstances. The DWP initially expected about 14,000 tenants, mainly in London, to be affected, but researchers in Cambridge quickly calculated that between 136,000 and 269,000 households would find themselves in 'severe difficulty' financially and would find 'it very hard or impossible to keep out of rent arrears or other debt' (Fenton, 2010, p 17). Many have had to move in order to try to find cheaper housing, but this is not straightforward or easy. Of these, 70,000 are families with children; 20,000 are over 60 (single people or couples) (Fenton, 2010). The worst-affected area is London and surrounding areas (Fenton, 2011), but the impact extends to other areas of England, Wales and Scotland.

The impact of these cuts in LHA is to corral private tenants into the cheapest and possibly the worst housing in an area. In some areas there are more private tenants claiming LHA than there are privately rented rooms, flats and houses in the cheapest third of the private rented sector (Fenton, 2011; Ramesh, 2012). Alex Fenton (2011, p 17 onwards) has calculated which boroughs are becoming unaffordable for LHA claimants in London. For his detailed research, he assumed that claimants could not manage a shortfall of more than £10 a week, given that their household incomes are very low. He found:

- from 2011, and certainly from 2016, 'almost the whole area of the traditional Inner London boroughs will be unaffordable except for LB Lewisham and the district of Bermondsey in Southwark';

- Hammersmith and Fulham, Wandsworth, Kensington and Chelsea, Westminster, Islington, Camden, Richmond, Barnet and Bromley will have 'few or no neighbourhoods which will offer rented accommodation affordable to benefit claimants'.

Barking and Dagenham, Newham, Bexley, Greenwich and Havering, as well as some boroughs in south and west London will still be 'affordable'. That said, many private tenants are being forced to move to unfamiliar areas where there may be private rented vacancies, but away from work, family ties, schools and familiar surroundings.

The government believes that its restrictions will drive down the cost of rents. It argues that these have become inflated because of the LHA, but there is no evidence to support this view. Evidence is also emerging (Beatty et al, 2012) that more private landlords are refusing to house people who rely on benefits. It is more likely that, as demand increases, with more people chasing fewer vacancies, rent levels will rise. This will restrict the options of people who rely on LHA even further. It is very unlikely that the private rented market will change positively to assist tenants who rely on the LHA. As an expensive, profit-driven sector, why should it? Unfortunately, this is a housing sector that the government is keen to see expand (see Chapter Seven).

Local authority building and improvement work ('the capital programme')

A local authority can undertake building or improvement work in connection with many of its functions, not just housing or housing-related services. As far as housing is concerned this work is part of the local authority's capital programme. This programme is undertaken in connection with services funded through the General Fund or the Housing Revenue Account, if the local authority still owns council housing.

Box 3.7: Definition: Capital funding

Capital funding is money spent on building new housing, facilities or infrastructure or improving existing buildings to substantially increase their value, extend their use or lengthen the life of the property or facilities.

Local authority capital spending in relation to housing services includes:

- building or improving council housing (if the authority still owns council housing);
- building or improving hostels or other temporary housing for people who are homeless;
- providing or improving pitches and sites for Gypsies and Travellers (if there is a need for this locally);
- private sector improvement work and dealing with empty property;
- building infrastructure (like roads) and new facilities (like schools and community centres).

The funding for this range of work comes from different sources, but mostly through borrowing or grants. Borrowing allows projects to go ahead that would otherwise not be possible to fund and it allows local authorities to spread the repayment costs over many years. Local authorities borrow from the Public Works Loan Board (PWLB), now established as an executive agency of the Treasury. The PWLB offers loans at lower interest rates than commercial lenders. Local authorities are not restricted to the PWLB. They can borrow from other lenders if arrangements offer value for money.

Given that the DCLG was the main casualty in the 2010 CSR, it is not surprising that the details that follow include sources of funding that have been severely reduced. The main sources of funding for new building or improvement work related to housing services are:

- 'supported' and 'unsupported' borrowing;
- using revenue to fund capital projects;
- 'useable' capital receipts from the sale of council houses and council land;
- the housing PFI;
- grants from central government and the Homes and Communities Agency (HCA).

Borrowing money to build or improve – 'supported' and 'unsupported' borrowing

As far as central government is concerned, overall figures for borrowing are set as part of each CSR and they contribute to the total Public Sector Net Borrowing. Following the Local Government Act 2003, central government does not need to give specific permission to local authorities to borrow (as in the previous system of 'credit approvals'), but it does indicate what the level of each local authority's *supported* borrowing will be. There have been Supported Capital Expenditure (Revenue) (SCE(R)) figures for different services in each local authority and there has been one for housing to cover the services provided through the General Fund. This is the level to which central government will pay subsidy to match a local authority's borrowing commitments. This is included as part of the RSG. Each local authority service usually works within the specific SCE(R) figure for its service because any borrowing above that level will not receive subsidy from government. The government decided in the 2010 CSR that it would not support any new borrowing within the SCE arrangements by local authorities until 2015 at the earliest. It prefers to provide specific grant funding for capital work.

Since 2004, an authority's borrowing (whatever the service) is also framed by the prudential borrowing regime (following CIPFA's Prudential Code for accountancy practice). This ensures that any borrowing that a local authority undertakes is affordable and represents value for money. There are specific guidelines to follow when borrowing is arranged, to ensure this.

Local authorities can still borrow outside of the SCE(R) figure, but if they do so they need to identify additional resources that they can use to pay back interest and principal over the length of the loan. They will not receive subsidy to pay for this. It might be possible to arrange 'unsupported' borrowing for General Fund projects that are likely to generate income easily, so that borrowing costs can be covered in this way with no additional subsidy, but this is not likely in housing services.

This difference between borrowing that is 'supported' (with subsidy covering it) and borrowing that is 'unsupported' (with no additional subsidy) had a particular impact on local authorities that own and manage council housing. The New Labour government expected local authorities to improve their council housing to the DHS. They were given until 2010 to do so. The government helped those that set up ALMOs, as can be seen in Box 3.8.

Box 3.8: ALMOs, 'supported borrowing' and HRA allowances up to 2012

'If a local authority had set up an ALMO to achieve the Decent Homes Standard, they would prepare to join New Labour's ALMO programme. A certain number of ALMOs that had achieved a high performance rating (having been inspected by the Audit Commission) were accepted on to the programme each year.

> Once accepted, the local authority was able to arrange its borrowing for the ALMO's work, secure in the knowledge that this would be "supported" borrowing, covered by government subsidy through the Housing Revenue Account [HRA]. The authority would also receive enhanced funding through the HRA major repairs allowance.
>
> Funding for 26 ALMOs for 2008–11 was announced as part of the 2007 CSR.
>
> • £2.4 billion was provided for 26 ALMOs, channeled through their HRA major repairs allowance;
> • £2 billion through SCR(R) was notified to individual local authorities. The costs of this "supported" borrowing were included in their HRAs through an ALMO allowance.'
>
> (Waite, 2009, p 90)

If a local authority decided not to follow the ALMO route (possibly because tenants did not want this or because it thought that it had sufficient resources) it would not be able to obtain 'supported' borrowing. If it wanted to borrow, this would have to be on an 'unsupported' basis. Before 2012 this might have proved very difficult because of the way the HRA worked then (see Chapter Five).

Revenue used to fund capital work

Garnett and Perry (2005, p 198) pointed out that the distinction between capital and revenue resources became increasingly 'blurred' under the New Labour government. Its preference was to channel funds for major repairs and improvements to council housing through revenue allowances in the HRA rather than via capital grants. The way that additional money for high-performing ALMOs was channelled through the major repairs allowance and the ALMO allowance shows this practice of using revenue allowances to fund capital works, as can be seen in Box 3.8.

The Coalition government retained the DHS capital programme set up by New Labour, but its emphasis changed. The HCA (which managed the programme) opened up the eligibility criteria. No longer was 'high performance' a necessary prerequisite for funding. Instead, local authorities that directly managed their council housing could bid for funds for the first time. However, any organisation applying had to have more than 10% 'non-decent' housing stock in order to be eligible to bid. Funding of £1.6 billion was made available for the four years to 2015 and allocated to bidders early in 2011 for an initial two-year period (HCA, 2011). Following the introduction of self-financing for local authority HRAs in 2012 (see Chapter Five) this 'Decent Homes backlog funding' was forwarded to local authorities (with or without ALMOs) as grants. This was credited to their HRA (for onward travel to their major repairs reserve). It could no longer be channelled through the major repairs allowance, as that allowance had been part of the old HRA subsidy system, which was abolished in March 2012.

An example of using revenue derived from 'efficiencies' (money saved in the borough's operations) is provided in the London Borough (LB) of Islington's HRA, detailed in Chapter Five.

'Useable' capital receipts

A local authority can sell its land or property (for example, redundant office buildings or council housing) but it cannot keep all of the proceeds of the sale. In some instances, a proportion of the sale price has to be returned to the HCA (formerly, directly to the government) or used to pay off any outstanding local authority borrowing.

The proportion of the capital receipts that the local authority can use depends on what is sold. A local authority can retain 30% of the value of a discounted council home bought under the right to buy. Since 2004/05, most money from council house receipts has to be returned (previously to the government, but now to the HCA) so that it can be redistributed to other housing programmes. Housing stock transfer receipts must be used to pay outstanding debt repayments. Any surplus can be retained, but the prospect of surpluses has declined with more recent transfers because of the quality of the housing (see Chapter Five). The money generated by the sale of council land to housing associations can be kept if the association has bought the land to build affordable housing.

'Useable' capital receipts (the proportion of the sale price that the authority can keep) can be put in an interest-earning account and used when required. Receipts help to pay for additional local authority building, or they might help to fund housing association new building (see Chapter Five).

The Private Finance Initiative – a hidden public liability

The first PFI scheme was established in 1992 under John Major's Conservative government, but the idea was taken up by New Labour in 1997. PFI involves a private consortium (or 'special purpose vehicle'), typically made up of a bank, a builder and a housing association. The PFI consortium invests in and manages a particular estate, selected by the local authority and leased to the consortium for up to 30 years. The capital that the consortium raises through borrowing in order to make improvements does not appear as public expenditure in the government's accounts as long as the PFI consortium can be seen to be taking on the project's 'risks'.

Longer term, the consortium manages the properties on behalf of the local authority for a fee. This service is usually provided by the housing association in the consortium. The cost of the fee is charged to the local authority's HRA. Up to April 2012, this was paid for by the government in the form of 'annual credits'. Although the subsidy system for council housing has changed to one of self-financing, these payments will continue, but in the form of grants to each local authority that has a PFI. As an example, LB Islington was the first local authority to agree a housing PFI contract. The impact of the PFI contract within Islington's HRA is described in some detail in Chapter Five.

PFIs have been very controversial, not least because they are an expensive private sector route to estate improvements and place large areas of local authority housing outside of democratic control (Whitfield, 2012, pp 154–7). Out of a total of about 800 PFI schemes running a wide range of public services, there are about 30 housing PFI schemes. The public liability for all PFIs has been estimated as £210 billion over 30 years, a far more expensive strategy than simply allowing public organisations to borrow directly to undertake the work. The National Audit Office (2010) cast doubt over whether they were good value for money and the programme was reviewed by the Coalition government and found wanting. Thirteen housing PFIs 'in procurement' were allowed to continue, 'subject to rigorous demonstration of value for money', but the rest were cancelled (CLG, 2010c). The government is looking now for a different model of involving the private sector in public sector projects.

Grants from central government – the private sector renewal budget

A long history of local authority-supported urban renewal ended in 2011 when the private sector renewal budget ceased to exist (see CIEH, 2013 for a detailed evaluation of the effects of this). The peak years for grant funding through this budget were 1983–84, when over £1 billion was paid in different grants to individual householders. By 2010, with a reduced budget of only £317 million, the types of help available to owner-occupiers and private landlords had been reduced substantially.

Many local authorities had supplemented this budget from their own resources and undertook group repair schemes, sometimes in areas with a mix of refurbishment and clearance. This work will be difficult to fund in the future. The Chartered Institute of Environmental Health (CIEH) surveyed local authorities in January 2011 and found that 80% of them were expecting reductions in urban renewal activity. Nearly 60% thought that their work would reduce substantially or disappear entirely (CLG, 2011). The CIEH is particularly concerned about the private rented sector where nearly 30% of the housing has serious hazards (CIEH, 2013).

Some local authorities have set up preferential loans schemes for local householders, available through a local building society or bank, and with local housing associations. It may be possible to obtain a supported loan for improvement work through equity release or a charge on the property. This is small-scale work in the face of increasing private sector disrepair and an ageing population who may not be able to undertake work of this nature because of the cost or complexity (see Chapter Eight). The only other grants available are not designed to deal with unfitness or hazards. They are:

- empty property grants – to bring empty property back into use – available from the HCA. Local authorities, housing associations, other providers and community groups can bid for a grant;
- handyperson work – small-scale repairs, often undertaken via a local 'care and repair' or 'staying put' scheme;
- disabled facilities grants – to help disabled people in England, Wales and Northern Ireland to pay for mobility adaptations to their homes. If householders satisfy particular eligibility requirements, the payment of a grant is mandatory (that is, the local authority has to pay it).

The ring-fenced disabled facilities grant budget was slightly increased by the government in the 2010 CSR (to £185 million in 2014/15), but this does not keep pace with inflation or with the need for help. Each local authority's entitlement is calculated by reference to the number of householders claiming specific disability benefits living within the authority's boundaries. It covers only 60% of the cost (up to a limit), so the local authority has to contribute to works from its own resources for each application. Unsurprisingly, there are long waiting lists for this grant work.

REFLECTION 3.3

'The end of local government as we have known it'

This chapter has detailed the likely impact of cuts to local government spending in relation to housing services. Local councillors will have been elected on the basis of their own manifestos. In this instance, is there a case for them to organise a local referendum with a proposal to increase local council tax to protect local services?

Further reading

To keep up to date on the position of local authorities it is important to check key websites, including the Local Government Association's website and a range of local authority websites.

The website of the Local Government Association – http://www. local.gov.uk/ – has discussion documents, reports and e-bulletins available on a wide range of local authority matters, including 'Finance and localism' and 'Environment, planning and housing'.

Each local authority will have available online all the revenue budgets for different departments and the capital programme for each year. There is a wealth of other information too. For example, in Sheffield the local authority gathers all of this information under 'Budgets and finance' on its website.

For commentary specific to local government see The Guardian Professional Local Government Network: www.guardian.co.uk/local-government-network/.

For general critical commentary, the Red Brick blog, a site for progressive housing debate, is useful: http://redbrickblog.wordpress. com/. It has posts commenting on current housing issues, with a great deal of information and connections to other sites.

FOUR

Owner-occupation

Introduction

In 1914 about 10% of the population owned or were buying their home (Malpass, 2005, p 49). For a short time, in 2001, this figure peaked in England at 70% (74% in Wales, but less in Scotland), although by 2012 it had declined to 65% and looks set to decline further (see Table 1.2). The New Labour government, believing that 90% of the UK's adult population 'aspired' to 'the dream of home ownership', had planned to extend owner-occupation even further down the income scale than had the Conservatives before them (DETR/DSS, 2000, p 30). New Labour wanted to enable lower-income households to build up 'wealth' through property ownership. They would benefit from ownership and their asset (that is, their home) would open the door to 'asset-based welfare' opportunities through opportunities for additional borrowing. The financial crisis of 2007 put paid to this prospect, but the astonishing growth – and more recent decline – of owner-occupation will be explored in this chapter, while Chapter Eight will focus on the implications of ownership for lower-income households, a solution to housing problems that the Coalition government continues to pursue.

A range of institutions with varying degrees of influence have been involved in the story of owner-occupation over the last 100 years. These include: private landlords, speculative house builders, building societies and banks, central and local government. Relationships between these bodies have waxed and waned over that time. Wider economic concerns have also played an important part: the rate and nature of formal employment; the availability of mortgages, and interest rates on loans; the extent and nature of financial regulation; and the development of transport links beyond the more central areas of towns and cities. These influences will be explored in five interlinked sections that will consider:

- the 1930s boom in owner-occupation, an early example of building societies' moving down-market;
- building societies and mortgage lending up to the early 1980s;

- the liberalisation of the financial services sector and the changing role of building societies and banks;
- the importance of mortgage interest tax relief (MITR) in the growth of the sector;
- the increasing financial risks of owner-occupation and the uncertain possibilities of 'asset-based welfare'.

The boom in owner-occupation in the 1930s

The 1930s was identified as the period when owner-occupation grew dramatically, with better-off working-class families buying for the first time. Peter Malpass (2005) has identified this period as one in which the origins of tenure restructuring or 'modernisation' were evident, with the growth of suburbia fuelled by people moving away from private rented housing in older, inner areas of towns and cities. This was neither gradual nor uneventful.

The Wall Street crash of October 1929 was followed by the worldwide Great Depression. The 1931 National Government, led by Ramsay MacDonald, had a Cabinet composed of a mix of Conservative, Liberal and Labour ministers. Domestic policy was largely dominated by the Conservatives. It was no surprise that in this decade, despite evidence of the need for more house building, general subsidies were cut and local authorities were redirected to slum clearance and rehousing. Growing lower-middle-class demand for housing was dealt with by largely uncontrolled, suburban house building for sale.

The Conservatives tended to look favourably on organisations which encouraged thrift and saving, strengthening the bond between citizens and property ownership. The economic circumstances of the time, with falling house prices and interest rates, were such that better-off working families in full employment and with a regular wage might be able to afford a mortgage if speculative house builders and the building societies that lent money for house purchases responded. The decade saw a boom in owner-occupation in parts of the country protected from the Great Depression, with a peak year for speculative house building in 1935, when 287,500 new homes were built.

By the 1930s, a multitude of small, locally based building societies had started to lend money to what John Burnett (1986) called the 'new' middle class made up of people working in new service and 'tertiary' jobs in management, teaching, senior administrative and clerical work. The mortgagor had to have a secure job and building societies continued to work on the principle that a family's housing costs (including the rates, a predecessor of the council tax) should be no more than 25% of net income. In practice, this meant 25% of the husband's salary (middle-class wives were expected to stay at home).

Many building societies had built up substantial funds from deposits by individual savers, due to competitive interest rates, but realised that they would have to change their lending practices if funds were to become accessible to the 'new' middle class or better-off working-class families. They did this by:

- extending the mortgage repayment period (hence reducing weekly repayments for mortgagors);
- charging competitive interest rates on loans – each society determined its rates and often undercut other local societies;
- reducing deposits from 25% of the purchase price (normal up to 1930) to 10%, 5% or even less by taking on collateral security: insurance policies, cash deposits from relatives or friends, local authority guarantees or 'builder's pool' collateral.

The 'builder's pool' involved the speculative builder of an estate of houses setting aside an amount of cash that the building society could use. This was based on the number of properties built and their value. If any mortgagor ran into payment difficulties or defaulted, the building society could draw an equivalent amount from the pool. In this way, building societies protected themselves from the possibility that some of their new borrowers might not be able to keep up mortgage payments.

But there were problems. Firstly, this system meant that building societies became involved with estate building rather than independent valuation. It was estimated that 40–70% of estates were built with builders' pools as collateral. Particular parts of the country saw the greatest increases in owner-occupation: the Midlands, the South and eastern England, so it was no surprise that well over one half of the leading building societies in the South-East in the late 1930s operated builders' pools (Craig, 1986, p 96). The existence of the 'pool' for collateral meant that the capital value of the house and the actual valuation might part company. Peter Craig commented:

> at its worst this type of agreement raised the possibility of collusion between builder and building society to defraud the purchaser. (Craig, 1986, p 96)

Many smaller builders were inexperienced, competition was fierce and they cut corners. Consequently, there was much criticism of 1930s suburban housing, especially the cheaper, speculatively built homes.

New homes might turn out to be 'the worst jerry-built monstrosities' (Aneurin Bevin's Parliamentary Private Secretary, quoted in Craig, 1986, p 105). This problem was highlighted by the famous case of Mr and Mrs Borders. In 1934, the couple moved into a new, three-bedroomed semi-detached house on an estate in Kent. What they experienced, led them to challenge the builder and the building society involved, eventually in court (Box 4.1).

Box 4.1: The Borders case and the mortgage strikes in 1937–38

The Borders and their new home

- In 1934 Mrs Elsy Borders and her husband, Jim, bought a house in the Coney Hall estate in West Wickham, Kent. The Borders had not seen the house before buying because no roads had been built. They chose it on the basis of its location.

- Unknown to the Borders, the house was covered by a pool agreement between Morrell's, which had built the estate, and the building society, the Bradford Third Equitable Building Society. Morrell's went bankrupt in the process.

- When the Borders moved in they found that the roof leaked, the house was damp throughout, the stairs and floors were unstable, interior woodwork including window frames was warped and the windows would not open, the woodwork and eaves were infested, new paintwork flaked within a few months, the foundations were crumbling, plasterwork disintegrated, the electric wiring was faulty, giving electric shocks to anyone who touched the walls and the chimneys were not properly lined, so smoke came through the brickwork when a fire was lit.

- The Borders, unsurprisingly, were not keen to sign the mortgage deed presented to them by the builder's agent until repair work had been completed. They signed it on the proviso that it would not be sent to the building society until this was the case. In January 1935 the building society wrote to them saying they had received the deed. Mrs Borders started paying the mortgage under protest, and three months in arrears.

- In June 1937 the building society started repossession action, citing payment arrears. Mrs Borders counterclaimed, claiming that the deed that the building society held was not the one she had signed and that legally it was invalid because she had not been told of the collateral security that Morrell's had paid. She further counterclaimed that the building society had acted fraudulently, as it had misrepresented the quality of the property they had bought.

Mortgage strikes

- 'The Borders case, rather than an isolated example of opposition to what was seen as building society malpractice was the spearhead of a campaign of mortgage strikes in the London area' (Craig, 1986, p 98).
- Some building societies, including Bradford Third Equitable Building Society, tried to create a situation close to renting for some mortgagors, in an attempt to prevent arrears and mass defaults. On the Coney Hall estate the builders employed mortgage collectors who visited people in their homes weekly to collect the payments due.
- Building societies were reluctant to reveal details of repossessions, but were known to deal harshly with people in arrears.
- On the Coney Hall estate 400 residents went on strike. The issues were the legality of the builders' pools and getting the defects repaired.
- Across the South-East at this time, about 3,000 people involved with different building societies and different builders, but all with the same problems, refused to pay their mortgages as part of this campaign. They paid up when repairs were completed.

Source: Craig (1986)

The case captured the public interest. Thousands of people went on mortgage strike in support, as they had experienced similar problems. The building societies viewed the mortgage strikes with 'great alarm'. The Borders case ended up in the High Court. Mrs Borders conducted her own defence in court and was articulate and effective (see Wilkes, 2001 for an interesting account). With the national press sympathetic, the building societies received a lot of criticism, publicly and privately. Although Mrs Borders lost some aspects of her case, the Borders Case proved to be a turning-point in the way that building societies conducted their business.

> The terms of the judgement in the Borders Case strengthened the case for protection of the borrower against malpractice. (Craig, 1986, p 102)

The prospect of government legislation, which had seemed to be distant, was strengthened when a Private Member's Bill was introduced in the House of Commons by Ellen Wilkinson, MP for Jarrow, which was far tougher than anything the government was considering at the time. This prompted government action. The Building Societies Act 1939 was not as strong as it could have been, but it contained clauses preventing collusion between societies and builders and enabled the establishment of a system of registered builders, with stricter arrangements in relation to builders' pools.

Peter Craig concluded that the inter-war years of building society expansion left an 'ambiguous legacy'. Attempts by building societies to push owner-occupation further down the income scale led to reductions in standards.

> What the marginal owner-occupier of the inter-war years got was in some respects more akin to a commodity than to a capital asset with a stable or appreciating value. (Craig, 1986, p 104)

In 1910, 1,723 building societies had advanced just over £9 million in mortgages. By 1939, this had increased to £137 million (Burnett, 1986, p 253). For some building societies, expansion had come at the price of financial stability. They were 'ill-equipped to bear the strains of hell for leather expansion' (Craig, 1986, p 103). One response from the building societies themselves came towards the end of the decade. With the volume of lending declining, they established an interest rate-fixing cartel which

> generally allowed for a sufficient inflow of funds to building societies, plus an adequate interest rate margin between borrowing and lending for most of them. (Ball, Harloe and Martens, 1988, p 134)

Unsurprisingly, the building societies also became the objects of increased scrutiny by the Treasury and the Bank of England. It became more likely that governments would intervene in building societies' affairs in the future. In the past, they had not done so, but the societies had grown substantially and government policy in relation to owner-occupation depended on them. Nevertheless, by 1939 some in government felt that the limits of owner-occupation had been reached and that the building societies would have to satisfy themselves with a more restrained role in the future. History proved them wrong.

Building societies and mortgage lending up to the mid-1980s

Owner-occupation is expensive relative to earnings, and usually householders borrow to pay for property, acquiring it after 20 or 30 years of steady repayments. Building societies provided the bulk of repayment mortgages up to the mid-1980s. They effectively borrowed short-term 'liquid' personal savings acquired from large numbers of savers and lent longer-term mortgages to mortgagors, with variable interest rates (to respond to short-term changes in general interest rates).

During these years, there was little competition with other organisations (such as banks) for individual personal savings. The building societies grew because they worked within these 'sheltered circuits of housing finance' (Ball, Harloe and Martens, 1988, p 131). The 1930s had seen the first signs of a possible mass market, but the 1950s, 1960s and 1970s were particularly important decades of steady growth because of the economic prosperity of most of that time (see Stephens, 2007, pp 202–5 for a more detailed account). Building societies developed an image that suggested that they were secure and friendly savings institutions.

Nevertheless, they continued to be conservative and cautious in their actual lending practices and this sometimes frustrated government policy in other areas. For example, in the 1970s there was evidence that building societies were 'red lining' inner-city areas, refusing to lend on property that they thought would not be a sound investment. This made it very difficult for residents and local authorities engaged in urban renewal work (Gibson and Langstaff, 1982, pp 122–3). Local authorities were able to circumvent these problems through offering mortgages themselves.

Competition between building societies on interest rates barely existed because of the cartel set up in the late 1930s, but as the decades passed, competition between them on other aspects of business grew. For example, they vied with each other in the provision of local branch services for customers. In 1968 there were approximately 481 building societies with 1,662 branches between them. By 1981 the number of branches had increased to 6,203, but mergers had reduced the number of building societies. Their business became concentrated in the hands of a small number of national societies. By 1981, out of 251 registered building societies, the 10 biggest held 71% of total building society assets (Ball, 1983, p 297, quoting Building Societies Association [BSA] figures). Ironically, the competition over who had the best branch network actually favoured the larger societies, as they had a bigger turnover and could afford all these small local offices.

Competition also occurred on savings accounts. Some societies started offering higher-interest accounts in order to gain the competitive edge over rival societies. Their mortgages might be more expensive as a consequence, with higher interest rates. This eventually led to the abandonment of the interest rate cartel that had been operational since the 1930s, but building societies were reaching a more important turning-point. By the mid–1980s they appeared to have saturated the market. Writing at that time, Michael Ball remarked:

> The societies have prospered with the growth of owner occupation but are now facing mounting problems as the expansion of owner occupation begins to falter and other financial institutions, particularly the clearing banks, take a growing interest in the mortgage market. Building societies are having difficulties both in getting sufficient money deposited with them and in lending it out as additional mortgages. (Ball, 1983, p 295)

A way would have to be found to increase their mortgage business. It was by no means clear in the early 1980s what that would be.

The liberalisation of financial services – 1986 onwards

Additional mortgage business in the early 1980s was provided in two different ways. With house price increases at the time, mortgagors had to borrow more. At the same time, the Housing Act 1980 precipitated the enormous growth in council tenants' right-to-buy purchases (see Chapter Five). Would this secure long-term building society growth?

By this time too, different organisations had started arranging mortgages, intruding on what had traditionally been building society business. Local authorities started lending in the 1970s, in the face of building societies' reluctance to invest in inner-city areas. Option mortgages were available to lower-income residents in these areas (see Karn, Kemeny and Williams, 1985). Endowment mortgages became available, linked to insurance policies, from insurance companies. Banks had started to lend to higher-income earners wanting to buy more expensive property.

By this time, it was clear that mortgage business growth went in cycles. It expanded in favourable economic times and declined when jobs and the economy faltered. Nevertheless, building society managers were no longer satisfied with cyclical growth. Many wanted permanent growth (Ball, Harloe and Martens, 1988, p 159). The solution to the problem of growth was provided by deregulation of the mortgage markets. The building societies themselves pressed for a change in their legal status. The Building Societies Act 1986 (subsequently amended by Acts in 1997 and 2000) and the Financial Services Act 1986 deregulated building societies and banks, enabling them to diversify and develop their services. For building societies, access to wholesale funds meant that they could respond more quickly to individual requests for mortgages. For the first time, they could provide banking services, act as estate agents, provide insurance brokerage and lend second mortgages on property. For the potential mortgagor, it was no longer necessary to be a saver with a building society before obtaining a mortgage.

The changes in the mid-1980s enabled some building societies to grow at an unprecedented rate. By 1986, building societies were providing 63–77% of mortgage lending, depending on the society and area in which they operated (Ball, Harloe and Martens, 1988, p 142, quoting BSA data). Nevertheless, deregulation proved a double-edged sword. Many were caught by privatising 'carpet-baggers' who wanted to reap profits from share issues if they could force building societies to privatise and become banks. Building society members (not renowned for radical action) sometimes anticipated these attempts and fought back, fearing the deterioration of their local service if their society was privatised, as can be seen in Box 4.2.

Box 4.2: Building societies resist carpetbaggers in 1999

Campaigners

'Campaigners opposed to building societies turning into banks have again called on Parliament to change the law after renewed threats to the large mutuals. So-called "carpetbaggers" hoping for windfall payouts have targeted eight building societies for conversion to banks: Britannia, Chelsea, Coventry, Portman, Skipton, Yorkshire, West Bromwich and Bradford and Bingley.

The first seven of these have received resolutions from Michael Hardern, a former royal butler, seeking conversion. Mr Hardern, who almost succeeded in forcing the Nationwide to demutualise last July, has also put himself forward for election to the boards of the societies ... For the resolution to be valid, the 50 members [needed to support it] must have been with the society for at least two years and have had minimum savings or mortgages during that time.

Members for Conversion, a group co-ordinated by Michael Hardern, believes members at the eight targeted societies would receive between £522 and £1,281 – at least – if conversions went ahead.

Asset-stripping

The mutual-to-bank campaign could lead to a flood of demands for new accounts from people chasing windfalls. Bob Goodall, co-ordinator at Save Our

> Building Societies, which opposes converting building societies to banks said the government must act to prevent what he called "asset-stripping". He argued that conversion would lead to worse service and rates for members. Building societies which are floated on the stock market and must make profits for shareholders cannot offer the same service or competitive rates as building societies which are answerable only to their members, he argued.
>
> "1999 could be a defining year for the building society movement," he said. "We will lobby MPs vigorously to introduce primary legislation to amend the Building Society Act 1986 to remove the section that allows for demutualisation." He added: "Carpetbagging is not a freebie but is in fact asset-stripping, legalised theft from future generations."
>
> The trend towards mutual societies turning into banks reached its peak in 1997 when the Halifax, Alliance & Leicester, Woolwich, Northern Rock and mutual insurer Norwich Union all converted.'
>
> (BBC, 1999)

The number of building societies in the UK continued to decline, not because of mergers but through de-mutualisation. They changed their legal status to become private institutions (see Stephens, 2007, pp 205–11 for a more detailed discussion). There are now only 47 UK building societies registered with the Building Societies Association (BSA). The sector is dominated by Nationwide Building Society. Bigger by far than all the other societies put together, it is the largest building society in the world, the result of countless mergers. The head office is in Swindon, Wiltshire, the county where one of its originating societies was based in the mid-1800s. It is the UK's third-largest mortgage provider and also provides current accounts, savings accounts, ISAs, investments, loans, credit cards and insurance.

Were building society members right to fear the changes brought about by deregulation? The building societies that remain have been able to provide a wider range of services and have become more responsive to their customers, but their market share of mortgage lending has declined dramatically from a peak in 1990. Table 4.1 shows that by 2007 building societies were dealing with a third of the volume of mortgages agreed in that earlier time. The BSA statistics on the market share of building societies as compared to banks and other institutions confirm these trends (see BSA, 2012).

The link between saving and borrowing for a mortgage was broken by deregulation. Finding a mortgage became a matter of 'shopping

Table 4.1: Number of mortgage advances per year in Great Britain, 1980–2011 (in thousands)

	1980	1990	1997	2000	2004	2007	2008	2009	2010	2011
Building societies	675	780	396	311	173	231	104	104	113	116
Banks	–	333	674	734	882	756	368	469	418	416
Insurance companies	18	26	–	–	–	–	–	–	–	–
Local authorities	16	8	–	–	–	–	–	–	–	–
Other specialist providers	–	–	116	68	205	269	44	24	44	61
Total	**709**	**1,147**	**1,186**	**1,113**	**1,262**	**1,260**	**516**	**598**	**575**	**593**

Source: Pawson and Wilcox (2013, p 160), Table 40.

Note: Specialist providers often concentrate on the buy-to-let market.

around' for a good rate over a reasonable term. This did not necessarily lead to realistic borrowing (see Chapters Two and Eight) or help building societies to retain customers. As house prices continued to rise, new institutions became involved in mortgage lending, increasing the scale of lending dramatically. (Chapter Two provides more information about the mortgage market in 2007.) Mortgage lending through banks became predominant, increasing from 1990 to the mid-2000s. It is noticeable that specialist lenders made an appearance in the field at this time as building societies' share declined. Their main interest was buy-to-let mortgages. By 2007 they were lending more than the building societies.

Since 2007, building societies have reduced their lending, but not on the same scale as banks. The banks have effectively withdrawn from new mortgage lending on any scale for house purchase, as can be seen in Table 4.1. Some may be concentrating on other, more profitable areas of work, while others are rebuilding their capital reserves through savings and other investments so they do not become so reliant on the wholesale market again. As banks have diverse possibilities for investment they are less reliant on the housing mortgage market.

Given the growth of the sector over recent decades, and its value, the fate of owner-occupied housing has become more closely linked to the state of the economy, arguably exacerbating economic cycles. This housing market volatility (with regular peaks and troughs of house prices) is colloquially described in terms of a 'boom and bust' cycle. There was a 'boom' in 1986–89, a 'bust' in the early 1990s, another 'boom' in the early part of the new century, followed by the global economic crisis in 2007 and another 'bust'.

Two aspects of this cycle of growth and decline in values will be explored in detail later. Making the most of housing as an 'asset' became a familiar feature of the 'boom' side of the sector from the mid-1990s. Dealing with financial risk is now most definitely part of the cycle's 'bust' side with the decline in property value which follows.

The importance of mortgage income tax relief (MITR) to owner-occupiers

Owner-occupation has been encouraged by different governments since the First World War in a number of different ways. Up to the early 1990s, the tenure was bolstered by the existence of MITR. Technically tax foregone, this has also been called a subsidy for owner-occupation. It was available for individual mortgagors, dependent on the size of their mortgage and earned income, and was subject to mortgage ceilings or limits which changed from time to time. Michael Ball concluded that up to the mid-1980s:

> The history of fiscal policies towards owner occupation can be summarised as being both haphazard and aimed generally at encouraging the tenure through tax reforms that removed adverse tax effects as they appeared whilst maintaining the beneficial ones as they grew in importance. (Ball, 1983, p 341)

MITR and what some have considered its corollary, Schedule A tax, can be considered in this light. Its existence enabled the substantial growth of the owner-occupied sector, a factor worth considering in any discussion of the costs of the current housing benefit system for tenants.

Mortgage interest tax relief and Schedule A tax

From the early part of the 19th century, no tax was levied by governments on the interest that had to be paid on any domestic loans. Money borrowed for house purchase was included in this exemption. Even by the early part of the 20th century, this provision benefited only wealthy families who paid income tax and owned their own home. The wider effects of this tax relief for owner-occupiers, in terms of the amounts of tax foregone (that is, not collected by the Inland Revenue) began to be noticed as owner-occupation grew, incomes and house prices rose and more homeowners started to pay income tax in the 1950s and 1960s. This exemption was abolished in 1969 for all except mortgage interest.

Balancing this tax foregone/subsidy had been a tax that owner-occupiers actually had to pay. Schedule A taxation had been (or was regarded as) a balancing measure against MITR. This measure had originally been aimed at private landlords. It was intended to tax the imputed rental income of owner-occupiers, that is, the monetary gain they experienced by occupying their home rather than renting it. The argument in support of the tax was that:

> as house-owners, owner occupiers implicitly derive rental income from themselves as house dwellers which like other non-money income should be taxed. (Ball, 1983, p 340)

The tax was calculated by reference to the property valuations used by local authorities in calculating the rates (the same records are currently used for council tax). By the mid-1960s, these figures had not been uprated for 30 years. Consequently, Schedule A payments were very small by then, but a new set of valuations was due to become operational in 1963. It was anticipated that many property valuations would triple or quadruple. The amount of Schedule A tax would substantially increase, as a consequence. The Conservative government decided to abolish the tax just before the general election, as a vote-winning measure. It lost the election, but the tax disappeared too. That left MITR as a clear financial benefit to owner-occupiers.

Forrest and Murie (1988, p 88) commented that in real terms the value of MITR increased 'by almost five times' between 1963/64 and 1985/86. More generally, the effect of MITR was regressive: the wealthiest benefited the most. They usually had the biggest mortgages and, until 1991, this tax relief was calculated against the highest rate of tax that a mortgagor paid.

The costs to government of the subsidy to owner-occupiers

Arguments for the abolition of MITR focused on the cost and whether it was right to subsidise individual mortgagors, especially when government investment in council housing was being substantially cut back (see Chapters One and Five). Others have argued that a tax foregone is not a subsidy. In this view, the long-term effect was as likely to be general house price inflation, encouraging homeowners to pay more than they might have done for an owner-occupied home (knowing that they would be eligible for MITR). Unsurprisingly, the value of MITR to individuals with mortgages was greater in areas where house prices were high (for example, some parts of London and the South-East). It may well have exacerbated periodic price 'booms' too (acting in relation to prices in a pro-cyclical way). MITR (or from 1983, MIRAS – mortgage interest relief at source) was finally abolished in 2000. By then, it had given a substantial financial advantage to owner-occupation and individual owner-occupiers, as compared to other tenures, and fuelled the sector's enormous growth.

The costs of MITR are shown in Box 4.3. The amount of this effective subsidy is far more than that for council or housing association rented housing or housing benefit costs. These figures also show a shift in policy direction away from the general consensus on housing policy priorities that was achieved between the two main political parties by the 1970s. By the late 1980s it had become clear that the Conservative government elected in 1979 was following a particular path in relation to owner-occupation and public expenditure on rented council (or housing association) housing. Forrest and Murie (1988, p 90) demonstrated that, in financial terms, there was a significant change of emphasis in housing provision away from *public* council housing and towards *private* owner-occupation. Subsidies shifted too, away from government bricks-and-mortar subsidies (to build council or housing association homes for rent) and towards individual income-based subsidies: MITR/MIRAS (for owner-occupiers) and means-tested housing benefit (for eligible council and housing association tenants).

Forrest and Murie also pointed out that the cost of these changes was less important to Prime Minister Margaret Thatcher than getting the direction and emphasis of policy that she wanted. This can be seen clearly in Box 4.3, where the detail shows that this regressive subsidy was far greater than that provided to tenants through the housing benefit scheme (see Chapter Ten).

Box 4.3: Mortgage interest tax relief

- By 1981 it was estimated that MITR cost £2,000 million in lost tax revenue, 'which was equivalent to all the central and local government housing subsidies to council housing, housing associations, new towns, rent rebates and rent allowances put together' (Ball, 1983, pp 339–40, quoting Treasury, 1981).

- By this time it was felt to be politically 'impossible' (Ball, 1983, p 340) to change this arrangement. Indeed, the mortgage ceiling above which tax relief could not be claimed was raised by the Conservative government in 1983 from £25,000 to £30,000. This cost £60 million in revenue foregone by the government (Forrest and Murie, 1988, p 89). At that time, the average price of a family home was £11,767, but the building societies and house builders wanted the mortgage ceiling for tax relief to be even higher, at over £50,000.

- Forrest and Murie (1988, p 88) commented that in 1985/86, the cost of this tax relief was estimated officially at £4,500 million (more than the housing programme, at £2,834 million, or capital expenditure, at £1,669 million).

- It was expensive to continue, but under Prime Minister Margaret Thatcher MITR/MIRAS could not be touched. Eventually, the Chancellor of the Exchequer, Nigel Lawson, adopted an incremental approach to reducing it, although there were dangers in this. Until 1988 unmarried couples and friends buying a property together could each receive MIRAS on the same property. This was abolished in 1988, but the Chancellor allowed a three-month lead-in time for the restriction. Many rushed to buy property before the deadline, boosting the amount lost by the Treasury. In 1988/89, MIRAS cost £5,400 million and this increased to £7,700 million in 1990/91.

- In 1991 MIRAS was limited to the basic rate of tax. Its phased abolition was then announced by the Conservatives in 1993 (three years after Thatcher's resignation as Prime Minister). This colossal subsidy reduced gradually: £6,100 million (1991/92), £5,200 million (1992/93), £4,300 million (1993/94), £3,500 million (1994/95) £2,700 million (1995/96), £2,400 million (1996/97), £2,700 million (1997/98), £1,900 million (1998/99) and £1,600 million (1999/2000).

- MIRAS was finally abolished by New Labour in April 2000, when most existing homeowners had actually already benefited from it.

Ironically, by the time MIRAS was finally abolished, its significance as a financial measure had changed. It was no longer important for middle-class borrowers with higher incomes and bigger mortgages. Instead, it had become most useful to lower-income families paying mortgages for homes with much lower values. When it disappeared, lower-income owner-occupiers found themselves paying more expensive mortgages.

Owner-occupation has been continuously promoted by recent governments as natural and appropriate for most households, although its growth was actively subsidised through MITR/MIRAS. The sector has been imbued with positive moral values and has been associated with self-reliance, hard work and financial foresight, but little thought appears to have been given to the financial risk associated with the excessive borrowing which is now required to buy a home. These features of owner-occupation are less a consideration when the economy is growing, when mortgagors are in full-time work and house prices are increasing. The 'feel good' factor tends to obscure the potential reality of repossession and homelessness if mortgage payments cannot be maintained. Mortgage arrears and repossessions tend only to be revealed as matters of public concern in times of economic downturn. Yet, permanent changes in the nature of paid work since the 1990s (Ford, Burrows and Nettleton, 2001) and in the current recession, linked to austerity measures, mean that high levels of arrears and repossessions are more likely to become a semi-permanent feature of the sector.

In 2000, when tax relief on mortgage interest was finally abolished, many low-income owner-occupiers with mortgages were left in a precarious position financially, though few noticed it at the time. There was little by way of a safety net of financial assistance from the welfare state if they became unable to pay their now more expensive mortgages. As Ford, Burrows and Nettleton (2001, p 80) remarked, abolishing MITR/MIRAS:

> fundamentally alters the balance of financial support given to households in different tenures [and] puts into sharp relief the limited support the UK government now provides to low-income home owners, relative to low-income households in other tenures. (Ford, Burrows and Nettleton, 2001, p 80)

The New Labour government had tended to put trust in the private sector (and mortgage payment protection insurance) to cover problems such as unemployment and ill-health. This proved to be ill fated.

The increasing risks of owner-occupation and uncertain possibilities of 'asset based welfare'

Owner-occupation as a sector is remarkably diverse. At one end of the scale, homeowners scrape by on low, erratic or fixed incomes. At the other end, there are multi-millionaires. The age, design and physical condition of their homes varies too: in Manchester alone, they range from the Victorian terraces of Cheetham Hill to the penthouse flats at the top of Beetham Tower. If an owner has purchased outright, has sufficient income for repairs and improvements and does not need or intend to move in the short term, they are unlikely to experience any financial difficulties related to their home. They can use it to borrow more funds if they choose.

At the same time, a number of features have combined over the years to make borrowing to buy a home a more risky business now than it was in past years. House price booms have been followed by sharp declines in house values (and negative equity) and have been marked by increasing home repossessions and homelessness. The early 1990s was one such period, in which many owner-occupiers who became unemployed in the recession became literally homeless. In 1991 over 75,000 homes were repossessed. In addition, 900,000 households were more than two months in arrears with their mortgage payments (Ford, Burrows and Nettleton, 2001, p 22). Local authorities have a statutory duty to assist homeless households in specific circumstances. In 1991, 12% of 60,000 homeless 'acceptances' by local authorities, and in 1992, 10% of 63,000, were for mortgage arrears, as compared to 3% and 2% for rent arrears in the same years. Negative equity (when the current house value falls to substantially less than the original purchase price) also appeared then as a large-scale problem for the first time.

The increasing risks of owner-occupation

The liberalisation of the mortgage market has meant that a wider range of people have been able to obtain a mortgage. This means that a large number of people are now buying their home when financially this is not a realistic option for them in the longer term (see Stephens and Quilgars, 2007). Housing shortages have led to house price inflation in most parts of the UK. Two full-time incomes are now needed to pay the mortgage (and other household bills). As recently as the 1980s, it was possible for a single person with secure employment to obtain a mortgage for 20 or 30 years on a property that might be the cheapest in the area – the so-called first-time buyer areas. That is not the case now. Although the number of single people living alone has increased (and will continue to do so), it is very difficult indeed for a single person to find housing at a price that is affordable with one income. That said, even for couples who may both be in work, the incidence of relationship breakdown, unemployment, redundancy and long-term illness is now more likely to seriously disrupt household finances – and the ability to keep up with paying the mortgage.

Many households have lived through their home being repossessed by their mortgage lender: 840,000 households between 1980 and 2010. Many more will have sold up before that eventuality (Stephens, 2011). To date, there has not been a repetition of the early 1990s' rate of repossessions, although official figures mask increasing levels of mortgage arrears and a new phenomenon, repossessions that are taking place because of credit card debt (Marshall, 2008). In 2011, 36,200 homes were repossessed (see the Council of Mortgage Lenders [CML] website for the most recent figures). The current recession and cuts in public spending are such that serious levels of repossessions and mortgage arrears will continue to be a feature of the sector for a long time.

The New Labour government insisted on lenders using a 'pre-action protocol' to avoid mortgage repossession and this has reduced the number of repossessions, but some banks are now clear that they would prefer to repossess property and sell it off, recouping some of their losses. They argue that it might be better for the mortgagor too: simply keeping up with interest-only payments with a repayment mortgage (the most usual mortgage product now) does not reduce the principal. At the same time, New Labour's mortgage rescue scheme involving housing associations has been made more restrictive by the Coalition government, which claims to be obtaining better 'value for money'. The grants available to housing associations for mortgage rescue have been reduced, the circumstances in which people can be helped have narrowed and the value of property considered eligible has been lowered. The Coalition announced a £19 million Preventing Repossessions Fund for local authorities in 2012. This money, distributed across all local authorities in England, is to be used for small, interest-free loans to homeowners. Without apparent irony, it was referred to as a 'safety net against repossession' by the then Housing Minister, Grant Shapps.

Conservative and New Labour governments alike have preferred not to provide an adequate financial safety net for mortgagors who become unemployed or are made redundant (see the detailed analysis in Wilcox, 2012c). New Labour did extend the help available for unemployed people who claim Jobseeker's Allowance or income support. The 'waiting time' of 39 weeks for Support for Mortgage Interest (SMI) was reduced to 13 weeks, after which the interest part of a mortgage payment can be paid as part of a householder's benefit entitlement, subject to a number of restrictions. Nevertheless, the Coalition government plans to restrict SMI from 2013. The justification for this is that it will make the system 'fairer to the taxpayer' (presumably those fortunate enough to have a job).

Conservative, New Labour and Coalition governments alike have relied on owners taking out insurance to protect themselves from the financial risks that they might face over the lifetime of mortgage repayments. Yet the reality of mortgage payment protection insurance is that it is a policy response that has failed: only one fifth of mortgagors are now covered by a plan, in part because it is recognised that insurers often refuse to help (see the detailed discussion in Ford, Burrows and Nettleton, 2001, chapter 4).

These arrangements are inadequate, given the numbers of low-income owner-occupiers who are still paying a mortgage. This will become increasingly evident as public sector job losses increase from 2013.

REFLECTION 4.1

Low-income owner-occupation and financial risks

What financial and practical assistance should be available from the welfare state for low-income households that have a mortgage?

What are the strengths and weaknesses of mortgage rescue schemes?

What are the realistic alternatives to low-income owner-occupation?

The housing dimensions of 'asset based welfare'

Despite the enormous increases in the value of most owner-occupied homes in the early 2000s, no government has considered charging capital gains tax on the increased capital value of a property if it has been used continuously as the owner's home. Most house sales are exempt. In a rising market, the idea of capital gains tax seems reasonable, not least because it would be one way of restraining the excessive and rapid increases in house prices. The idea seems more problematic when a market is declining. It has also been suggested that such a tax would inhibit labour mobility (Stephens, 2011).

Given that there seems to be little prospect of this tax being extended to include owner-occupation, many homeowners who have paid their mortgages off are now living in an 'asset' worth a great deal of money. Their 'equity' is the value of the property. A third of homeowners are still paying a mortgage, but even for them, as time passes, their 'equity' increases as their mortgage payments decline either absolutely or relative to the assumed increasing value of the property. In the past, so-called 'equity release' has been seen when owner-occupiers:

- sell their property and move to a cheaper home. Assuming that they do not have to repay any other loans, the difference in price is theirs to use as they wish;

- have sold up and moved into a different tenure. An older person might sell their home so as to move nearer to their family. A middle-aged couple might split up, each moving to a private rented flat;
- have sold their home to pay for residential care costs. This is a very unpopular policy but continues because no recent government has been prepared to take on the substantial costs (see Chapter Eight).

By the early 2000s, a different situation had emerged. Homeowners could borrow additional funds using the increasing equity of their homes as security. This became known as 'equity release' or 'equity withdrawal', although it was actually simply more personal borrowing (or more debt). Homeowners could use the money borrowed for whatever they wanted, as this borrowing was no longer linked to MITR/MIRAS.

> Mortgage market deregulation has increased the importance of the distribution of housing wealth, since it has also made housing wealth more liquid. The ability to convert housing equity into income (equity withdrawal) has blurred the relationship between wealth and income. (Stephens, 2007, p 214)

This idea was taken up by New Labour, surprisingly keen on homeownership in its Green Papers *Quality and Choice* in 2000 and *Homes for the future: more affordable, more sustainable* in 2007. The Housing Minister, Yvette Cooper, made it plain that it was a matter of 'social justice' that homeownership extended even further down the income scale (quoted in Davis and Wigfield, 2010, p 16). Citizens with modest incomes would be able to obtain 'assets' or housing wealth through homeownership just like other owner-occupiers. Critics believed that the prospect was hazardous for poorer households (Davis and Wigfield, 2010, p 17). The policy ignored the likely financial situation of poorer households (erratic, low-paid work and possible spells of unemployment) and the possibility that poorer owners might have bought lower-value property which might decline rather than increase in value over time.

Nevertheless, many owner-occupiers had been borrowing substantial sums of money against the equity in their homes. They had literally been 'spending the home' (Smith, Cook and Searle, 2007, p 4). It was believed that the government felt that these assets could be used to unlock additional household resources that could be used to provide welfare services (Malpass, 2005, p 144) – but was that the way in which this borrowing was being used?

Research found that households might use the extra money for private healthcare, private education or expensive holidays. They had also used borrowing like this in emergencies, such as redundancy or relationship breakdown, when no other source of money was available. Only about a half of the gross equity released had been reinvested in housing (Smith, 2005, p 7).

The housing-related areas where these funds were used included:

- major repairs or improvement, especially as government grants for this declined and then disappeared (see Chapter Three);
- paying off more expensive debts to ensure that the mortgage could be paid;
- contributions to alterations that might improve the physical layout and/or facilities for a homeowner or family member with a disability (see Chapter Three);
- part of a mortgage-rescue strategy employed by the local authority or housing association to prevent repossession.

Given that the New Labour government seemed to be thinking of wider uses, more recent research has tried to find out what owner-occupiers' attitudes are towards possible government intervention in relation to equity withdrawal (Smith et al, 2007). Most of the 150 owners interviewed did not want any government intervention, for two different kinds of reasons. They:

- had worked hard to pay their mortgage; surely it would not be right for the government to tell them how to spend any equity-based borrowing?
- had paid for repairs and improvements with the extra borrowing; some were an investment, with owners taking the financial gamble that the improvements would increase the value of their home over time. Why should any government interfere with that?

There was concern about the possible mis-selling of financial products. Regulation to deal with the uncontrolled growth of these was looked on favourably. There was also concern about 'equity leakage': using money secured against the equity in the home on lifestyle or luxury items unconnected with the home. While this had boosted consumer spending (and helped economic growth), it had also increased personal debt (see Smith, 2007 for more detailed analysis of the interviews).

Since 2007, the financial crisis and recession have severely dented consumer confidence, and equity-based borrowing has declined substantially. However, there are still questions to be asked. Is it appropriate that owner-occupied housing should be used in this way? Can a house be an asset (and treated as such) when it is simultaneously and first and foremost someone's home? More generally, has this blurring of equity and money simply hidden a long period of virtually static earnings for most? Borrowing like this has been the mechanism which has until recently kept the economy growing, but at what cost in terms of personal debt? More than that, while working households may borrow against equity with some degree of confidence (assuming that they are not made redundant), what of older homeowners who need residential care?

The idea of 'spending the home' is an interesting way of describing what other commentators have termed the growing 'financialisation' of citizens. Citizens are being expected to borrow for welfare needs (instead of the state raising taxation and providing for needs more generally). Lending institutions of various kinds see welfare needs as another potentially profitable area to turn into a 'market'. There are limits, of course, mortgage protection insurance being one good example of market failure to provide help when required. Chapter Eight looks at this issue in a different way. Who are the owner-occupiers who may find that their home is not an 'asset' but a liability?

Further reading

The website of the Council for Mortgage Lenders is at: www.cml. org.uk/cml/publications/research. The CML provides commentary and research from the perspective of mortgage lenders. The CML produces 'Market commentary', analysing the current state of the mortgage market. It is available at: www.cml.org.uk/cml/publications/marketcommentary. It also produces research and other reports. A useful evaluation of the current mortgage market from the lenders' point of view is provided by CML (2012a) *Where do we go from here? How UK mortgage lenders see the UK market – past, present and future*, London: CML.

There are a range of publications available generated by the Housing Market Taskforce, set up by the Joseph Rowntree Foundation, at: www.jrf.org.uk/work/workarea/housing-market-task-force. These include:

Mark Stephens and Peter Williams (2012) *Tackling housing market volatility in the UK: A progress report*, www.jrf.org.uk/publications/housing-market-volatility-progress.

Christine Whitehead and Peter Williams (2011) 'Causes and consequences? Exploring the shape and direction of the housing system in the UK post the financial crisis', *Housing Studies*, vol 26, no 7-8, pp 1157-69.

FIVE

The changing fortunes of council housing

Introduction

The number of local authorities that own and directly manage council housing has declined dramatically since 1997. About 200 local authorities in England, Scotland and Wales now own and manage council housing. In Northern Ireland, the Northern Ireland Housing Executive manages all the council housing there on behalf of local authorities, but changes to this arrangement are likely too. The focus in this chapter will be on England, given the limitations of space.

The most significant feature of council housing in recent years is its numerical decline from 4.9 million properties in 1976 to 1.7 million in 2011. From a tenure that represented 29% of the housing stock in England in the late 1970s (and higher in Scotland), it now represents less than 7.6% of the total. This chapter will explore how politicians have set in motion the processes that have led to this situation, not least establishing the right to buy and large-scale stock transfers. Neither of these processes could have happened to the extent that they did if the reputation of the sector had not declined too. Years of under-investment, enforced by tightening government control of local authorities' HRAs, produced a situation where councillors were often responsible for council property that had increasing problems of disrepair, outdated fixtures and fittings, and poor local facilities. Council tenants saw landlord services decline year on year, despite paying their rents. At the same time, tenants were not immune to the attractions of the right to buy. Wanting to own your own home was promoted as natural and profitable. Consequently, the themes to be discussed in this chapter will cover:

- achieving a much-reduced council sector: the right to buy and stock transfer;
- tightening government control over council housing management through HRA subsidy arrangements;

- providing a housing management service under New Labour: a detailed example from LB Islington;
- evaluating whether the Decent Homes Standard has been met;
- the prospects for council housing under 'self-financing'.

Achieving a much-reduced council sector

In many areas of the country local authorities no longer own or manage council housing. The process of reduction (through individual sales) and transfer (to housing associations) has been continuous since 1980. Conservative and New Labour governments alike have worked to turn local authorities into 'enablers' rather than have them continue in a direct landlord role. However, replacing a direct, democratically controlled landlord role with 'enabling' does not seem adequate. In practice, local authorities have been equally as effective as housing associations in housing management, and the process of transfer certainly results in a democratic deficit. It is no surprise that these sales policies have become very controversial measures. Many local authorities, with the support of tenants, have campaigned to keep the service.

Against this background the Audit Commission (2009) found that most local authorities had not developed their 'enabling' role. Although it was promoted by successive governments, it was not a local authority priority in the years under New Labour. Unsurprisingly, this is one aspect of local authorities' work that is more than likely to disappear as a result of Coalition government reductions in the RSG for local authorities (see Chapter Three).

Nevertheless, governments' promotion of 'enabling' – creating the circumstances in which it might be seen as preferable, and the means to achieve the 'enabling' local authority – have led to a much-reduced sector. Table 5.1 shows the effects. One consequence of New Labour-supported right-to-buy sales and housing stock transfers is that council

Table 5.1: Dwellings by tenure in England in 1997 and 2011

England only	1997	Percentage of total stock
Housing association	985,000	4.8
Local authority	3,401,000	16.5
England only	**2011**	**Percentage of total stock**
Housing association	2,255,000	9.9
Local authority	1,726,000	7.6

Source: Pawson and Wilcox (2013, pp 122-3, Tables 17a and 17b)..

housing as a tenure diminished from an average of 16.5% of all housing in England in 1997 to just 7.9% in 2010 (and now stands at less than 7.6%). During the same time, the proportion of housing association rented homes grew from 4.8% to 9.6% and continues to grow.

The right to buy and housing stock transfer were the two main ways in which the council sector was effectively halved in size by a New Labour government over 13 years. Both measures had been inherited from the previous Conservative government.

The right to buy

The Conservative government's Housing Act 1980 offered tenants the chance to buy their council homes with very generous discounts on the sale price. As a consequence, 1.3 million council homes were sold to tenants in England from 1980 to 1997. The New Labour government that followed also envisaged a much smaller role for local authorities than had ever been the case before, with the right to buy (and council stock transfers to housing associations) used to secure this objective. Right-to-buy sales continued, with nearly 500,000 completed up to 2010. The same pattern occurred in the other countries of the UK.

Right-to-buy receipts of just over £40 billion were recorded by local authorities in the period 1980–2009 (£22 billion under the Conservatives up to 1997 and £18 billion under New Labour up to 2009, the latest figures available – see Pawson and Wilcox, 2011, Table 60). These capital receipts (see Chapter Three) had to be used in different ways by local authorities: to repay borrowing, to invest in repairs and improvements to council housing locally or, when 'pooled' nationally, to reduce public expenditure on housing. Capital receipts represent only the discounted sale price of council housing. The value of the accumulated discounts is not known. The average discount on a valuation of a council house in England was 50% (53% in London) in 1998/99. It would have been higher in previous years. This gives an indication of the large amount of public money spent in subsidising nearly two million tenants' desire to be owner-occupiers.

After 2002, right-to-buy discounts became less generous in some areas, following press stories of abuse of the system. It also became harder for tenants to obtain a mortgage, especially after 2007. In 2010 just under 3,000 council homes were sold under the right to buy, a considerable decline from the early days of Margaret Thatcher's policy, when half a million properties were sold in the five years to 1985 (Pawson and Wilcox, 2012, Table 20a, p 125).

The Prime Minister David Cameron has proposed a new initiative on the right to buy in the Coalition's *Housing Strategy* (DCLG, 2011c). The details were confirmed and launched in April 2012. The 'new' scheme simply has more generous discounts of up to £75,000 in order to revive sales. It is not yet known whether sales will increase but the government has spent nearly £1 million advertising it. In order to deflect criticism that selling off council houses/flats is irresponsible in a time of extreme housing shortages, the government has insisted that homes lost to the sector through sales can be replaced by new council homes for rent. The reality may turn out differently for a number of reasons, not least that the replacement council home has to be built within the Coalition government's 'affordable rent' programme (see Chapter Six for housing associations' responses to date).

Building new council housing to replace losses from the right to buy?

There never has been a 'like for like' replacement programme for rented homes sold to tenants, under either the Conservatives or New Labour. (The only exception has been that announced for the future by the Coalition, but it is hedged with difficulties.) Instead, subsidy for new council house building declined rapidly under the Conservatives from 1979 and under New Labour from 1997. The effect on the number of new homes built can clearly be seen in Table 5.2.

New Labour began to think differently about what local authorities might do, in its housing Green Paper *Homes for the future: more affordable, more sustainable* (CLG, 2007). Under a new Prime Minister, Gordon

Table 5.2: The decline in numbers of council homes built each year from 1980 to 2010

Year	Number
Conservatives, 1979–97	
1980	67,337
1991	For the first time, fewer than 10,000 (8,051)
1995	For the first time, fewer than 1,000 (782)
1997	290 (part of the Conservative legacy)
New Labour, 1997–2010	
1998	250
1999	For the first time, fewer than 100 (50)
2007	250 (a slow, steady increase)
2010	790 + 1,775 in 2011 (part of New Labour's legacy)

Source: Pawson and Wilcox (2012, p 119, Table 19b).

Brown, local authorities were encouraged to build, albeit with 'special purpose vehicles' and in partnership with other organisations. Numbers were still very small but the best results of this change of policy came just after the 2010 general election. The number of new council homes completed in that year continued a slow but positive change of direction that had been evident from 2007.

The Coalition government's alternative 'affordable rent' programme has been used by a handful of local authorities to start building new council homes again. This remains on small scale; most building for rent is still being undertaken by housing associations (see Chapter Six).

Local authorities may encounter difficulties if they try to replace council homes sold under the revived 2012 right to buy. The actual value of the capital receipt that they retain is likely to be very small. Several council homes may need to be sold in order to generate sufficient receipts to enable the local authority to borrow at a reasonable rate to build one new property for rent. In these circumstances, local authorities are not likely to be able to provide many replacement homes, and certainly not on a 'like for like' basis. If the receipts cannot be used in this way, the government has determined that they should be returned to the HCA to be recycled into other housing programmes. This may indeed be the Coalition's preferred objective, rather than providing replacement council housing. Through announcing the replacement programme, the Coalition government has deftly shifted responsibility for the decision about whether to build replacement housing onto the local authority (in an apparent example of localism).

If local authorities are to build council housing again on the scale required, they will need a range of different ways to finance this work. The 'affordable rent' programme does not work in most parts of the country, so different approaches will be needed to suit each local authority. This is beginning to be seen, following the move to 'self-financing' in 2012, and will be considered later.

The right to buy enabled the continued growth of owner-occupation, albeit often marginal owner-occupation (see Chapter Four). Over the same time, stock transfer transformed many local authorities and the housing association sector too (see Chapter Six).

Council housing stock transfers

Large-scale transfers under the Conservatives and New Labour

Initially, council stock transfers to housing associations were encouraged by the Conservative government following the Housing Act 1988, but relatively few were arranged. Housing associations were reluctant to be seen by local authorities as potentially predatory (Malpass and Mullins, 2002). Most of the 52 local authorities that showed an interest in transfers set up their own associations to receive the 245,000 homes that were transferred. These large-scale voluntary stock transfer associations (LSVTs) continued to be regarded as the 'local' association, in the early days at least. Few partial transfers were arranged in this period. Most transfers were in the south and west of England and involved small district councils. Table 5.3 shows the total housing stock involved and the costs during the Conservative governments of 1988–97.

Table 5.3: Large-scale stock transfers in England under the Conservative government, 1988–97

Financial years	Dwellings	Gross transfer price (£ million)	Partial transfers	Whole-stock transfers	All transfers	Loan facilities at transfer (£ million)	Set-up costs (£ million)
1988–1997 totals	245,705	2,292.2	9	52	61	4,041.5	114.6

Source: Data from Pawson and Wilcox (2011, p 182, Table 68a), drawing on the HCA's stock transfer dataset.

When New Labour came to power in 1997, £19 billion of repairs and improvement work were estimated to be outstanding, following years of council housing being deliberately starved of resources for political ends. The Conservative government from 1980 onwards had exercised increasing control over the diminishing resources available to local authorities to run their housing management services (outlined in the next section). New Labour's response to this problem was to devise a policy that continued stock transfers but linked them to what became known as the Decent Homes Standard. The New Labour government believed that the way of achieving the DHS in council housing would be primarily through stock transfer.

This policy and approach did not give local authorities genuine choice about their future. Stuart Hall has called this way of designing social policy New Labour's 'double shuffle' (Hall, 2003). Ostensibly, it appeared to be about tackling the repairs backlog in council housing; in reality, it was about the privatisation of public assets.

New Labour's first housing Green Paper *Quality and Choice* (DETR/ DSS, 2000) described a programme of annual transfers of up to 200,000 council homes. These would be supported by the government if tenants voted for the transfers. Conservative administrations had never attempted such an ambitious and politically difficult programme, but Tony Blair's view was that directly managed council housing was a 'flawed model' (Malpass, 2005, p 194).

The government argued that stock transfer would be likely to achieve the objective of the DHS by 2010, with relatively little impact on public expenditure. Housing associations could buy the housing stock and obtain private finance to undertake the repair and improvement work required. This investment would not be counted as public expenditure, given their status as private bodies. If local authorities wanted to retain and manage their council housing directly or their tenants voted against transfer, the DHS-related repair and improvement costs would have to be paid for from their own resources, not through government 'supported' borrowing, grants or an enhanced major repairs allowance in the HRA (see Chapter Three).

Table 5.4 shows what happened when New Labour established stock transfer as the main plank of its housing policy and set up a transfer programme with ambitious annual targets. The timing of transfers was carefully controlled by the DCLG, as sufficient money had to be available from lenders in the market when needed. It is worth noting

Table 5.4: Large-scale stock transfers in England under the New Labour government, 1997–2010

Financial years	Dwellings	Gross transfer price (£ million)	Partial transfers	Whole-stock transfers	All transfers	Loan facilities at transfer (£ million)	Set-up costs (£ million)
1997/98	32,982	259.7	11	5	16	682.2	14.1
1998/99	73,900	483.9	14	10	24	1,239.3	20.6
1999/00	97,385	658.7	13	13	26	1,512.4	48.6
2000/01	134,219	795.0	2	16	18	1,892.0	37.7
2001/02	35,390	377.7	1	7	8	647.5	15.7
2002/03	167,270	545.9	9	15	24	2,114.3	73.3
2003/04	38,635	140.8	3	7	10	409.5	16.5
2004/05	101,511	200.4	6	10	16	1,231.5	44.0
2005/06	46,653	114.8	11	8	19	807.0	15.3
2006/07	75,753	105.7	12	10	22	1,354.0	45.5
2007/08	93,594	244.1	13	18	31	3,183.9	38.8
2008/09	41,961	8.0	5	4	9	1,337.7	16.0
2009/10	23,575	5.6	3	3	6	447.7	8.9
Total	**962,828**	**3,940.3**	**103**	**126**	**229**	**16,859**	**395**

Source: Data from Pawson and Wilcox (2011, p 182, Table 68a), drawing on the HCA's stock transfer dataset.

that 126 local authorities transferred all their housing stock to new bodies: LSVTs or housing companies.

The housing company model was introduced so as to involve more councillors and tenants on the boards of transfer organisations as a way of building support for the transfer. New Labour later added ALMOs and the housing PFI to the range of organisations that it would consider acceptable for this work (see Chapter Three). This was another way of circumventing continued reluctance on the part of many local authorities, MPs and council tenants (House of Commons Council Housing Group, 2010).

Partial transfers under New Labour

By the early 2000s, whole stock transfers became politically difficult to achieve (especially in areas where a Defend Council Housing campaign group was active). A different approach emerged: piecemeal and specific to particular areas. This is evident in the number of partial transfers (103) that were undertaken. These often involved large council landlords (metropolitan authorities or London boroughs). These landlords preferred to use a range of alternatives to achieve the DHS. This might mean a number of partial stock transfers to new or existing associations or companies, a housing PFI and ALMOs. Direct management might be retained, but on a smaller scale than before. The example of LB Islington in this chapter is illustrative of this approach.

In total, nearly 1 million council homes were transferred to housing associations or housing companies under the New Labour government. The cost of transfer was nearly £4 billion to these new organisations, but they then went on to borrow over four times as much (£17 billion) to fund repairs and improvements, often beyond the somewhat basic DHS (Table 6.4).

'Overhanging debt' payments and 'gap funding' for large transfers

When a local authority sold its council housing it had to use the capital receipt from the sale to repay its outstanding housing debt and pay any 'breakage penalties' to the Public Works Loan Board for early repayment of loans received in the past. Some had to pay a Treasury levy on the sale too. This was a 20% surcharge payable by some local authorities to 'compensate' the Treasury for anticipated income foregone. By the end of 2008, more than £475 million had been 'creamed off' by the Treasury from transfer receipts in this way (Pawson and Mullins, 2010, p 63). Wealthier authorities, with smaller stocks of council housing, might find that they still had a large capital receipt left. They could use this for other local authority capital projects. Larger metropolitan authorities in the North and Midlands were not usually in this position. Many of these authorities found transfer not only politically unpalatable but also financially problematic.

The local authorities that remained as large direct landlords in the mid-2000s often had particularly poor-quality housing stock and its value might be very low. This affected them in different ways if they planned a stock transfer. There were problems:

- where the valuation of the council stock was lower than the amount of debt held by the local authority (that is, the repayments of principal and interest due on loans taken out to build council housing in the past). This was 'overhanging debt';
- where the finance needed to buy, improve and maintain the (former) council housing over the period of the LSVT's business plan (often calculated over 30 years) was more than the anticipated income from rents and any other income due over that time. 'Gap funding' was needed here.

New Labour had started to deal with the problem of 'overhanging debt' in 1999. Determined to achieve its policy objectives, the government extended these payments to partial transfers in 2004 on a pro-rata basis. By 2006, payments to clear remaining local authority housing debt had become relatively common and by 2008 totalled £3.6 billion in England alone (Pawson and Mullins, 2010, p 65).

Box 5.1: 'Overhanging debt' payments by government

By 2008, government had paid £3.6 billion in overhanging debt payments. Some of the biggest were:

- Liverpool £721 million;
- Bradford £183 million;
- Wakefield £149 million;
- Glasgow £909 million + £196 million in breakage costs + £27 million for the local authority's preparation, paid for by the Scottish Executive;
- All transfers in Wales by this time had involved overhanging debt payments and breakage costs totalling £323 million.

Source: Pawson and Mullins (2010, p 66)

'Gap funding' was introduced by New Labour in 2004 for housing stock transfers approved in the period 2004–06. By 2008 the government had paid over £600 million in 'gap funding'. Box 5.2 shows a number of large settlements that enabled transfers to proceed (Glasgow's being particularly expensive and contentious).

Box 5.2: 'Gap funding' by government

- Preston £48 million in 2005;
- Liverpool £130 million in 2008;
- Glasgow £787 million in 2003;
- In Wales, gap funding of £28 million had been paid to seven transfers by early 2009. This was handled by the Welsh Assembly Government. Forward projections indicated that £821 million would be needed. Payments were agreed for the first five years of each LSVT. Future requirements are subject to negotiation.

Source: Pawson and Mullins (2010, p 66)

The New Labour government's justification for the stock transfer programme was identified by Hal Pawson and David Mullins in DCLG sources:

> central government has pointed to the perceived benefit to the public purse of transferring risk to the private sector. Also [these sums] have been argued as justifiable in principle because of what are considered to be the benefits of separating the local authority strategic role from that of housing delivery. (Pawson and Mullins, 2010, p 65)

Table 5.5 shows the aggregate figures for stock transfers under the Conservative and New Labour governments.

Table 5.5: Stock transfers under Conservative and New Labour governments, 1988–2010

Financial years	Dwellings	Gross transfer price (£ million)	Partial transfers	Whole-stock transfers	All transfers	Loan facilities at transfer (£ million)	Set-up costs (£ million)
Grand total (from Tables 5.3 and 5.4)	1,208,533	6,232.5	112	178	290	20,900.5	509.6

Source: Data from Pawson and Wilcox (2011, p 182, Table 68a), drawing on the HCA's stock transfer dataset.

The amount of private finance that had to be borrowed by the new LSVTs was substantial. Over £6 billion was borrowed to buy the housing from local authorities (including the payment of over £500 million in fees for the consultants and professionals involved). Over £20 billion was raised (in loans and bond issues) to improve up to and beyond the DHS (Table 6.4).

LSVTs that were set up in the 1990s will have dealt with their promised programme of DHS-linked improvements and may have embarked on building programmes which would not otherwise have been possible if the local authorities concerned had not sold their council housing. Transfer organisations set up more recently will be focusing on DHS and energy-efficiency improvements to the exclusion of much else. LSVTs and housing companies have transformed the housing association sector, which has more than doubled in size in 13 years and now contains a very diverse mix of organisations. In that sense, government can no longer expect one policy response from this sector (as will be seen in Chapter Six).

Nevertheless, New Labour's justification that it was necessary to transfer 'risk' from public local authorities to private housing associations to undertake the work required is debateable. With 'supported' borrowing, many local authorities could have maintained. and improved council housing without the need to transfer it to new organisations. The issue for government was more one of what counted as public expenditure. It is not known how much government spending was devoted to this programme. The 'overhanging debt' and 'gap funding' problems discussed here were artificial and expensive creations of the transfer process. These payments were necessary only in order to ensure that transfers took place despite financial circumstances that would ordinarily have stopped them from proceeding. The ALMO programme outlined in Chapter Three showed that the New Labour government itself recognised that a local authority could ensure that the DHS was achieved albeit at 'arm's length'. But was it right that local authorities that managed their council housing directly received no additional financial help to achieve the DHS?

REFLECTION 5.1

Transferring council housing to associations and companies

New Labour's stock transfer policy was very controversial. What are its long-term implications for council housing?

Tightening government control over council housing management through HRA subsidy arrangements

Council housing survives, despite the incursions that the sector has faced since 1980. This section will look at how the housing management service has been financed within local authorities. Over the years, this has changed, usually in ways designed by central government to enable it to exercise more control over expenditure. The HRA has been central to these considerations. Income and expenditure related to the management and maintenance of council housing has to be recorded in this account. It is a ring-fenced account within the General Fund specifically dealing with this local authority service.

Changes that were wrought by the Conservative governments of 1979–97 will be considered first. These made it more difficult for many local authorities to maintain and improve their council housing. These financial arrangements provide one answer as to why some local authority council housing deteriorated to the extent that it did. New Labour built on the Conservatives' framework, establishing a tightening system of financial control between each local authority and central government. Its deficit subsidy system was complicated to administer and to understand and became unjustifiable as more authorities fell into 'negative subsidy' and had to pay large sums to the Treasury each year.

From April 2012, council housing in England has become 'self-financing'. The degree of control that central government exercised in the past has now disappeared. The prospects for council housing under these new financial arrangements will be considered later in this section.

The Conservatives' tightening control

The Housing Act 1980 subsidy system

The Housing Act 1980 introduced a subsidy system for council housing that was 'simple, elegant and difficult to oppose' (Malpass and Murie, 1987, p 194). The new subsidy system overlay a multiplicity of rents charged at that time for different properties in different local authorities. In the Conservative government's use of notional rent increases to tighten control, Malpass and Murie thought the new system represented 'an unprincipled attack on general subsidies' for council housing (Malpass and Murie, 1987, p 194).

At this time, local authorities could decide the council rents they wanted to charge on different properties and any annual rent increases. Councillors also might decide to supplement the HRA with money from the local rates (a predecessor to the council tax) to keep rents low or to invest in additional improvements to the housing stock (see Chapter Nine). The 1980 system simply gave the government power to assume specific rent increases (that is, they used notional rents not the actual rents charged by local authorities). These notional rents were then used in the calculation of the amount of subsidy that a local authority would receive. Authorities that did not want to keep up with these notional rent increases found that the amount of subsidy they received each year to help run the service gradually declined (as the government was using them to calculate the subsidy due). By the mid-1980s, many local authorities received no subsidy from central government at all. Their council housing service became reliant on rental income and any contribution that might be made from the local rates. Many local authorities struggled to undertake essential repairs, maintenance and improvements to their stock (Mullins and Murie, 2006, pp 161–3). During the 1980s, differences between Labour- and Conservative-controlled local authorities became more noticeable. Often, Labour-controlled authorities tried to be more financially creative so as to avoid the worst restrictions of Conservative antagonism towards expenditure on council housing, but there was only so much that could be done within the financial system operating at the time (Davis and Wigfield, 2010).

The Local Government and Housing Act 1989 subsidy system

The Local Government and Housing Act 1989 was the Conservative government's solution to what Prime Minister Margaret Thatcher interpreted as Labour councils' defiance of spending limits. This Act was important, as it reintroduced the central government control over HRAs that had been lost when local authorities moved out of subsidy under the previous system. It established the ring fence around the HRA, which is still in place today. This legislation introduced a single HRA subsidy system and gave central government more control again by changing how subsidy was calculated. This can be seen in Box 5.3, where the housing part of the subsidy (that related to the housing management service itself) and the rent rebate part (government reimbursement of housing benefit payments made by the local authority to council tenants) are clearly separate. This separation was introduced with the 1989 legislation. Why was this important?

> ## Box 5.3: The 1989 Act and a single HRA subsidy system
>
> - The HRA subsidy was made up of a 'housing element' and a 'rent rebate element'.
> - The 'housing element' of the subsidy was calculated by the government each year. It was based on standard allowance figures for management and maintenance, plus payment for any outstanding debt charges arising from borrowing by the authority for council house building in the past. From 2001 onwards a major repairs allowance was included.
> - The 'rent rebate element' was simply reimbursement for housing benefit payments made to council tenants each year by the local authority.

The 1989 Act enabled the Conservative government to identify those local authorities that were generating rental 'surpluses' by charging rents that were higher than the levels expected by central government. It could do this because the two elements that made up HRA activity – transactions in relation to housing management and transactions in relation to rent rebates (housing benefit) – now had to be separately identified in the HRA. Given the Conservative government's determination to exercise more control over local authority expenditure (especially where the local authority was Labour controlled), the ability to identify rental 'surplus' was central.

The new arrangements meant that any local authority raising rents above the limits that the government wanted would be bound to generate a 'surplus'. The government decided that this amount could now be deducted from the 'rent rebate element' before the amount of money reimbursed to the local authority was paid. This was extremely controversial and did not go unchallenged. Why was this?

- Local authorities paid housing benefit to eligible council tenants but this was a welfare benefit, locally provided on behalf of the DSS (now the DWP). As such, local authorities expected to be reimbursed by the government in full.
- The deduction of any so-called 'surplus' from the amount of housing benefit due to be reimbursed to the local authority meant that better-off council tenants who paid the rent and did not claim housing benefit were actually paying the costs of housing benefit due to those tenants whose incomes were lower and who did need housing benefit. They were effectively paying an amount for housing benefit reimbursement that should have been paid by the government, as the scheme was provided for out of general taxation.

- Tenants launched the Daylight Robbery Campaign to change this 'tenant tax'.

The 1989 Act was also important because it introduced a ring fence around the HRA. What did this mean in practice? The ring fence operated so that if the HRA generated any surplus at all (even after the deductions against the rent rebate amount), then that surplus had to be passed over to the General Fund. It could be used for general services; it could not be used to improve the housing management service for council tenants. At the same time, the ring fence meant that the local authority could no longer make any contribution to the HRA from the rates.

Box 5.4: The 1989 Act and the ring-fenced HRA

- Payments could not be made into the HRA from the General Fund. In some local authorities, councillors had always contributed money from the rates to the HRA to pay for repairs or to keep rents low. This was no longer possible.
- Surpluses had to be transferred to the General Fund. If there was any money left in the HRA at the end of the financial year, it could not be left in the HRA to be used the following year.

As can be seen, the way in which this ring fence worked did not protect the housing management service. It operated to restrict council spending on the housing management service more effectively, and practically led to the deterioration of services to tenants. The Conservative government wanted this new system because it gave it greater ability to control and reduce public expenditure on housing; the system implicitly encouraged council tenants to buy, as they were certainly being squeezed as tenants. This new subsidy system particularly adversely affected larger urban authorities that might have a lot of housing, significant disrepair problems but less to spend on repairs and improvements. Many local authorities in the South, with fewer problems and under Conservative or Liberal Democratic control, decided at this time that transferring the council stock was the way to go. Their argument was that stock transfer might protect council housing from further right-to-buy sales, provide improvements for tenants and increase the amount of rented housing available locally through new building. It might also generate a healthy capital receipt for the local authority that could use it to build other facilities.

In 1996 the Conservative government introduced new ways in which the 'rent rebate element' was to be calculated in the HRA. This was through a system of 'rent rebate subsidy limitation' (Box 5.5). Up to that point, local authorities still had some leeway in deciding what their council rents should be, but this system of guideline rents acted as another centrally imposed restraint.

> ### Box 5.5: Rent rebate subsidy limitation
>
> • This was made up of a series of guidelines for rents for different kinds of property.
> • Local authorities received the rent rebate element of the HRA subsidy in full only for those rents that were at or below the central government-determined guideline rent levels.

Local authorities that charged more than the guideline amounts would not receive subsidy for the 'excess', even if tenants were being paid full housing benefit by the local authority for the rent at this level. From this time and in these circumstances, local authorities really had little choice but to keep within the government's guideline figures when setting their rents each year.

New Labour's tightening control

Moving the 'rent rebate element' from the HRA

New Labour inherited this system. Surprisingly, it kept it for some years, gradually developing it through financial regulations. It finally consolidated all of these and developed the subsidy system further in the Local Government Act 2003. Two significant changes were introduced in this Act.

The first related to the 'rent rebate element' of the HRA subsidy system. This was housing benefit reimbursement from the DWP to the local authority. The New Labour government wanted to correct the impression that better-off council tenants were helping to pay for the housing benefit of poorer tenants. Housing benefit was moved out of the HRA calculations (Box 5.6). In that sense, the Daylight Robbery Campaign had succeeded.

> ### Box 5.6: The 'rent rebate element' moved to the General Fund
>
> • The 'rent rebate element' of the HRA subsidy system was transferred out of the HRA.
> • It was moved to the General Fund for accounting purposes.

- Council tenants were now to be treated, for rent rebate reimbursement, in the same way as private tenants.

Establishing a deficit subsidy system

The second change had the most impact on the HRA. A deficit subsidy system was established to enable central government to control 'surpluses' and redistribute them between local authority landlords. The 2003 deficit subsidy HRA system was supposed to be clearer and fairer, but there were always disagreements about the distribution of 'positive subsidy' between local authorities each year. For example, London boroughs often felt that the government was using calculations that favoured the North or, alternatively, that the government was squeezing local authority subsidies to favour housing associations. Box 5.7 provides a bare outline of the system, based on central government 'notional' calculations of what each local authority required.

> ### Box 5.7: A 'deficit subsidy' calculated through a 'notional' HRA
>
> - From 2003 onwards, central government used a 'notional' HRA calculation each year, rather than actual local authority HRA figures in accounts, to calculate the subsidy entitlement of each local authority.
> - Local authorities were told by the DCLG in December of each year what their entitlement would be for the forthcoming financial year, in time for budgets to be prepared.
> - If a local authority was in surplus in the notional HRA, it was expected to pay that surplus to central government from its actual HRA. This amount was called 'negative subsidy'.
> - If a local authority was in deficit in the notional HRA, it received a 'positive subsidy' amount from government that was credited to its HRA and was treated as income for that year.

For those unaware of the intricacies of the subsidy system, it was easy to claim that 'efficient' councils were subsidising those that were 'inefficient', but there was more to the situation than this. Guideline rents used by the government in the notional HRA calculations increased each year much faster than management and maintenance allowances. This pushed increasing numbers of local authorities into surplus in their 'notional' HRA calculations. In reality, this meant that tenants in these local authorities were paying steadily increasing rents but not seeing improved services locally, as the 'notional' surplus calculated for their authority became a very real 'negative subsidy' payment to the Treasury each year.

It also encouraged a simplistic view that those authorities that were 'debt free' and paying 'negative subsidy' were subsidising those authorities that received 'positive subsidy' and that were assumed to be profligate with resources. This argument revealed ignorance of history. It is easy to forget, in the current climate, that many local authorities were the major builders of rented housing in the past, encouraged by Conservative as well as Labour governments to borrow and build on a scale unimaginable today (see Chapter One). Any 'debt' figure is the cumulative cost of borrowing and represents the costs of investment in rented housing, which has varied depending on a local authority's circumstances. The purpose of this subsidy system was to ensure that the historic costs of council housing could be met by all local authorities, with those with more needs being assisted by those with fewer. Unfortunately, its complexity, and the reality of the majority of authorities paying 'positive subsidy' each year despite some pressing local needs, undermined its legitimacy. It became increasingly hard to justify it and New Labour started investigating alternatives from the mid-2000s. These will be considered in the last section of this chapter.

A local authority's HRA in the mid-2000s

The London Borough of Islington's (LB Islington) HRA from 2006/07 is used in this section as an example of the way that a local authority might fund its housing management service in the mid-2000s under this deficit subsidy system. It gives a flavour of the complexity and range of issues that had to be considered in financing a council housing management service, including the issue of 'positive subsidy'. The service was affected by many aspects of New Labour's approach to council housing. At this time, Islington had a three-pronged housing strategy: working with an ALMO and a housing PFI and undertaking a partial stock transfer. The detail drawn from accounts is presented here with discussion afterwards, focusing on the DHS, the attainment of which was particularly important at this time.

Arm's-length management – Homes for Islington

In 2006/07 the ALMO Homes for Islington provided the management service to the 25,500 council tenants in the borough. It was established in 2004 in the third round of the government's programme. At the time, it was one of the biggest ALMOs, at 39,278 properties. In that year it obtained an additional £156 million from the government's DHS programme to undertake DHS work: new kitchens and bathrooms, new windows and roofs, improved home security and damp-proofing and insulation work. The local authority had also received funding for the ALMO's work through the Major Repairs Allowance (MRA) in the HRA. The MRA was introduced in 2001/02 and represented the estimated long-term average amount of capital spending necessary to keep a local authority's stock in reasonable condition. Each authority had a different stock profile and this allowance reflected that. Although it was paid as part of the subsidy arrangements for the HRA, it was effectively a capital resource to be spent on building repairs and improvements each year.

The private finance initiative

The first housing PFI in LB Islington was set up in 2006 to refurbish 2,900 rented and 1,200 leasehold homes. This included many of the borough's 'street properties', scattered across the borough in mixed-tenure streets and roads outside of its large council estates. These were very popular but in serious disrepair. At the time, the contract was for repairs and improvements to achieve the DHS by 2010/11 and to manage the properties for the next 16 years. That contract was worth £165 million. A number of different PFI contracts are now running and the contractors will be providing management and maintenance, including planned maintenance, for council tenants within these contracts for the next 30 years.

A number of PFI contractors will also be undertaking major external repair work on leaseholders' property. Islington's leaseholders are former council tenants. They live in blocks of flats that require regular planned maintenance work. Leaseholders are protected from such expenditure for the first five years of their ownership. That period has now expired for many, and major repair work is due. They will have to pay for this work and will be billed for it, or it will be reflected in increased service charges. The leaseholders may find the cost of the work problematic.

Generally, the PFI contracts will prove very expensive for the government in the long term. The revenue payments due from local authorities that have PFI contracts with the private sector will have to be acknowledged as public expenditure, even if the initial capital investment by the PFI contractor is 'off balance sheet' and invisible to public accounts.

Partial stock transfer

The local authority also transferred some of its estates to housing associations in partial stock transfers. These properties needed a range of remodelling, demolition and new building, which associations could undertake more effectively. The way in which this might be done by housing associations will be considered in Chapter Six.

Islington's budget

The detail in Islington's budget that is illustrated in Table 5.6 will have appeared in the ALMO's accounts, as it managed the service on behalf of the authority up to 2012. The authority's HRA will have recorded the ALMO's management fee for this work (which is subsumed here in the 'general management' item of expenditure in this detailed record).

That said, this financial detail was made available in this form for the general public to understand what was being funded, and it provides

Table 5.6: LB Islington's HRA budget for 2006/07, including rents, service charges and other fees and charges

HRA – Main Account	Budget 2006/07 (£000s)
Expenditure:	
General Management	51,683
PFI Payments	13,289
Special Services	4,193
Repair and Maintenance	26,328
Rents, Rates, Taxes and Other Charges	2,412
Revenue Contributions to Capital	19,101
Capital Charges,	74,315
Contingencies, Bad Debt Provision and Smoothing Fund	3,199
Growth	1,000
Gross Expenditure	**195,520**
Income:	
Dwelling Rents	(100,120)
Unpooled Service Charges	(7,971)
Reception Centres – Rents	(1,374)
Income from Commercial Rents	(4,540)
Heating and Hot Water Charges	(1,547)
Leaseholder – Service Charges and Major Works	(11,830)
Other Charges for Services and Facilities	(5,594)
HRA Subsidy (including PFI Credits)	(61,489)
Interest Received and General Fund Shared Costs	(1,055)
Gross Income	**(195,520)**
In Year (Surplus)/Deficit	**0**

Source: Islington LBC Service and Financial Plan 2006/07–2008/09, integrated into annual Statement of Accounts available online. All years' accounts and other supplementary documents are available online. See Islington LBC (2011a).

an insight into the work in the borough. A commentary on specific items follows.

HRA expenditure – points to consider

General management

The sum of £51.7 million included the £1.8 million fee to the ALMO, Homes for Islington (HFI), that ran the service on behalf of the council at that time. It included staff salaries and offices and equipment to manage council housing in the borough. The cost of providing the service increased each year by a specific inflation figure, but generally costs were contained for the duration of the contract with HFI. General management costs declined in some years as contracts for part of the stock were allocated to other budget headings, depending on the work being undertaken.

PFI payments to PFI contractors and payments to the Smoothing Fund

The payment of £13 million to the three PFI contractors was possible because government approved these schemes and made PFI credits available to meet these revenue payments via the General Fund. A contribution of £1.8 million to the Smoothing Fund in 2006/07 was to build up a surplus at the beginning of each PFI contract. The Fund will be used to deal with anticipated deficits in future years that are due to changes in the profile of payments, income and savings.

Repairs and maintenance

In Islington this figure fell, compared to previous years, as there were fewer properties to maintain in 2006/07. Some stock had been transferred to other landlords, there were right-to-buy sales and property was transferred to the PFI headings in anticipation of DHS work starting. Planned maintenance on 5,000 homes in two PFI contracts was the responsibility of the PFI contractor.

Revenue contributions to capital

Homes for Islington, the local authority's ALMO, received money through the MRA to undertake improvement work to ensure properties met the DHS. It also had a contractual obligation to the council to raise money through revenue 'efficiencies'. These funds were used to pay for minor infrastructure work on estates.

Capital charges

This £74.3 million was the payment of principal and interest due for the historic costs of borrowing to build and improve the council stock.

Contingencies and bad debt provision

These were reduced in 2006/07 because collection of rent arrears had improved. An amount was set aside to deal with the rising costs of gas and electricity for heating and hot water provided in the communal areas of some schemes.

HRA income

Rents

The rents paid by council tenants were the main source of income for the HRA, at £100.1 million. In 2006/07 the average rent increased by £3.43 a week from £70.65 to £74.08 (an increase of just over 4%), in line with the government's rent restructuring formula (see Chapter Nine). In Islington, 74% of tenants were claiming full or partial housing benefit. The increase raised an additional £2.7 million for the HRA.

Unpooled service charges

Islington 'unpooled' its service charges in April 2003, so from that time tenants paid for services as separate items. They paid for caretaking and estate services if they received them. There were charges for heating and hot water for some tenants. In 2006/07 the charges for most services increased by 3.2%. Heating and hot water increased by 4.9%, reflecting the council's costs to purchase electricity and gas.

Leaseholder service charges and major works

Leaseholders were former council tenants who had bought their council home (usually a flat or maisonette). They paid service charges, insurance and for major works (for example, a contribution to the replacement of the external cladding on a block of flats). Islington was undertaking a programme of major works to improve these properties, with the assistance of the PFI contractors. Service charges would increase once works had been completed.

Other rents

Reception centres and commercial properties (like shops on estates) also generated rental income for the HRA.

Other charges

Short-life users with minimal rights to occupy paid a fee in Islington for their occupation of housing that would otherwise be empty. Most was due to be refurbished or demolished in the near future, when they would leave. Garages and parking spaces also generated income for the HRA.

Positive housing subsidy

The annual HRA subsidy settlement for Islington of £61.4 million in 2006/07 was recorded in this Plan as 'poor'. The 'positive subsidy' amount represented a reduction of £0.5 million over the previous year because assumed rental income exceeded management and maintenance allowances in the 'notional' HRA calculations. At the same time, the amount that the government paid through 'positive subsidy' in recognition of Islington's debt was increased. PFI credits were also included in this amount. Support for the capital programme, undertaken by Homes for Islington, also fell because of reductions in the MRA. The MRA was one route through which government channelled support for ALMOs' work to achieve the DHS (see Chapter Three).

The DHS achieved in part

The example of Islington shows the different ways in which local authorities pursued the objective of achieving the DHS for council tenants by 2010, the target date set by New Labour. It was not alone in using a variety of strategies to do so. It set up an ALMO and housing PFIs, and arranged selective transfers to local housing associations of stock that it could not realistically refurbish. Many larger local authorities have followed a similar path.

More generally, Table 5.7 shows the progress made by local authorities in working to comply with the DHS by 2009 (the most recent figures

Table 5.7: English housing conditions – the Decent Homes Standard

| | Unfitness based* | | | HHSRS based* | | |
| | 2001 | | | 2009 | | |
	Decent	Non decent	All	Decent	Non decent	All
Local authority	58.2	41.7	100.00	72.9	27.1	100.00
All social sector	61.1	38.9	100.00	76.8	23.2	100.00

Source: Derived from Pawson and Wilcox (2012, p 130, Table 23b), using the English House Condition Survey Headline Report and the English Housing Survey Headline Report 2009–10.

Note: * To meet the fitness standard, properties had to be in a reasonable state of repair, have reasonably modern facilities and services and provide a reasonable level of thermal comfort. This standard was replaced in 2006 by the Housing Health and Safety Rating System (HHSRS), which considers the level of hazards in a property.

available). It is clear that although a lot has been achieved, by 2009 some 27% of the stock still needed to be modernised to the DHS standard. The date for achieving this standard has retreated to 2015, and may be met by then. Further allocations of funding for council landlords in 2011 and the possibilities of 'self-financing' make this more likely.

Referring back to the example of Islington, it is likely that it could have undertaken much of the DHS work itself, but the way in which funding options for DHS work were structured by the New Labour government prevented this. LB Islington was not alone in its approach. At their peak, there were nearly 80 ALMOs working in 66 different local authorities. As can be seen from Table 5.8, the additional funding available to ALMOs made it easier for them to reach the target. It was also much easier for them to enhance the basic DHS with additional work because they received additional money through the MRA and the local authority could also arrange 'supported' borrowing to pay for the work that was needed (see Chapter Three).

Table 5.8: Views on the standard of 'Decent Homes' work by comparison with actual DHS criteria

Social landlord type	Similar (%)	A little higher (%)	Much higher (%)
ALMO	8	70	23
Local authority with retained council housing	50	35	15

Source: Derived from Pawson and Wilcox (2012, p 63, Table 2.2.1), using data from the National Audit Office (2010).

ALMOs no longer have protected additional grant funding for DHS work. Any landlord with more than 10% 'non-decent' stock awaiting repair and improvement work could bid for funds from the Decent Homes Backlog programme run by the HCA in 2011 (see Chapter

Three).The programme declined substantially: the 2010 CSR set aside £1.6 billion over the years to 2014/15. Those landlords that were unsuccessful or that had less than 10% of poor-quality stock (and so could not bid for extra funds) will have to fund the work from their own resources. The HRA is now self-financing, so there is a better prospect that they will be able to do this.

Given the financial constraints within which all landlords are currently working, LB Islington decided to terminate the ALMO contract and bring the management function (and staff) back in-house. The original contract with Homes for Islington was due to run until 2014, but was ended in April 2012 after consultation with tenants, leaseholders and staff. This saved the authority £1.8 million in management fees each year. However, the real catalyst for this decision was the introduction in 2012 of a 'self-financing' regime for all local authorities that still owned and managed council housing (Islington, 2011b). The prospects for local authorities as direct landlords looked brighter: as Islington's press office announced: 'Islington Housing Comes Home'.

'Self-financing' – the future for council housing

By 2007 it had become clear to the New Labour government that the HRA deficit subsidy system had become discredited, over-complicated and unsustainable in the long term. Two-thirds of local authorities were in 'negative subsidy', making contributions to the Treasury each year. It was calculated that the realignment of council rents, following rent restructuring, would mean even fewer 'positive subsidy' authorities in the future. Politically, this was unsustainable.

New Labour's proposals

In 2009 the New Labour government announced its provisional consultation proposals (CLG, 2009a). Many thought that they were generous, though some authorities were not happy about the way in which outstanding debt (borrowing secured for council house building in the past) was treated in this consultation. Local authorities were given many months to calculate whether or not the proposals would work for them. During this period the Local Government Association (LGA) and some local authorities determinedly campaigned for the accumulated debts to be written off by the government. They argued that this had been done for LSVTs (the 'overhanging debt' payments), and so should be done for councils that still managed council housing.

Box 5.8: New Labour's 2009 consultation proposals

- The debt (outstanding borrowing) held by local authorities would be redistributed between all local authorities that retained council housing. Each authority would be expected to agree to take over debt that was manageable for them, on the presumption that they would need to borrow in the future to build or improve their housing.
- There would be an increase in MRA that would help those local authorities still working to achieve the DHS.
- There would be an increase in 'supported' borrowing to enable the achievement of the DHS.
- There would be increased funding through the HCA's Affordable Housing Programme for new council house building.

Source: CLG (2009a)

By 2010, local authorities had responded individually and collectively, through the LGA, the Chartered Institute of Housing (CIH) and the House of Commons Council Housing Group (HCCHG). Tenants responded too, through tenants' federations, the CIH and Defend Council Housing (DCH). The majority of local authorities felt that New Labour's self-financing proposals were acceptable. They offered a positive future, especially in relation to building more council housing and refurbishment. The HCCHG and DCH accepted them too, although they would have preferred a complete debt write-off. This was never an option for New Labour, possibly because of the cost and the country's worsening economic situation.

The consultation period was followed by a prospectus, *Council housing: A real future*, in March 2010 (CLG, 2010a). A more detailed self-financing model was provided.

Box 5.9: New Labour's 2010 self-financing model for council housing

- Councils would keep their rental and service charge income.
- Councils would keep their capital receipts in full and the interest derived from investing the receipts from right-to-buy council house sales and sales of land.
- Councils would be expected to build council housing again on a reasonable scale. They would be enabled to obtain loan finance for this through a recalculation of the value of their existing stock.

Source: CLG (2010a)

Local authorities had to accept their share of what was then calculated to be £25 billion of outstanding debt associated with borrowing in the past to build council housing, but rental income would increase. The government specified that rent restructuring would continue, with convergence occurring between council and housing association rents in 2015/16, increasing council rents to near market levels. Management, maintenance and major repair allowances would increase up to 2012, giving local authorities more money in the short term. However, New Labour decided to retain the power to restrict local authority borrowing. Local authorities would not be able to exceed the borrowing levels calculated in this proposed 'once and for all' settlement (a reflection again of government concern about public expenditure).

This self-financing model gave local authority finance staff the opportunity to make detailed calculations for their authorities. Councillors then decided whether or not the local authority should agree to this set of proposals. It was assumed that New Labour would move quickly to institute the new arrangements if there was consensus, but the general election intervened. Would this mean the end of all this hard work and consultation activity?

The Coalition government's approach

The Coalition government inherited the review, including the self-financing proposals. It decided to extend the review period and then reach its own decisions about the future, although it indicated that it was inclined to look favourably on 'self-financing', as this appeared to accord with its emphasis on 'localism'. A consultation paper on social housing, *Local decisions: A fairer future for social housing*, was published in November 2010 (CLG, 2010b) but the consultation period was only six weeks. This was followed by an implementation paper in 2011 (DCLG, 2011b). The main differences between New Labour's proposals and those of the Coalition were:

- an increased debt figure to be distributed among local authorities still in the system;
- the retention of the ring fence around the HRA;
- a lack of emphasis on new council house building.

In the event, the Coalition pursued its model determinedly. Local authorities with council housing became 'self-financing' from April 2012. The details are contained in Box 5.10.

Box 5.10: The Coalition's 2012 self-financing model for council housing

- The redistribution of £30 billion of 'debt' between local authorities as a 'once-and-for-all' redistribution has been completed. Some authorities have taken on more 'debt', while others have less.
- Most local authorities borrowed from the PWLB to buy out the historic borrowing ('debt') held collectively in the system by the government.
- The HRA remains ring fenced.
- Local authorities are now self-financing but their borrowing is limited by a government cap.
- Capital receipts money from council house sales will be split between the government (75%) and the local authority (25%*).
- It is not assumed that there will be much new council house building in this model.
- Management, maintenance and major repairs allowances payable in the last year of the old system were increased by the government to cover historic less-than-inflation settlements in the past.

Source: DCLG (2011b)

Note: * This is now 30%.

Local authority HRAs became 'self-financing' in April 2012 and the 171 involved can now plan their borrowing and new building independently of some of the constraints of the old system. The government worked out which local authorities should be allocated 'debt' and which not by considering the current level of support being provided within the old HRA system and the detail of an authority's 30-year business plan. A decision was then made as to the level of debt that the local authority could support in the new system (see DCLG, 2011b; CIH, 2011b). This was a very important calculation for the local authority. A majority (136) took on more debt than before: they have their existing borrowing to service, and the new amount that they took on when debt was redistributed between all the local authorities in the system in 2012. The 35 local authorities that are now 'debt free' may not have had any debt before and they have not been given any as part of this settlement.

Local authority HRAs now work to 30-year business plans. There are plans involving more detail covering shorter periods of time approved by councillors. In reality, each local authority has a different profile. Many are now responsible for greater borrowing (more 'debt') than they had in the old subsidy system. Far fewer authorities have less borrowing or none. This will affect what they can do in the short and longer term. How are different local authorities responding to these changed circumstances? It is impossible to generalise. There are some differences already, relating to rents policy and new building.

Local authorities still have to work within the rent-restructuring regime that is due to see convergence of rents between housing associations and local authorities for similar property by 2016. The debt settlement in April 2012 used that system to calculate estimates of future rental income. However, the Retail Prices Index (RPI) in September 2011 was 5.6% so individual settlements may have over-estimated the likely income from rents as inflation has fallen since then. That said, the system of rent restructuring will still lead to rent increases that are in far in excess of the increases in personal or benefit income that most tenants can expect.

Rental income is of paramount importance now. A local authority will need to agree rent increases each year that enable it to manage the service effectively. Whether it will then be possible to generate additional borrowing (for example, for outstanding DHS work) will depend on the level of revenue (mainly but not exclusively derived from rental income generated each year) and the local authority's specific borrowing cap (see Box 5.10).

If local authorities have some leeway to borrow additional funds in this way, each one then will have to make its own decisions about priorities, for example, the need to finish DHS work or to provide enhancements to that work (for example, in relation to energy efficiency). Others may want to build more council houses as quickly as possible so as to respond to growing homelessness. Given that authorities had prepared detailed business plans, it was unfortunate that the Prime Minister announced the enhancement of the right-to-buy scheme only a few weeks before the changeover to 'self-financing' in April 2012. The potential loss of income represented by more council house sales (lost rental revenue) and increased discounts (minimal receipts for the local authority) has meant less confidence for local authorities in their financial plans. These moves may lead to some local authorities deciding to transfer housing stock to housing associations, cooperatives or community-owned organisations (this being a favourite of the Coalition government under the 'Big Society' banner), but for the present this trend appears to be declining. Instead, local authorities are still working out what may be possible under the new arrangements.

Further reading

To keep up to date on the position of local authorities it is important to check key websites, including the Local Government Association's website, local authority websites and the Red Brick blog for current commentary on a range of housing issues.

The website of the Local Government Association – www.local.gov.uk/ – has discussion documents, reports and e-bulletins on a wide range of local authority matters, including 'Finance and localism' and 'Environment, planning and housing'.

Each local authority will have available online all HRA Statement of Accounts and other papers that are useful. For example, in Sheffield the local authority gathers all of this information under 'Budgets and finance' on its website. The HRA information is available on: https://www.sheffield.gov.uk/search-result.html?queryStr=HRA. This includes the Statement of Accounts for the HRA and papers such as 'The future of council housing' (from 14 June 2012), detailing the planning required to bring an ALMO back in-house.

For discussion on the prospects of local authorities building council housing again see:

John Perry (2012) *Let's get building – the case for local authority investment in rented homes to help drive economic growth*, Scarborough: National Federation of ALMOs with ARCH, CIH, LGA and in association with CWAG.

John Perry and Ben Taylor (2013) 'A resurgence in English council housebuilding?' in Pawson, H. and Wilcox, S., *UK Housing Review 2013*, Coventry: CIH, Heriot Watt University and the University of York, pp 21-8.

The Red Brick blog is a site for progressive housing debate: http://redbrickblog.wordpress.com/. It has posts commenting on current housing issues, with a great deal of information and connections to other sites.

There are a number of other organisations that provide information and advice but membership is required to obtain these services. These include the Chartered Institute of Housing, Housing Quality Network and CIPFA.

SIX

Housing associations

Introduction

The term 'housing association' covers a wide range of organisations. It can include small associations and housing trusts (like York Housing Association), large-scale voluntary stock transfer organisations (like New Charter Housing Trust) or, increasingly, groups of associations that appear to be independent of each other but that are in fact linked. For example, Your Housing Group has resulted from the merger of Arena Housing Group (with six subsidiaries) and Harvest Housing Group (which included seven other associations in its group structure). Associations may be small: 30% have no paid staff and 80% have fewer than 100 homes to manage. A relative few are very large: 1% have over 10,000 homes. Stock transfer associations (or companies) are likely to be big, with more than 500 staff. In the late 1980s there were approximately 475,000 association homes for rent. Now the figure is just over two million.

The work of housing associations will be considered by looking at:

- some key financial features of associations and the tension between commercial and welfare-oriented values;
- housing management in Leafy Glades Housing Association (Leafy Glades HA) – a medium-sized housing association working in 2011/12;
- financing new rented homes and the changing relationship between public grant and different kinds of private finance or private contribution.

Some key features and principles

Can they still be 'moulded' by governments?

Until 1988 many associations occupied a semi-public position, working closely with local authorities, but Conservative Prime Minister Margaret Thatcher wanted them to become part of a new 'independent rented sector'. Following the Housing Act 1988, which enabled associations to use private finance as well as public grant to develop housing, the Conservatives' 'independent rented sector' was made up of housing associations and private landlords.

Twenty-five years later, the sector is made up of housing associations, transfer housing companies and private developers. The way associations have been described has changed too – from 'housing associations' to 'registered social landlords' (RSLs) to 'registered providers' (including private sector developers) to 'private registered providers' (including registered social landlords and large private landlords that provide social housing).

In the 1970s, 1980s and 1990s it was clear that governments of different political persuasions all felt that they could 'mould' associations. They shaped them via legislation and by changing grant availability for new building in ways that fitted with their own political view of what was required: small-scale urban renewal in the 1970s, a slowly growing and less expensive 'independent rented sector' in the 1990s and, from 2000 onwards, a larger independent rented sector with LSVTs.

Today, the big associations now operate largely beyond the wishes of government. Others see themselves as social enterprises, using their surpluses for wider social objectives in addition to the provision of rented housing. Within this variety, what are some of the key features of associations?

Growth

Most of the growth of housing associations since 1989 has been driven by stock transfer (53%), not new house building (see HCA/TSA, 2011, p 10). New house building remains at a very low level, mainly because successive governments have not seen this as a priority.

The scale of surpluses

'Surpluses' (profits) amounted to £609 million in 2009/10 for associations with over 1,000 properties. Accumulated surpluses up to and including that year amounted to £5.5 billion (Pawson and Wilcox, 2012, Table 71a). Some surpluses have been invested and used later to help to pay for new rented housing.

Designated and restricted reserves

These amounted to £1.6 billion in 2009/10 for associations with over 1,000 properties (Pawson and Wilcox, 2012, Table 71a). An association will have a sinking fund to pay for major repairs and this will be a 'designated reserve'. A 'restricted reserve' is one that can be used only for a specified purpose. A good example of the use of a restricted reserve is where a developer's financial contribution to the association in lieu of building rented housing in a new housing estate (which may be a planning requirement) is placed in such a reserve until it is needed to build rented housing somewhere else.

The tension between commercial and welfare values

There has been a noticeable shift away from a 'welfare ethos' and towards a commercial or private sector culture. In this environment, associations take more notice of the markets in determining priorities than of anything else. As the Coalition government's planned reductions in tenants' housing and welfare benefits take effect (see Chapter Ten) the tension between the associations' financial interests and the survival of many of their tenants will become palpable.

The 'eye of the storm' will be rents. There are two significant and retrograde changes to the housing benefit system that the Coalition has introduced and that will seriously affect association tenants and associations as landlords: actual reductions in housing benefit and the abolition of rent direct.

Reductions in housing benefit entitlement

Although association rents are expensive, housing benefit helps with paying them. Nevertheless, the Coalition's housing benefit cutbacks will leave many tenants living far below the poverty line. This includes some tenants with jobs, as low and erratic wages (including below the minimum wage) are endemic for many tenants. How long can tenants and their families continue without building up rent arrears and other debts? This will vary between different households and depending on the amount of benefit that has been withdrawn. If households cannot pay the rent because they literally have no money to do so (unless they go without food and/or stop paying fuel bills), what will they do? Will the association help them or evict them?

Rent direct

Many tenants arrange for their housing benefit to be paid direct to their landlord. This has provided associations with a secure rental stream. Because of these stable rental streams, banks and building societies have favoured associations with good borrowing terms for the loans that they need in order to build new housing. The universal credit system that the Coalition government plans to introduce will not allow for direct payments (except in extreme circumstances). Only Northern Ireland will be exempt from this change. Tenants, as well as associations themselves, have protested about the change, but to no avail.

It seems likely that levels of rent arrears will rise as tenants struggle to make ends meet as a result of reductions in housing benefit/ universal credit. Associations may have to spend more on their housing management service in order to collect rents. They will probably increase the amounts that they set aside for 'bad debts'. Equally important to associations, will their borrowing become more expensive, or more difficult to obtain, if lenders think that their rental income streams are potentially insecure?

How will associations deal with these situations?

If associations put the interests of the association as a financial body to the fore, they will evict tenants who fall into arrears as quickly as possible, acting as if they were private landlords. They will change their lettings or allocations criteria so as to ensure that in the future they house people in paid work who are in reasonably well-paid jobs.

If associations put the welfare of their tenants to the fore, as responsible landlords, they will move affected tenants to smaller properties (dealing with the so-called 'bedroom tax' – see Chapter Ten). They will actively help tenants and their family members to find better-paid work. They can review the rents set on properties of different sizes, ensuring that those with 'box rooms' are not counted as having bedrooms that they do not have (or are not counted as such in benefit calculations). They can set up emergency funds to help those worst affected so that they do not end up with ever-increasing rent arrears (this would supplement the discretionary fund to which the local authority will have access). The same issues are occurring within local authorities, but the difference here is that tenants are more likely to be organised so can represent their interests more effectively.

Association boards will have to decide where their principles lie. Are they welfare-oriented organisations or commercial developers?

Housing management in Leafy Glades HA – a typical medium-sized association

This section uses an example of a medium-sized association, Leafy Glades HA (a pseudonym), to show the range of services provided and costs of housing management. The different sources of revenue for the services will be considered, as well as the costs of providing some of them. The subsequent discussion will focus on rents, service charges, support and maintenance and will outline a number of issues associated with them.

Leafy Glades HA has 3,000 homes in management and 121 staff. It works across two local authority areas in Yorkshire. It was established 40 years ago and has grown slowly. It is used as an example here because it is relatively easy to see how it raises and spends money to provide a housing management service and build property. Large associations, especially those in group structures, are more complex. Leafy Glades HA does build a small number of new homes each year and engages in a range of markets (for example, student housing).

Leafy Glades provides 'general needs' housing for families and has some flats for single people and couples. Some tenants need 'housing-related support' in order to maintain their tenancies. This is provided by the association with directly managed supported housing and sheltered housing, as well as a 'floating support' scheme. Indirectly, housing support is also provided by eight managing agents. These provide a range of support services to residents in hostels, dispersed tenancies and shared homes. Leafy Glades works with them and maintains the property that they use, while the managing agent independently provides the housing management and support. Leafy Glades HA employs money advice and benefits workers to help tenants (1,600 tenants are likely to be affected by benefit reductions and 440 will be affected by the 'bedroom tax' alone – see Chapter Ten).

A range of activities

Leafy Glades demonstrates the point made earlier, that associations are likely to be engaged in a variety of activities. Its main business is rented housing (with or without additional support services), but it also develops student housing and housing for shared ownership. In terms of the business, this means that there are different risks that have to be evaluated and dealt with on a regular basis. Financial Note 1 from the association's Annual Accounts shows the range of activities of Leafy

Glades HA and their cost (Table 6.1). The figures are for the period to the end of March 2012.

Table 6.1: Financial note 1: Turnover, operating costs, cost of sales and operating surplus

	Turnover* £000s	Operating costs** £000s	Operating surplus/deficit £000s
Income and expenditure from social housing lettings			
Housing accommodation	7,524	6,033	1,491
Supported housing and housing for older people	4,078	3,016	1,062
Shared ownership accommodation	248	132	116
	11,850	**9,181**	**2,669**
Other social housing activities			
Supporting People contract income	1,311	1,311	–
First tranche shared ownership sales	68	60	8
Asset management and development services	–	178	(178)
	1,379	**1,549**	**(170)**
Non-social housing activities			
Lettings – student accommodation	350	68	282
Other – commercial property	83	28	55
	13,662	**10,826**	**2,836**
Operating surplus analysed			
Social housing lettings			2,669
Other social housing activities			(170)
Non-social housing activities			337
			2,836

Notes:

* The turnover is the total income that the association receives over a given time. It is made up of the income from tenants and leaseholders, other service income, revenue grants and sales proceeds for first-tranche sales of shared ownership properties.

** The operating costs are what it costs Leafy Glades HA to provide the housing management and other services. They show what it costs to run the housing management service for tenants.

The housing management service

Financial Note 2 from the Annual Accounts shows a detailed breakdown of Leafy Glades' income that has enabled it to provide a management and maintenance service to its tenants over the financial year (Table 6.2). This Note also identifies the different costs that Leafy Glades HA has incurred and which have to be met in providing a service.

Interest on loans that have been taken out to build or improve housing is not included in this Financial Note. Interest is not tied to

Table 6.2: Financial note 2: Income and expenditure from social housing lettings

	General needs housing £000s	Supported housing and housing for older people £000s	Shared ownership £000s	Total 2011 £000s
Income from social housing lettings				
Rent receivable net of identifiable service charges	7,278	3,256	238	10,772
Charges for support services	–	115	–	115
Service charges receivable	246	454	10	710
Net rents receivable	**7,524**	**3,825**	**248**	**11,597**
Other revenue grants	–	253	–	253
Total income from social housing lettings	**7,524**	**4,078**	**248**	**11,850**
Expenditure on social housing letting activities				
Service charge costs	306	528	–	834
Management	1,635	1,327	83	3,045
Routine maintenance	1,587	420	–	2,007
Planned maintenance	1,176	366	–	1,542
Rent losses from bad debts	16	17	–	33
Depreciation of housing properties	1,219	358	49	1,626
Impairment	–	–	–	–
Other costs	94	–	–	94
Total expenditure on social housing lettings	**6,033**	**3,016**	**132**	**9,181**
Operating surplus on social housing lettings	**1,491**	**1,062**	**116**	**2,053**
Void losses	84	49	–	133

either turnover or operating costs, but in accounting terms is regarded as a separate business item.

A large part of the association's surplus from housing management (£2,053,000) is used to repay interest each year on the money it has borrowed. Income generated from other activities helps with this too. In 2011/12, Leafy Glades HA paid £2,066,000 in interest on loans and bank overdrafts.

Leafy Glades HA expenditure – points to consider

General management

The costs of providing the core housing management service for general needs housing (£1,635,000) and supported housing (£1,327,000) include staff salaries and the running costs of offices, costs of letting and managing properties, paying for IT and financial services, computer costs and support costs such as accountancy and legal fees. Housing management costs tend to be higher than those in equivalent local authorities because associations usually cannot create economies of scale unless they operate in large group structures.

Repairs and maintenance

The association spent £1,587,000 on routine maintenance in 2011/12 for its general needs housing and £420,000 for supported housing. For the general needs housing, this is nearly as much as it spent on general housing management.

Planned maintenance

It spent a further £1,176,000 on planned maintenance for general needs housing and £366,000 for supported housing. The trend in associations is to try to plan as much maintenance work as possible so that costs can be negotiated and possibly reduced by creating economies of scale.

Rent loss because of bad debts and voids

At £16,000 and £84,000, respectively, for general needs housing these figures are negligible at 1.4% of the total rental charges due, but note that these losses are quickly written off, so the accounts figure here remains low. This amount may increase in the future, due to benefit reductions (see Chapter Ten).

Rent arrears

For the year 2011/12 the gross arrears as a percentage of the rent and service charges were stated as 1.3%. This is very low. In a study of rent arrears management practices in housing associations, Pawson et al (2010) found that the average proportion of rent lost through bad debts or arrears was between 5.5% and 6%. This amount may increase in the future, due to benefit reductions (see Chapter Ten).

Voids

Leafy Glades HA lost £84,000 in 2011/12 because of voids (empty property awaiting a new tenant) in its general needs stock. The equivalent figure for supported housing was £49,000. This is a slight improvement over the previous year. Associations will be under considerable pressure to reduce re-let times to an absolute minimum, so as to avoid rent loss.

Leafy Glades HA income – points to consider

Rents

The association expected over £10 million from rental income from general needs and supported housing in 2011/12 (see Chapter Nine for more discussion on rents).

Service charges

Leafy Glades HA received over £700,000 from its tenants in service charges in 2011/12. Housing associations have traditionally charged for communal services separately from the rent that tenants pay. This practice dates back to the introduction of fair rents.

Support charges and other revenue grants

Leafy Glades HA provides additional support to tenants in its sheltered housing and directly managed hostels. It also provides a 'floating support' service for individual tenants who need help to manage independently.

The association has listed supported housing and older people's housing separately. Its total income from the management of this housing in 2011/12 was just over £4 million. Most of this was made up of rental income, but £115,000 came from individual charges for support. Support services were paid for mainly by Supporting People contract income of £1,311,000.

Leafy Glades HA also works with managing agents who provide services directly to residents: homeless people, people with alcohol problems, women leaving domestic violence and young people. Independently of Leafy Glades HA, these agents receive Supporting People contract income to pay staff to support residents. Leafy Glades provides and maintains the building(s) that they use.

The importance of rental income

The most important income for an association is the rent paid by tenants. This can be seen in Leafy Glades HA (and in LB Islington in

Chapter Five). The rent that can be charged for a property has been calculated in different ways over the years, with varying amounts of control by the association itself. Currently there are four different types of rental charge: fair rents, assured rents, intermediate rents and 'affordable rents'. Not all associations will charge all of these, but more details can be found in Chapter Nine. Leafy Glades charges fair, assured and intermediate rents.

There have been profound political consequences for associations as landlords since 1988, arising from the increasing use of private finance in new building and steadily increasing rents. Since 1988, they have moved from being a small but steadily growing sector working to complement local authority housing to becoming dominant 'private registered providers'. Their rents have become increasingly expensive. This has been encouraged and only slightly restrained by successive governments. Even though they had encouraged higher rents in 1988, the Conservatives finally introduced a rent-influencing scheme in 1996, designed to curb association rent increases.

In 2000, the New Labour government decided to tackle rents in a different way, proposing 'rent convergence', which generally meant that local authority rents increased while associations had smaller increases or reductions over the period to 2011/12 (see Chapter Nine). In some parts of the country, rents in both sectors have increased to near-market levels. Unsurprisingly, expenditure on housing benefit has risen, despite additional restrictions on entitlement. The Coalition government's cutbacks of housing benefit entitlement, especially from 2013, will be discussed further in Chapter Ten.

Service charges and support

Service charges

Service charges may include payment for items such as cleaning and decorating shared areas in blocks of flats (like stairs and landings), the maintenance of door-entry systems, gardening/landscaping work and additional lighting in specific housing schemes. Service charges are paid by tenants in addition to the rent. Leaseholders (for example, those in leasehold schemes for the elderly) also pay service charges. They may be fixed over the year or may be variable, depending on the actual costs of providing a service (which may be unknown at the beginning of the financial year). Charges have to be reasonable. An association will not usually charge for 'support' of various kinds in its service charge to tenants.

Housing-related support

Housing-related support is paid for through the Supporting People programme, now paid through local authorities' RSG. An association can bid for a contract from the local authority to provide Supporting People services. People may need support on a short-term basis (in a crisis or to settle into a tenancy) or over the longer-term (a good example being support provided for people with learning difficulties in shared homes). Reductions in Supporting People funding from 2004 and the removal of its protective ring fence in 2009 have created problems for providers and residents (see Chapter Three). Debate about the impact on sheltered housing and other groups is captured in detail in the Parliamentary Select Committee's proceedings (CLG Commons Select Committee, 2009, chapters 2 and 6).

The decline of Supporting People funding has led to other changes. There has generally been a reduction in accommodation-based schemes like hostels or shared homes, with more emphasis now on 'floating support'. Support staff visit people wherever they are living. With budgets being cut, in order to maintain the same level of service staff may be expected to support more residents over a wider area. Support may also be time limited and targeted (or rationed). For example, women who have left violent partners may receive specialist support if they are considered to be 'high risk', but otherwise may be expected to obtain support from generic support schemes.

Housing association providers of services will be trying to financially reposition their services. Some 'client groups' may be eligible for social care funding for vulnerable adults rather than relying on Supporting People contract payments. For example, people with learning difficulties who need intensive support to live in the community may be better served by the association linking the service to a social services budget, which is less likely to be substantially reduced. Ironically, these budgets are also becoming insecure as a funding stream, but for different reasons. They may be reduced by the trend for 'individual budgets' or 'personalisation', where money for support is paid directly to the 'client', who can then make their own choice of support provider (see Dunning, 2011 for more detail).

These trends are reflected in association accounts by changing levels of grant from year to year, and possibly increasing levels of charging for support. In the example of Leafy Glades HA, the association receives over £1 million in Supporting People contract income from the local authority. It also receives £115,000 in charges paid by tenants for support each year.

Responsive and planned maintenance and the DHS

Leafy Glades HA spends nearly as much again on maintenance as it does on general housing management. It also spends a lot on planned maintenance.

Planned maintenance can include boiler replacements, the replacement of single-glazed with double-glazed windows, kitchen upgrades, fitting new baths and showers, replacing doors and improving paths and boundary walls and replacing fascias, soffits and roofs.

Associations transfer an amount each year from their surpluses into sinking funds set up to deal with a range of major work, including large-scale improvements and repairs and energy-efficiency and carbon-reduction improvements to their housing stock.

Box 6.1: Definition: A sinking fund

This is an account set up to receive funds reserved for major repairs that will be needed in the future. The money ultimately comes from the rents that tenants pay.

All social landlords, including Leafy Glades HA, were expected to ensure that their housing met the DHS by 2010. Traditional associations were expected to use their own resources to complete this. Most did so, although some associations took the opportunity to sell redundant offices or difficult-to-modernise property so as to raise additional capital to invest in order to achieve this objective. LSVTs were in a slightly different position: attaining the DHS was an integral part of their business plans devised to convince tenants of the worth of transfer from the local authority as landlord. Most borrowed to undertake this

Table 6.3: English housing conditions – the Decent Homes Standard

| | Unfitness based* | | | HHSRS based* | | |
| | 2001 | | | 2009 | | |
	Decent	Non decent	All	Decent	Non decent	All
Housing association	66.9	33.1	100.00	80.3	19.7	100.00
All social sector	61.1	38.9	100.00	76.8	23.2	100.00

Source: Derived from Pawson and Wilcox (2012, p 130, Table 23b), using the English House Condition Survey Headline Report and the English Housing Survey Headline Report 2009–10.

Note: *To meet the fitness standard, properties had to be in a reasonable state of repair, have reasonably modern facilities and services and provide a reasonable level of thermal comfort. This standard was replaced in 2006 by the Housing Health and Safety Rating System (HHSRS), which considers the level of hazards in a property.

work, although some LSVTs obtained gap funding for their transfers (see Chapter Five), part of which was spent on DHS work.

Not all associations reached the DHS by 2010. In 2009, 20% of associations' stock was still below the standard (the most recent figure available). The need to complete this work will be reflected in association priorities over the next few years (see the DHS discussion in Wilcox, 2012b, pp 68–70).

The DHS is only a minimum standard and some landlords have worked to higher standards (Table 6.4). LSVTs have tended to do this more than traditional housing associations. They have also been more likely to demolish stock that is difficult to improve and unpopular (some system-built schemes, for example). Large associations (mainly LSVTs) demolished 45,000 homes in the 10 years from 2001 (HCA/ TSA, 2011, p 10), as they were too expensive to repair or improve.

Table 6.4: Refurbishment standard adopted, compared to the Decent Homes Standard in England

Social landlord type	Similar (%)	A little higher (%)	Much higher (%)
Stock transfer housing association (LSVT)	9	50	41
Traditional housing association	22	62	17

Source: Derived from Pawson and Wilcox (2012, p 63, Table 2.2.1), using data from the National Audit Office (2010).

Financing new homes: the changing relationship between public grant and private contributions

The financing of house building and improvement work has changed profoundly since the 1970s. Most associations were small organisations then and reliant on grant for this work, which successive governments made available. Grant funding was administered in national programmes by government quangos. The Housing Corporation administered the Approved Development Programme up to 2007. The HCA took over this role and administered the National Affordable Housing Programme from 2007 to 2010. It is now managing the Coalition's Affordable Homes Programme from 2011 to 2015.

This section will focus on different aspects of funding new building for rent that associations have been working with since the 1970s. The level of grant from government has changed significantly since then and this issue will be explored first. The varieties of private finance and private contributions to associations' rented housing will then be discussed. The Coalition's new Affordable Rent programme expects associations to build new homes using increased private borrowing and cross-subsidy, tapping into surpluses generated by charging 'affordable rents' of up to 80% of the equivalent local market rent. In this way, there is minimal or no need for grant. This programme will be considered later.

The changing significance of grants

The relationship between public funding and private finance has changed since the 1970s. There were three combinations of public and private finance used to build rented homes from 1974 to 2010. These were:

- housing association grant, available following the Housing Act 1974, with minimal private borrowing;
- 'fixed' housing association grant and the 'mixed funding' regime, established after the Housing Act 1988, with the grant gradually reduced by the mid-1990s to cover about 50% of the cost of producing homes;
- social housing grant, available following the Housing Act 1996, steadily reduced to 30–40% of the total costs until it was ended by the Coalition government in 2010.

The thread running through these different arrangements was the changing balance between publicly funded grant and private finance. In the 1970s, the Labour government assumed that public investment raised through general taxation would be needed by associations to build rented housing. A Conservative government thought differently, and from 1988 associations trod a different path, using grant and increasing amounts of private finance. New Labour inherited this system and kept it, reducing grant to 30–40%, levels not considered viable when the system was first established in 1988.

Reducing grant may have meant that more housing could be achieved with a given amount of programme funding, but there were wider implications to the ever-reducing public contribution. The precise costs of building specific types or numbers of properties became the focus, and associations started thinking about how to build housing schemes that would maximise rental income from a piece of land. When they built with higher levels of grant, a wider range of housing could be produced. Today, many housing associations build mainly two-bedroomed flats (HCA/TSA, 2011, p 18). These have value only to smaller families. The issue of what can be built with different levels of grant contributing to overall costs will be flagged up at different points in the discussion that follows.

Housing association grant, 1974–88

In the early 1970s most associations were 'very minor players', as compared to local authorities (Malpass, 2000, p 162) and could not raise finance in the commercial markets to undertake building or improvement work. Peter Malpass believed that the Labour government of Harold Wilson adopted them to lead on urban renewal in the 1970s not because of any association pressure or because of their reputation in this field. As he put it:

> it was the government consciously adopting associations as instruments of housing policy, despite doubts about their competence and capacity to expand into a significant force. (Malpass, 2000, p 161)

The Housing Act 1974 provided a new grant regime with Housing Association Grant, and signalled a new regulatory role for a government quango, the Housing Corporation. No association could receive grant unless it was registered with the Corporation and subject to its regular inspections. In this way, the government ensured that public money was spent appropriately.

Housing Association Grant (HAG) represented the amount that was available to associations to build or improve homes for rent. Each housing scheme's building costs had to receive prior approval from the Housing Corporation and there were a series of cost limits for different kinds of property in different parts of the country. Over 95% of eligible costs were paid for by HAG. If a building project exceeded the cost limits because of unexpected circumstances, the Housing Corporation could increase the grant payable by a small amount. This flexibility protected associations from extra costs that might be incurred in developing difficult inner-city sites where the risk of cost overrun was high.

Grant covered all the agreed capital costs, apart from a small amount which had to be paid for by the association. It usually borrowed this. The fair rent set by the Rent Officer was the key to the amount of grant available.

> ## Box 6.2: Calculating Housing Association Grant
>
> - Total annual rental income *minus* 4% voids = A
> - Total annual management and maintenance allowances* for the scheme = B
> - A *minus* B = the amount left to use to pay for a (residual) loan
> - HAG was the agreed capital cost of the building works minus the amount covered by the residual loan.
> - HAG was paid in three 'tranches' at different points of the building process. The final payment was made after the fair rent had been set by the Rent Officer, when the property was completed.
>
> Note:* Set amounts, which varied by scheme type and location, published by the government annually.

The availability of grant enabled associations to grow slowly during the 1970s and 1980s. Some worked in Housing Action Areas and Renewal Areas. Others built new family homes, sheltered housing for older people or 'special needs' housing (as it was called) like hostels for homeless people or shared homes for people moving from institutional care to live independently (Gibb and Monro, 1991, pp 113–15; Hills, 1991, pp 116–21).

Fixed Housing Association Grant 1988–96

The Housing Act 1988 introduced a new way of funding association building. HAG was now available only in predetermined fixed amounts that were paid at the beginning of the building works. This was known as 'fixed HAG'. The funding regime was called 'mixed funding', as the fixed HAG needed to be supplemented by private loans and/or other financial contributions.

The amount of grant paid by the Housing Corporation varied, depending on the type of scheme and its precise location (as in the pre-1988 system). That aside, there were significant differences between pre-1988 and post-1988 HAG. 'Fixed' HAG was a set amount. It was also a one-off payment, to be received by the association at the beginning of the work. Once it had been paid, the association had to raise the rest, usually by borrowing from banks and building societies. The association now had to deal with any cost overruns too. The Conservative government made it clear that fixed HAG would decline as associations became more experienced in raising private finance. It had issued a consultation paper in 1987, *Finance for housing associations: the government's proposals*, outlining that it wanted to:

increase the volume of rented housing the associations can produce for any given level of public expenditure. (Department of the Environment, 1987, para 2)

The consultation paper also stated that the government wanted to 'create new incentives' for associations in order to encourage them to be cost-effective. Some changes achieved this:

• Initially, fixing HAG at 70% of the total costs (compared to 95% or more in the 1974 system) provided an incentive to minimise costs so that the amount that needed to be borrowed was kept to a minimum.
• Eligible costs in HAG changed. For example, there was only a fixed percentage allowance for interest charges on loans taken out to fund building work. Previously, the whole amount had been eligible. Associations speeded up building work where possible so as to reduce interest charges.
• Associations now needed to work in a way that minimised their financial risks: estimates had to be accurate and work had to be finished on time.

The Conservative government had promised that housing benefit would be paid on the more expensive rents that had to be charged because of the borrowing costs of private finance. For now, the rents increased dramatically but 'took the strain'.

John Hills (1991) referred to this new financial regime as the 'brave new world'. Drawn from Aldous Huxley's dystopian novel of the same name, this is an ambiguous and ironic comment well suited to the new reality. This financial regime was not as rosy as it first appeared. Worries about the extent of their private borrowing and whether these loans could be repaid from rental income were for the future. Associations had to compete for grant and were encouraged to try to develop housing using less grant and more private finance. The more successful they were in this, the more the Housing Corporation reduced grant rates. More rented homes were built, but not on the scale needed to deal with growing waiting lists (Table 6.5).

Table 6.5: Housing association completions in England, 1980–97

	1980	1985	1990	1991	1992	1993	1994	1995	1996	1997
Housing associations	19,299	11,298	13,821	15,295	20,789	29,779	30,848	30,888	27,025	20,966

Source: Davis and Wigfield (2010, p 10), using statistics from Wilcox (2008, p 99, Table 19b).

There were other features of this period that were far from positive:

- rent levels were often not affordable for households living on low wages, especially in London;
- building standards declined, especially in relation to space and storage;
- risky inner-city improvement work declined, to be replaced by less risky greenfield new build schemes;
- the number of large family houses built declined because of the grant rate and resultant rents that had to be charged. More two-bedroomed houses and flats could be built on the same amount of land;
- specialist housing (shared homes, refuges, small hostels) declined because of the costs.

The Housing Act 1996 was one of the last pieces of legislation enacted by John Major's Conservative government before it lost the general election in 1997. It introduced the Social Housing Grant (SHG) to replace HAG. This more generic name was appropriate, as the legislation also enabled different organisations to register with the Housing Corporation for the first time. Private shareholder-based companies could now register, but not bid for grant. Nevertheless, opening up registration to them paved the way for this in 2008. From 1996, associations registered with the Housing Corporation were to be known as 'registered social landlords'. Ten year later, the Housing and Regeneration Act 2008 renamed them 'registered providers' (which included private shareholder companies too), thus completing the long journey to creating the 'independent rented sector' first envisaged in 1988.

Social housing grant 1997–2010

The early years of the New Labour government were a disappointing time for many who had expected increases in investment in local authority and housing association housing (Davis and Wigfield, 2010). In the first five years there was less spent on social rented housing than the Conservatives had planned.

The average grant rate did increase in 2001/02, from 54% to 60%, to reflect some increased association costs and to cushion the effects of the introduction of the rent restructuring regime (see Chapter Nine), but it was only in 2003/04 that the Approved Development Programme nearly doubled to £1,236 million (from £687 million in 2000/01). This marked increased New Labour government expectations of associations in relation to producing rented housing and low-cost homeownership homes for sale.

Despite this, the number of new homes built by associations up to 2006 was disappointingly low (Table 6.6). Grant rates continued to fall as associations competed with each other to win SHG. In this environment, associations began to wonder about the level of borrowing that they were taking on and whether home sales (including shared ownership sales) could be maintained. Some associations used profit from sales to cross-subsidise the rented homes built, reducing the amount of private finance needed, even though the grant rates kept on falling.

Table 6.6: New association rented housing built in England, 1997–2006

	1997	1998	1999	2000	2001	2002	2003	2004	2005	2006
Housing associations	20,966	19,901	17,775	16,681	14,502	13,309	12,882	16,604	17,535	20,660

Source: Drawn from Davis and Wigfield (2010, p 14), using statistics from Pawson and Wilcox (2011, p 115, Table 19b).

Note: A proportion of the association properties were built for sale, not rent. It is not possible to distinguish the funding source (for example, what derives from mixed funding, including housing association grant/social housing grant, planning gain, or building using an association's own resources).

New Labour's approach changed when Gordon Brown became Prime Minister in 2007. The 2007 Green Paper *Homes for the future: more affordable, more sustainable* proposed £8 billion over the following three years for:

> a major programme of building new social housing, including stronger roles for local councils as well as housing associations and the private sector. (CLG, 2007, p 73)

Associations were expected to build 155,000 new properties in 2008–11, building 45,000 homes by 2010/11, increasing to 50,000 in 2011. Social rented housing would make up two-thirds of this total (with £6.5 billion in grant funding); shared ownership the remaining third (with £1.5 billion in grant funding). Associations were expected to match this public funding with £12 billion raised from private borrowing or the use of their own resources (surpluses).

Grant funding for this larger National Affordable Housing Programme was available from the HCA, which took over this role from the Housing Corporation (which had been abolished). In 2008 the HCA allocated the majority of funding through a competitive bidding system, emphasising 'value for money'. Up to this point the grant rate had continued to decline. The average grant for housing schemes was now 44% (according to the HCA), but the government expected further reductions. HCA research had concluded that associations could invest more of their own surpluses or borrow more to help pay for the expanded building programme. The government thought that 61,000 more homes could be built from the same amount of public money if grant was squeezed to 24–34% of scheme costs.

Most SHG in 2008 was allocated to large associations like London and Quadrant Housing Group (£120 million), Accent Group (£65 million), Affinity Sutton Group (£58 million), Swan Housing Association (£53 million) and Riverside Housing Association (£63 million). These worked with partner associations and house builders on programmes covering several years of work, building homes agreed in advance by the HCA. The HCA set aside some funds that associations could bid for at a later date. This was intended to introduce a degree of flexibility for associations: if opportunities arose, the HCA was anxious that they should quickly take advantage of them, given the problems that had resulted from the 2007/08 global financial crisis.

Individual associations might negotiate a higher grant rate on a scheme-by-scheme basis. This was needed to fill funding gaps previously filled by private finance. This had become difficult to obtain (or 'draw down'), even though loans might have been agreed with banks months before. In *Building Britain's Future* (HM Government, 2009), Gordon Brown committed an additional £1.2 billion in 2009/10 to build an additional 20,000 homes and create 45,000 construction jobs. This was one part of a growth package of measures to avoid the complete collapse of the housing market and to revive economic performance. It did enable more rented housing to be built by 2010 than in the previous two years (Table 6.7), possibly with increased grant rates, although that remained a subject for private negotiation within the HCA. In the event, associations completed (or acquired) 25,000 new homes in 2008 and 2009 – nowhere near 45,000 but a creditable achievement in the face of the worst financial crisis since the 1930s. The years 2010 and 2011 were better and may be considered as part of Gordon Brown's legacy.

Table 6.7: New association rented housing in England, 2007–11

	2007	2008	2009	2010	2011
Housing associations	22,100	25,650	25,260	39,443	33,915

Source: Drawn from Davis and Wigfield (2010, p 14), using statistics from Pawson and Wilcox (2011, p 115, Table 19b).

Up to 2010, social housing grant steadily declined in value and reduced as a proportion of the costs of development. This was always the intention of the Conservatives when they introduced this regime in 1988, but New Labour's continued adherence to the idea of declining grant was a surprise. As the grant rate steadily declined, associations built more two-bedroomed houses and flats, much like the private sector. Relatively few family homes were built (HCA/TSA, 2011). This was and remains a serious public policy issue. Homes built with public investment should be suitable for all those who need them, not just families with one or two children.

From 2010, the Coalition government changed arrangements for grant funding. It effectively abolished any SHG contribution to new rented housing produced by associations or local authorities. The HCA only honoured the payment of SHG for schemes that were already agreed and committed on the ground (which had been scheduled for 2011). The Coalition government established its own 'affordable rent' regime for new building. This will be considered later.

Private finance, rather than grant, now holds the key to the immediate future of housing associations' house building for rent, shared ownership and other low-cost homeownership initiatives. What are the principles and prospects here?

Private finance – loans, derivatives and bonds

Private loans

Private loans were a very important source of funding for associations up to 2010. Associations typically borrowed £6 billion a year from the private sector. Most recent surveys indicate that they will now need slightly less, at £4 billion–£5 billion a year as building rates fall during the recession (HCA, 2012) and many associations decline involvement in the Coalition's Affordable Rent programme because of the financial risks involved.

To date the main lenders for associations have been Lloyds Bank, Barclays Bank, Nationwide Building Society, Santander (formerly Abbey) and the Royal Bank of Scotland.

Associations use their property portfolios or rental streams as security for borrowing. In the early 1990s, associations tended to take out short-term loans, but as banks became familiar with the sector they were happy to arrange longer-term loans with lower interest rates. Since the global financial crisis of 2007–08 onwards, that trend has reversed. Recently some banks have tried to re-price loans, increasing the interest due on existing loans when associations have asked for new borrowing. Others have reduced the length of their loans, so that they can raise interest rates more quickly. The number of lenders in the market has also declined and loan finance is more difficult to secure.

In the past, associations were regarded as relatively low risk investments by banks and the larger building societies. There were a number of reasons for this. Associations:

- have had stable cash flows (rental income) from well-managed properties;
- generally have had better-quality property than local authorities and private landlords;
- have been closely regulated by the Tenant Services Authority (TSA) and its predecessor, the Housing Corporation;
- have been trusted with government funds (SHG) for building and direct payments of housing benefit for rent.

None of these assumptions will hold true for much longer. The HCA has taken over the economic regulation of housing associations from the TSA. It produces quarterly reports on the financial health of the sector as far as borrowing to build is concerned. An example of the situation of associations up to the end of 2012 is provided in Box 6.3. This is the purely commercial side of association activity. The contrast with the welfare side – and the cutbacks in their housing benefit that are being experienced by association tenants – could not be starker.

Box 6.3: Private finance and housing associations

- By Q3, 2012, associations had borrowed £55.3 billion. £11.6 billion had been agreed but not yet 'drawn down' (that is, actually used).
- In Q3, associations arranged £1.3 billion in new borrowing. This was in the form of bank loans and bonds.
- Retail bank loans are gradually being displaced by bonds arranged on the capital market with institutional investors that provide longer-term finance.

Source: HCA (2012)

Derivatives

Associations have also used derivatives to try to control expenditure on interest rates on their borrowing. In the financial markets, derivatives were developed as financial instruments trading on future events. There are now derivatives that trade by offering 'swaps' in cash flows based on the movement of interest rates in the future.

> ### Box 6.4: Definition: What is a derivative?
>
> - Any derivative is a complicated financial hedging instrument.
> - It can be designed to trade in future movements of interest rates.
> - Associations have agreed 'swap' contracts with financial institutions to protect themselves, especially from falling interest rates.
> - There is an element of risk here as the 'hedging' involves anticipating the future – and that is, to a degree, unpredictable. This is particularly the case now as the markets are very volatile.
>
> *Source:* HCA (2012 onwards):

The HCA reported in 2012 that there were 50 associations using derivatives, mostly arranged with commercial banks and other financial institutions. Most were 'long-dated' and 'free-standing' swaps, according to the HCA (2012) – that is, the movement of interest rates was usually to be considered some time into the future and only covers part of any association's financial operations. As an example, in 2013, Astor Group (a group of associations trading as an 'ethical social enterprise' with 27,000 properties across the South West) has around £730 million in bank debt, £140 million of which is hedged by 'swaps'.

The essence of these contracts is to 'hedge' interest rate movements. Associations try to predict which direction interest rates will take in the future. Where an association has entered this sort of arrangement, the 'swap' might protect them from falling interest rates for a specific time but if rates move beyond those specified in the contract, the association will have to make payments to the financial institution/ organisation they have swapped with.

The HCA reported that 'swaps' covered a total of £9.8 billion of associations' cash flows at the end of 2012 but the HCA as regulator was not entirely happy. The HCA has insisted that total collateral of £1.6 billion (mainly in property rather than cash) be set aside by a number of associations in case they are called on to make payments to the institutions they have 'swapped'/contracted with.

The TSA had a rigorous approach to financial regulation, but it was abolished by the Coalition government. The Coalition wanted 'lighter touch' regulation. 'Economic regulation' of associations is now dealt with by a committee in the HCA and inspections of associations are non-existent (the new arrangements were enshrined in the Localism

Act 2011). This may not be wise. For example, in May 2012 the US bank JP Morgan Chase lost $2 billion in swap deals organised from its London office (Nasiripour, 2012) and $30 billion was wiped off its share price. Are associations any better at managing these risks?

Bonds

Another way of raising private finance, increasing in use by the larger associations, is to raise money from the capital markets through bond issues.

> ### Box 6.5: Definition: What is a bond?
>
> The London Stock Exchange says that a bond is:
>
> 'a tradeable security, issued by a borrower (the bond issuer) and representing a formal agreement between the issuer and the lender (the bondholder) that the issuer will repay to the lender the full amount borrowed plus interest over the lifetime of the bond.'
>
> *Source:* London Stock Exchange, 2010, p 3

Financially strong organisations like large housing associations or local authorities can issue a bond independently. A bond is for a given sum of money. There are 'wholesale' bonds and 'retail' bonds. 'Wholesale' bonds are tradeable in units of £50,000 or more. 'Retail' bonds are tradeable in smaller units, like £1,000. An association will need a minimum funding requirement of about £150 million in order to issue a public bond in its own name. The Housing Finance Corporation has acted on behalf of groups of smaller associations in arranging bond issues for them.

How do bonds work? The investor (for example, a pension fund) agrees to pay the sum sought by the association to use over a period of time. The association then pays the interest rate due over that time (the 'coupon' on the bond) to the lender(s), usually on an annual basis. At the end of the term, the association repays the amount lent to it (the principal) by the investor. Bonds have become more popular as private loans have become more expensive, but the capital markets are increasingly volatile. Association involvement with bonds has waxed and waned accordingly.

Cross-subsidies of various kinds and private contributions

Building for sale

The financial model used most by associations in the 1990s involved a combination of grant and private finance. By 2000, many associations were investing some of their own surpluses in new rented house building. This financial model is more complicated, as it has involved grant, private finance and what is known as a cross-subsidy, provided by the association itself from its surpluses.

Association surpluses have been built up in different ways: from rental income, sales of low-cost homes (if associations build these), right-to-buy receipts and 'asset management' sales (sales of empty property or redundant office buildings). Investing money from the association's own surpluses does two things. It reduces the amount of private finance that has to be raised (which reduces costs). Just as importantly, by 2010, cross-subsidies were hiding the fact that the grant rate had become ridiculously low in the last days of the New Labour government.

Build for sale and shared ownership sales were used by associations to increase their surpluses. Although many associations have dabbled in this market, it has been most successful in London and the South-East, where it has helped first-time buyers on low incomes. Building for sale represented over 40% of association development activity in 2008/09 (HCA/TSA, 2011, p 6) but it is slowing as the recession continues. Most property sales have been in London and the South-East (60%), where the market for homeownership remains relatively strong, despite the recession. One- and two-bedroomed flats made up 50% of all sales in 2008/09 (HCA/TSA, 2011, p 18).

The global financial crisis of 2007–08 created serious problems for associations that were heavily involved in building for sale. The crisis seriously compromised their ability to cross-subsidise rented housing. By October 2008, the number of properties that associations could not sell peaked at nearly 10,000. Many had to be temporarily converted to rental housing (with so-called 'intermediate' rents, just below market rents). This enabled at least some income to be generated from what would otherwise have been empty property. Under a newspaper headline 'Model is broken say mega-associations' (Dowler, 2008), London and Quadrant's Chief Executive David Montague suggested that the government should bring forward the whole of the unspent National Affordable Housing Programme (budgeted to run to 2010/11). Associations could then be allocated additional SHG, ensuring less reliance on private borrowing and property sales. This was not the comment of an association that was being 'moulded' by government.

The problem continues, as market conditions are still difficult. About 10,000 homes are produced for sale each year (HCA, 2012), although some are not sold for many months, a sign that first-time buyers are still finding it difficult to get a mortgage. The amounts generated by association sales are not small. For example, in the last three months of 2012 associations had total asset sales of £562 million (HCA, 2012). This generated a profit of £159 million over those three months. Nevertheless, although nearly 2,500 sales (including shared ownership sales) were completed during this period, over 3,500 properties remained unsold (and over 1,500 had been on the market for over six months). The level of expected surpluses is still restrained for some associations, as a consequence.

Capital contributions through 'planning gain'

Planning gain is another form of cross-subsidy that has been important in producing more rented housing. It is a private contribution to social house building. A developer is expected by the local (planning) authority to mitigate the potentially negative consequences of their development by making either a contribution in kind (for example, providing some affordable housing) or a financial contribution to the local (planning) authority.

If the developer agrees to provide some social rented housing (if they are building housing), the ownership of these homes and their management is transferred to a housing association. The alternative for the developer (especially if their development is non-housing) is to agree a sum that is paid to the local authority in mitigation. In the planning agreement, it is specified how and when this money will be used by the local authority (see Chapter Three).

> **Box 6.6: Definition: Planning gain: Town and Country Planning Act 1990, section 106**
>
> A financial or other contribution made from the profits that a developer makes on a private development that requires planning permission.
>
> A financial contribution can act like a grant, although it is not really a grant at all.

> Alternatively, a developer sets aside a number of units for social housing and finds an association that is willing to buy them at a reduced price for use as social housing.

This approach has had its critics, but developers' criticism needs to be set in context. Up to 2010, only 6% of planning permissions granted to developers in England expected any contribution by way of planning gain. However, those that did:

> were substantial ... including funding roads, schools and new affordable housing in England. [Contributions] have risen from £2 billion in 2003–04 to £4 billion in 2005–06 and to £5 billion in 2007–08, of which half in each year was for new affordable housing. (Burgess et al, 2011, p 3)

Burgess et al found that housing associations had increasingly benefited following the financial crisis and recession.

> Some [local planning authorities] had seen increased amounts of affordable housing delivered as developers sold whole developments to RSLs since the downturn. Some schemes that had a proportion, for example, 30 per cent, of the housing agreed to be affordable in the s106 were being sold to RSLs so in fact they will be 100 per cent affordable. Some developers were building the affordable housing first to help their cash flow. There were a few instances of reducing the amount of shared ownership units as these have become more difficult to sell recently and instead increasing the amount of social rent, or exploring Rent to Buy. (Burgess et al 2011, p 7)

A more principled criticism of 'planning gain' is that this was another example of New Labour's over-reliance on the private sector. Contributions from the private sector have substituted for what would have been provided through planned investment through public expenditure in different times. These private contributions are piecemeal and essentially unpredictable. The quality of the homes made available is often poor and they tend to be small (Burgess et al, 2011; HCA/TSA, 2011).

About 25,000 homes are acquired through section 106 each year, the majority in the South, where most development is located; but the continued contribution of planning gain is likely to be undermined in a number of ways:

- developers may still mothball entire schemes because of the recession. That said, in 2012 (and in line with its *Housing Strategy*), the Coalition government announced that it would change planning law to enable developers to drop social housing contributions on private house building sites that are currently stalled, so that the developer can make a profit.
- the new discretionary Community Infrastructure Levy has first call for developers' contributions, but these will probably not be used for housing (DCLG, 2011a).

The Coalition's New Homes Bonus will not be able to match the contribution made through section 106 agreements. The value of section 106 housing recently provided through 'planning gain' has been worth £2.5 billion each year (Burgess et al, 2011, p 3). The New Homes Bonus (NHB) scheme is expected to be worth only about £1 billion to participating local authorities up to 2014/15.

The Coalition government's new Affordable Rent model

The Coalition hopes that about 80,000 homes will be produced within the so-called Affordable Homes programme, mainly using its 'Affordable Rent' funding model. Shared ownership housing and other types of provision will contribute to the larger overall total. It is worth noting that Affordable Rent is not a model that is being followed in Wales, Scotland or Northern Ireland.

The proposals for this funding change were published on 22 November 2010. The government clearly not wanting to engage in protracted discussion ensured that the consultation period (for what turned out to be major change) was excessively short, the deadline being 17 January 2011. The paper itself was brief, vague and contradictory in parts. An appendix detailed the 'new funding model for affordable housing'. From April 2011, it said, 'registered providers' would work with the HCA to create a 'bespoke delivery agreement' that would maximise their contribution to producing rented housing through efficiencies, use of cross-subsidy and s 106 contributions (CLG, 2010b).

The model of funding that would be used was to be based not on grant but on rents and additional borrowing.

The rents charged on properties built under this programme may be set at up to 80% of the market equivalent for the property. These are called Affordable Rents. It is expected that these higher rents will also be charged on an agreed proportion of association re-lets. It is anticipated that by charging rents at this level additional surplus and/ or an increased rental stream against which to borrow will be created. Associations in the programme are expected to let the new 'affordable rent' tenancies (plus the agreed re-lets) as 'flexible tenancies' (short-term tenancies of between two and five years in length). These 'flexible' tenancies have reduced security of tenure and it will be easier to evict any tenants with rent arrears. The government's proposal continued:

> The introduction of the Affordable Rent tenancy is a key element of the new delivery model. It will give registered providers the flexibility to increase the revenue that is available to them through rents … In the future, providers will be able to reach an agreement with the regulator/investor, allowing them to convert a proportion of their empty properties into the new tenure. The higher rents charged will generate additional revenue and debt servicing capacity for registered providers … with surpluses, generated by applying flexibilities, used to generate new supply at higher rent levels and lower grant. This ongoing process of conversion and higher rent levels on new stock will build in long term sustainability for the new funding model. (CLG, 2010b)

A 'framework document' with more details was issued later in 2011 (CLG/HCA, 2011). The main proposals did not change in the intervening period, despite substantial criticism from a wide range of housing organisations. The main concerns focused on the issue of charging rents of up to 80% of market value and the reduced security of tenure associated with 'flexible tenancies'.

In reality, for associations in the North, there was not much difference between charging their current rents and 80% market rents. They felt that the amount of private finance that they would have to borrow in order to build with minimal or no subsidy would be far too great. Many expressed concerns about financial risk and the association's viability if it used this model to build. The picture was different for associations in the South. Many were concerned about the level of rent being proposed, especially associations in London, where market rents are probably double association rents on social housing. If they were to increase their rents, they would generate surpluses, but there was a wider issue. Whom would they be housing (National Housing Federation, 2011)?

More generally, there was concern that associations' rental streams would increasingly be linked to the market. Market pricing is volatile and association rental streams would mimic this volatility. This would mean losing one of the advantages that banks and building societies have always identified with associations: their secure rental streams, which are ideal for paying off debt. The CIH and Savills thought that banks might increase interest rates on loans, to reflect increased risk to cash flows (CIH/Savills, 2011).

The CIH felt that it would not be possible to develop supported housing or larger housing with this revenue-based model of funding (CIH, 2011a). Rents for these would be difficult to fix, as there are no private sector comparables. The trend to smaller units would be reinforced as associations tried to maximise income from sales and rents.

Associations will have access to very little (if any) grant in this Affordable Rent model. The HCA advised associations and other bidders for Affordable Homes Programme funding that their bids should be for the minimum grant necessary to make the development viable (see the House of Commons Library, 2011 for a good summary of this programme). The government's belief is that eventually rents of up to 80% of market levels will raise sufficient revenue to substantially increase association surpluses. In the shorter term, the government believes that higher rents will enable more private finance to be obtained as cash flows increase. Either way, building homes will now be dependent on revenue surpluses and private finance rather than on capital grant.

The programme was taken up by 146 different organisations that bid successfully for inclusion in 2011. By August 2012, just over 100 had signed firm contracts with the HCA (about one year later than the government had planned). It was expected that about one quarter of the 80,000 affordable homes to be provided will be produced through s 106 planning agreements with private developers. The rest will be built mainly by housing associations. A recent overview of the Affordable Homes programme is contained in Table 6.8 (see Chapter Seven for a discussion on 'affordable rents').

A breakdown of investment by HCA 'operating area' reveals that London and the South-East take the lion's share of the money available for Affordable Homes, with 48.86% of the total (£857.6 million). If the South and South-West's indicative allocation is added to this, the clear southern bias of the programme becomes even stronger, with 62.61% of the indicative programme being allocated in the South, South-East

Table 6.8: Number of new affordable homes by HCA operating area

HCA operating area (OA)	Affordable rent homes	Affordable home ownership homes	Total affordable homes	OA %
East and South-East	10,874	3,558	14,432	18.04
London	16,130	5,726	21,856	27.32
Midlands	10,647	2,898	13,545	16.93
North-East Yorkshire and the Humber	7,286	849	8,135	10.17
North-West	8,320	991	9,311	11.64
South and South-West	9,697	3,024	12,721	15.90
Grand total	**62,954**	**17,046**	**80,000**	**100.00**

Source: HCA Affordable Homes website (August 2012).

Note: All figures are subject to change through the contracting process.

and South-West (£1,098.9 million). By comparison, Yorkshire and the Humber and the North-East have received indicative allocations of 10.35% (£181.6 million) for an enormous stretch of the country with significant and enduring housing problems.

In some senses, this simply reflects northern associations' concerns. In terms of investment, however, the geographic bias to the south and London is a trend that was evident in New Labour's time. Research has shown that in 1991/92, 58% of investment went to London and the southern regions. This figure increased to 68% in 2008/09 (HCA/TSA, 2011, p 6).

The future?

Large associations may be able to build using surpluses and borrowing based on increased rents, so-called Affordable Rents. The most obvious areas where this might produce housing are London and the South-East, where there are relatively large differences between associations' current rents (calculated through rent-restructuring formulae) and the equivalent market rent. But even here, some associations are not planning to charge the higher end of the range. There is increased financial risk. Some associations have borrowed to their limit – or are very close to this – so additional borrowing is not possible. The potential to cross-subsidise is also more limited now.

Public subsidy was first made available for local authorities to build council housing on a large scale in the 1920s. Housing associations have never had such a significant role, even though they have been given priority for government funding since the 1980s. In the early part of the 20th century the extent of government investment was far higher than anything that has been recently contemplated. Public money can ensure quality housing and rents within the reach of low–income households, but the government has to believe in and want to make this investment. It shows no signs of wanting to do that now.

REFLECTION 6.1

Building new homes for rent with truly affordable (that is, low) rents

Is it realistic to simply rely on associations' borrowing, their surpluses and some 'flexibilities' to build good-quality rented housing for all those who need and want to rent? Will such homes be affordable?

Further reading

CLG (2007) *Homes for the future: more affordable, more sustainable,* Cm 7191, London: The Stationery Office, www.communities.gov. uk/documents/housing/pdf/439986.pdf.

CLG (2010b) *Local decisions: A fairer future for social housing,* www. communities.gov.uk/documents/housing/pdf/1775577.pdf.

National Housing Federation (2011) *Radical reform: real flexibility,* NHF: London.

Cathy Davis and Alan Wigfield (2012) *Let's build the houses – quick!* Nottingham: Spokesman Books.

Hal Pawson and colleagues (2010) *Rent arrears management practices in the housing association sector,* London: Housing Corporation, www. tenantservicesauthority.org/upload/pdf/Rent_arrears_management_ practices.pdf.

Housing association annual accounts (obtainable by request if not on the websites) are another useful source of information about how these organisations work. They are usually read in conjunction with the Annual Report.

The National Housing Federation (the trade body for housing associations) has useful information and reports (www.housing.org. uk/). Much of this is available to non-members.

The Red Brick blog, a site for progressive housing debate, has useful commentary. It is available at http://redbrickblog.wordpress.com/. It has posts commenting on the Affordable Rent programme, with a great deal of information and connections to other sites.

SEVEN

The private rented sector

Introduction

The private rented sector was in decline for most of the 20th century. The Housing Act 1988 and deregulation of the financial services sector are being claimed as the keys to its apparent phoenix-like recent growth. Some commentators are now focusing on private renting and identifying potential for it to play a significant role in housing low-income households, as the Coalition government wants. But is this new private rented sector any different from the old one, which was notable for badly managed, poor-quality and expensive housing? This chapter will examine this in a number of ways:

- rent control and selective decontrol: the decline of private renting in the 1930s;
- early 1950s London: the problems of decontrolled rents and uncontrolled landlords;
- the 1960s and the 'fair rent' solution for a 'regulated' market;
- the Housing Act 1988 and the 'independent rented sector' with rents and tenancies that are now 'assured';
- a focus on growth: buy-to-let mortgages and homeowners renting out their home because they cannot sell;
- 25 years of deregulation – expensive rents, poor living conditions and limited security. Can private rented housing provide a long-term home?

Rent control and selective decontrol in the 1930s

The idea of rent control – administratively fixing rents in private lettings at a particular level rather than allowing the landlord to do so – has been discussed in Chapter One. There have been different forms of rent control. Their impact has been much exaggerated. Rent control or, most recently, rent regulation, has affected private rented housing in different ways depending on the landlord arrangements (resident or non-resident), type of letting (furnished or unfurnished) and/or the rateable value of the property. Unsurprisingly, its more general impact has varied depending on the nature of the local private rented sector.

Rent control was first introduced by George Asquith's war-time coalition government in 1915 because private landlord profiteering triggered rent strikes during the First World War (Melling, 1983 and Chapters One and Nine). It was intended to be a temporary measure but, once peace came, it was clear that rent control would be very difficult to remove. Lifting control would inevitably lead to large rent increases because landlords would 'catch up' on rent increases that they had been unable to levy earlier. Tenants would be likely to find it difficult to pay, leading to arrears and evictions on a scale that would have political implications for any government. An incremental approach was adopted instead.

- In 1923 when a tenant living in a controlled tenancy moved on, the tenancy became decontrolled, that is, the landlord could set the rent at the level they decided for the new tenant.
- Legislation in 1933 and 1938 extended decontrol in the private rented sector, but rent control remained for the cheapest lettings, in properties with low rateable values.
- With the threat of war in 1939, Neville Chamberlain's Conservative government decided to reintroduce rent control for every new private tenancy.

Commentators have expressed different views about the impact of rent control on the private rented sector. One view is that control stifled landlord investment in new building for rent and in repairs and maintenance. Was there any truth in that?

Up to the Second World War it had become clear that the sector was declining. In 1914, about 90% of the population was living in a private rented room, flat or house. Gradually, over the course of the 1920s and 1930s, this figure declined to about 60%. Particular cities and towns – and specific parts of the private rented market – were affected by rent control and subsequent decontrol in different ways.

At one end of the spectrum, decontrol in the 1930s of more expensive rented property led to new building for private rental in London and along the south coast. Property developers and finance companies now found it profitable to invest in the expensive, high-quality end of the market (Kemp, 2004, quoted in Lowe, 2011, p 74). This mini-boom accompanied the growth of the suburbs in the South-East.

Poor-quality, low-rent private rented housing at the other end of the spectrum, in the North and in some parts of London, was quite different. Here, the sector's decline was related to the fact that private landlordism as an investment had become obsolete. Owning and renting out a small number of houses might have been profitable in Victorian England, but 40 years later this was far from the case. Most landlords owned one, two or three houses and had never made much money, whether or not the rent was controlled. George Orwell's discovery of the small landlord in the North in the 1930s is telling.

Box 7.1: The road to Wigan Pier: the private landlord in the 1930s

'I found – one might expect it, perhaps – that the small landlords are usually the worst. It goes against the grain to say this, but one can see why it should be so ... it is the poor old woman who has invested her life's savings in three slum houses, inhabits one of them and tries to live on the rent of the other two – never, in consequence, having any money for repairs.'

(Orwell, 1989, p 52)

There was little incentive to improve. This was not necessarily because there was not enough money to do so because of rent control. Tenants' incomes were low. They could not pay more. Demand for poor-quality private rented houses far exceeded supply in many areas. This was even the case where local authorities were making little impact with slum-clearance programmes. Landlords did not need to do repairs in order to let their property.

Box 7.2: The road to Wigan Pier: poverty and the housing shortage

'[T]he central fact about housing in the industrial areas [is] not that the houses are poky and ugly, and insanitary and comfortless, or that they are distributed in incredibly filthy slums around belching foundries and stinking canals and slag-heaps that deluge them with sulphurous smoke – though all this is perfectly true – but simply that there are not enough houses to go round ...

[I]n the industrial areas the mere difficulty of getting hold of a house is one of the worst aggravations of poverty. It means that people will put up with anything – any hole and corner slum, any misery of bugs and rotting floors and cracking walls, any extortion of skinflint landlords and blackmailing agents – simply to get a roof over their heads ...

> [S]ome people hardly seem to realise that such things as decent houses exist and look on bugs and leaking roofs as acts of God; others rail bitterly against their landlords; but all cling desperately to their houses lest worse should befall.'
>
> (Orwell, 1989, pp 46–7)

In other areas, where local authorities tackled slum clearance with vigour, private rented slums were disappearing, and with them, the landlords. Their former tenants moved into new council housing. Outside of these areas, the 'window' of decontrol during part of the 1930s presented the landlord with another opportunity to sell up – and many did. As Stuart Lowe put it, landlords were leaving the sector 'in droves' during this time (Lowe, 2011, p 74).

Early 1950s London: the problems of decontrolled rents and uncontrolled landlords

By the early 1950s, both owner-occupation and council housing had grown as tenures but the private rented sector generally was still declining. London was one exception to this, but in the capital the housing shortage, exacerbated by in-migration nationally and internationally, had become acute. Shortages and, for some, the 'colour bar', distinguished the sector, not the controlled rent. Thousands of tenancies were outside of the Rent Acts, especially if someone rented a room or set of rooms in a house where there was a resident landlord. The niceties of rent control were non-existent.

One of the most notorious areas for private landlordism in London was in north Kensington and surrounding areas. It was partly redeveloped in the 1970s and is now known as Notting Hill. In the 1950s, it was an area filled with long terraces of large Victorian mansion blocks, some converted into hotels, some run as boarding houses where rented rooms or part-rooms were available. Overcrowding, dilapidation and racial discrimination were the order of the day for many residents. The area was well known for prostitution and intermittent fascist and Teddy-boy attacks on black people (who were blamed for the poor conditions).

> Black and white working class families lived in squalid, overcrowded slums. Black and white tenants alike were exploited, bullied and harassed by racketeering slum landlords. (Fryer, 1984, p 378)

Michael Heseltine was one landlord out of the 'hundreds' operating boarding houses in the area. He later played a major part in Margaret Thatcher's Conservative government as Secretary of State for the Environment. The money to be made from letting rooms was considerable, as this account shows.

Box 7.3: Being a boarding house landlord in 1950s London

Michael Heseltine's first career was as a private landlord. When he left university, with a cheque for £1,000 left him by his grandfather, he bought 39 Clanricarde Gardens with an associate. His friend Julian Critchley recalled:

'In 1955 there was no security of tenure, no rent restrictions. [The property was in] a cul-de-sac on the northern side of Notting Hill Gate ... Tall and narrow, gloomy and dilapidated, the house was divided into eighteen rooms; Heseltine lived in two of them and let the rest at two or three guineas a week ... Should any of his tenants fall behind with the rent, due on a Friday, Michael would fit a lock to the outside of their doors and await their return. An agreement to pay was arrived at; no one was ever put on to the street ... Life in Clanricarde Gardens was pretty sordid but it provided an income and a roof over his head.

He sold this property after a year, making a profit, and with his associate bought another, the New Court Hotel in Inverness Terrace. This was run as a boarding house, not a hotel. It was sold after about a year to a Colonel Sinclair, an associate of Rachman's, at a handsome profit.

Heseltine used his share to buy another boarding house in Tregunter Road (and set up a property company, Bastion Constructions). In Tregunter Road Michael lived a life of luxury. His drawing room was dominated by an enormous chandelier, his bathroom would not have disgraced the Colby's and the flat was partly warmed by electrically charged carpets ... He bought a two litre Jaguar and employed a chauffeur. The Lad had arrived.'

(Critchley, 1987, pp 21–3)

Note: One guinea was £1 1s (£1.05). Two guineas were £2 2s (£2.10) and so on. Using Measuringworth.com and annual RPI rates, in 1955, 16 rooms let at a minimum weekly rate of £2 guineas would generate an annual income for the landlord before deductions of just over £1,747 in 1955 values. The average wage in that year was £434. In 2010 values (the most recent available), Clanricarde Gardens would have generated minimum rental income of £35,776 a year before deductions. 'The Colby's' were a multi-millionaire family in a soap opera of the same name that appeared on BBC TV in the 1980s.

Perec Rachman, who operated in the area, owned several hundred mansion blocks/houses let out as rooms. Boxers and wrestlers with Alsatian dogs for 'protection' were employed as weekly rent collectors. Rachman paid for people to threaten and intimidate long-standing, controlled tenants out of their homes. He packed properties with people who had no tenancy protection. Most were African Caribbean migrants, newly arrived in Britain. They usually faced the discriminatory 'colour bar' when trying to find a home (see Short, 1963, for a retrospective account).

Very controversially, it was against this background that the Conservative government decided to decontrol rents (Donnison, 1967). It believed that landlords needed a free rein to decide rents for themselves so they would have sufficient rental income to undertake repairs and make private landlordism a profitable concern. The Rent Act 1957:

- introduced the immediate decontrol of properties with a higher rateable value (£30 outside of London and £40 within London);
- decontrolled tenancies as soon as a controlled tenant left;
- enabled landlords to increase controlled rents to twice the gross rateable value – that is, twice the 1939 market rent level. Rents could increase by 150% overnight (Malpass, 2000, p 88).

It is worth emphasising that decontrolled tenants had no protection in the courts against eviction. The 1957 Act extended their notice period from one to four weeks, but this was academic. In London, many landlords wanting vacant possession simply evicted tenants or put sufficient pressure on them to leave. Rents charged by landlords increased dramatically after 1957. Officially, they were much higher than equivalent council rents even though conditions were usually very poor. There was no rent allowance scheme in place (a precursor of housing benefit/local housing allowance) to help the poorest. If the rent could not be paid, tenants had to leave. Outside of high-pressure London, tenure-wide implications became apparent.

- Private landlords decided to sell as soon as their controlled tenants died or left. This was a gradual process in many places. In inner-city areas, in the 1960s and 1970s many of these properties were bought by first-time buyers looking for a relatively cheap 'rung' on the so-called 'ladder' of homeownership.

- Sitting tenants also took the opportunity of buying the property from their landlord. Mortgage payments might be cheaper than decontrolled rents (see Chapter Four).

The 1960s and the 'fair rent' solution for a 'regulated' market

The controversy about the likely impact of the Rent Act 1957 did not die down, but the extent and nature of racketeering in the private rented sector in London was not fully exposed until Rachman's activities came to light during the Profumo scandal in 1963. The Conservative government felt obliged to investigate. In August 1963 it set up the Milner Holland Committee (under the chairmanship of a lawyer, Sir Edward Milner Holland). In 1956 the private rented sector had been made up of about 5 million tenancies. By the mid-1960s, this figure had declined to 3.75 million. It was estimated that about 700,000 controlled tenancies remained.

The Milner Holland Committee's report was published in March 1965. The Committee had not been asked to prepare proposals, but recommended that tenants' security of tenure be improved. Seven years had passed since the Rent Act 1957. Thousands had been evicted or had left their homes. During that time too the government had changed. In 1964 the Labour government of Harold Wilson had been elected. What was its approach to the private rented sector?

In 1956, the Labour Party's annual Conference had agreed a motion committing the party to the municipalisation of the private rented sector. In this period, conference votes were a significant influence on subsequent party policy and government action, but in 1956 the Labour Party was not in power. By 1962, a similar motion failed. The mood had changed: municipalisation was too expensive to contemplate. Instead, a motion was passed for a discretionary programme of compulsory purchase of poor-condition private rented housing by local authorities. Now in power as part of the newly elected Labour government, Richard Crossman, the new Minister of Housing and Local Government, had to decide what to do about the private rented sector: tackling illegal harassment and rents was the key.

To start, Crossman found the Milner Holland report 'extremely good'. Amongst other things, it disposed of what Milner Holland called 'hypotheses' and what Crossman renamed 'Tory legends' about the causes of the housing shortage in London.

Box 7.4: Some 'Tory legends'

Milner Holland's report disposed of what Crossman called 'the four legends' about housing shortages in London. These were that housing shortages:

- were created by rent restriction in the private rented sector. The Committee found that it was not rent control as such that created shortage, but a combination of political and economic circumstances facing the private landlord. It suggested that private landlords should be given loans or subsidies to enable them to improve their property;

- were created by the way that London's council housing was managed, with under-occupancy and better-off tenants blocking the rehousing of poorer private tenants. The Committee could find no evidence of under-occupancy. Council tenants were found to have incomes below those in the private rented sector;

- were a result of 'immigration' – the Committee found that people who were recent migrants were not the cause of the problem. They were often the victims;

- were the result of empty housing – while there might be empty property in some parts of London, it was not to be found in the council sector. Empty property might be located in the private sector but, as Crossman remarked to the House of Commons, it was not sufficient for Conservative MPs to expect poor private tenants to buy it.

Source: Richard Crossman, comments during debate on the Milner Holland Report in the House of Commons, *House of Commons Debates*, 22 March 1965, vol 709, cols 52–181. Available at: http://hansard.millbanksystems.com/commons/1965/mar/22/housing-milner-holland-report.

Milner Holland showed that in Greater London 190,000 households were in urgent need of housing and another 61,000 single people were living in housing that had no sinks or stoves. These were higher than official figures from the early 1960s and showed that the situation had deteriorated. Crossman pointed out that many of these households were low paid, would have been refused or been ineligible for a building society mortgage and could not wait 'five or six years' for a council house. They were:

compelled to accept what the private landlord can provide in furnished or unfurnished accommodation. The one kind of housing which is in desperately short supply, outside the council estates, is just that accommodation which these lower paid families or migrants can afford. (House of Commons, 1965)

He argued that the housing shortage in London had been made worse by Conservative policies with:

- an overemphasis on owner-occupation and restriction of local authority activity on slum clearance;
- slum clearance then giving private developers opportunities for making profits by building luxury flats at £300–£400 a year (in 1965 prices), offices and shops.

The Milner Holland Committee had not been able to find one developer across Greater London who was building for the lower end of the private rented market. Many local authorities were compounding the problem by not rehousing those displaced by slum clearance (recently arrived single people and families did not command high priority on waiting lists).

Crossman had already begun work on what became the 'fair rent system' for the unfurnished private rented sector, but he persuaded the Milner Holland Committee to publish its report before his Bill was tabled in the House of Commons. In this way, the report and its comments about fair rents were used to add weight to the Bill (see Crossman, 1976, p 186, diary entry for 21 March 1965). Crossman later regretted not including furnished tenancies within the Bill's remit. Nevertheless, it was a challenge devising this new 'administrative rent' for the unfurnished private rented sector and steering it through a civil service with its own ideas of what was possible (Crossman, 1975, pp 89–90, diary entry for 7 December 1964) as well as an initially hostile Standing Committee for the Rent Bill, which considered it clause by clause (1976, pp 221-3, diary entries for 17 and 18 May, and p 231, for 26 May 1965). The Committee was an important stage in the Bill's progression through Parliament before becoming law. (See Chapter Nine for the details.) As Malpass summed up:

The scheme overcame the rigidity of rent control by allowing for periodic reviews of fair rents, and for increases to be phased in over a run of years. This amounted to a

> system of moderated market rents, but allowed prices to move more or less in line with inflation and incomes. The fair rent system was introduced in the Rent Act 1965, but it spread only slowly through the sector at a rate dependent upon applications from tenants and landlords ... the concept of fair rents survived as a cornerstone of policy in relation to private renting until 1989, and in the meantime provided the basis for a major expansion of the housing associations. (Malpass, 2005, p 93)

Despite the care taken in devising the fair rent system, it only ever covered a part of the private rented sector: unfurnished property where landlord and tenant were happy to see a 'fair rent' set. Controlled tenancies with very low rents gradually disappeared (see Chapter Nine), but so too did furnished private rented housing as the private rented sector continued to decline relative to other tenures. Small landlords with one or two properties (always the majority of the sector) continued to leave the sector, selling to sitting tenants, first-time buyers or housing associations undertaking house improvement work in Housing Action Areas and Renewal Areas in the 1970s and 1980s (see Chapter Eight). In 1971 the tenure had represented less than 19% of all dwellings. By 1989, this figure had declined to 7.7% and the sector appeared to be in terminal decline.

The problem of boarding houses remained. Mainly a London issue, many were demolished as part of borough clearance and renewal programmes in the 1970s. For example, many of Rachman's multi-occupied slum mansion houses disappeared in this way and the remainder were gentrified. Down-at-heel bed-and-breakfast hotels emerged as another variation of the sharp end of the private rented sector from the 1970s onwards. They were used as permanent housing by many who could find nowhere else to live and by homeless people sent to these places by local authorities, which used them as a form of temporary emergency accommodation.

The 1970s was a time when local authorities had growing responsibilities for homeless people, especially after the enactment of the Housing (Homeless Persons) Act 1977. 'Bed and breakfast' had to be used because of a lack of alternatives: insufficient council housing was being built to respond to people who could not afford mortgages or private rents. It was estimated that local authorities paid hotel owners over £18 million for bed-and-breakfast rooms in the period 1971–77 (Bailey, 1977, p 30). This increased as their use peaked in March 1987, when 47% (England) and 59% (London) of statutory homeless households were housed in this way (DCLG, 2012e, p 10). For bed-and-breakfast owners, the trade in homeless residents was very lucrative indeed and has continued into the 21st century (see Chapter Three).

The Housing Act 1988 and the 'independent rented sector' with rents and tenancies that are now 'assured'

New regulated tenancies and fair rents ended with the Conservative government's Housing Act 1988. The Act introduced 'assured' and 'assured shorthold' tenancies and 'assured' rents to replace them. These changes were designed to:

- remove fair rent regulation in relation to rents in the private sector. Some landlords had never used fair rents, but now all landlords could decide the rent that they wanted to charge, up to the market level;
- enable landlords to end tenancies more quickly and easily than in the past.

The Conservative government's purpose was made even clearer when the position of assured and assured shorthold tenancies was reversed in the Housing Act 1996. The assured tenancy had been the main or default tenancy created in the Housing Act 1988. This was reversed in 1996 legislation when the assured shorthold tenancy became the main or default tenancy. Its length was reduced from 12 to 6 months. Notice could be served two months before the end of the contract in order to obtain possession. If a landlord wanted to create a longer-term assured tenancy under the 1988 Act, a specific notice detailing this intention had to be issued to the tenant before the start of the tenancy (see Cowan, 2011, pp 279–82).

In this way, the Conservatives ended any vestige of rent regulation. The relationship between landlord and tenant was now firmly weighted in favour of the landlord. The government thought that this would revive what it called the 'independent rented sector'. Another 'essential step' in the government's determination to expand the private rented sector was:

> to enable private landlords to charge rents on new lettings at a level that will give them a reasonable return. (Department of the Environment, 1987, para 3.4)

The government was keen to emphasise the importance of the sector in providing quick and easy access to housing for people who needed to move for a new job (assuming that they could pay the rent and deposit). Yet, with less security of tenure and more expensive rents in prospect, it was by no means clear which new groups of people would be interested in renting privately. Cowan makes a telling point, which should have been particularly important for the New Labour government that followed:

> If one aim of housing policy is to improve the quality of the housing stock and, more specifically, to ensure that the vulnerable are not taken advantage of, the ease with which a landlord can take possession may not assist either aim. (Cowan, 2011, p 281)

So there was a question mark in relation to future demand. The other side of the equation was supply. The sector continued to be dominated by small landlords who owned one or two properties, rather than by large-scale investors. Now that rents and tenancy conditions were stacked in their favour, would potential new investors be persuaded to provide more property to let?

In the event, the sector has grown, but not quite in the way envisaged. Table 7.1 shows the details, with data divided into two periods. The effects of Conservative legislative changes gradually emerged in the period 1988–97. The Conservatives also tried unsuccessfully to secure larger-scale investment, for example through the time-limited Business Expansion Scheme. From 1997, New Labour continued the Conservative's neoliberalist approach to the sector but introduced some additional regulation to improve conditions. It also tried to harness parts of the sector for local authorities to use in dealing with increasing numbers of homeless households in the mid-2000s. Unsurprisingly, this had costs (Davis and Wigfield, 2012, pp 13–16).

The figures for 2007/08 were the last collected in this form (Pawson and Wilcox, 2011/12, Table 54a). (The Survey of English Housing was amalgamated with the English House Condition Survey in April 2008.) They update those provided in Table 7.1 and follow the same trends. The total number of tenancies in the private rented sector as a whole had increased by 2007/08. There were now 2,770,000 private sector tenancies but this was not the whole picture:

- 2,204,000 were let as assured tenancies;
- 127,000 lettings were with resident landlords (and there were 14,000 'other' lettings);

Table 7.1: Number of private rented homes in England, 1988–2004 (thousands, percentages in brackets)

Year	All tenancies	Regulated	Not accessible to the public	Unregulated active market
Conservative government				
1988	1814	1071 (59)	508 (28)	235 (13)
1990	1787	590 (33)	482 (27)	715 (40)
1993/94	2132	371 (17)	379 (18)	1382 (65)
1994/95	2197	311 (14)	431 (20)	1381 (63)
1995/96	2254	272 (12)	427 (19)	1555 (69)
1996/97	2280	242 (11)	416 (18)	1622 (71)
New Labour government				
1997/98	2255	205 (9)	349 (15)	1701 (75)
1998/99	2247	188 (8)	387 (17)	1672 (74)
1999/2000	2305	154 (7)	444 (19)	1707 (74)
2000/01	2186	122 (6)	382 (17)	1682 (77)
2001/02	2129	117 (5)	308 (14)	1705 (80)
2002/03	2221	127 (6)	354 (16)	1741 (78)
2003/04	2350	138 (6)	347 (15)	1864 (79)

Source: Mullins and Murie (2006, p 119), using data from Office of National Statistics *Survey of English Housing* (2004).

Note: 'Regulated' tenancies were self-contained, unfurnished tenancies let under the Rent Act 1977. Most were not likely to have had a fair rent registered on them because tenants would be wary of potentially undermining a good landlord–tenant relationship. The 'unregulated active market' in 1988 included unfurnished self-contained accommodation let by the landlord using a licence agreement to circumvent the Rent Act 1977 provisions which protected tenants from summary eviction. From 1993/94 these figures are inclusive of non-private lodgers (lodgers of people who were owner-occupiers or tenants of social rented housing). The figures for the active market also included resident landlord and 'other' lettings (a small figure unspecified in the original data). Lettings 'not accessible to the public' included tied tenancies, lettings of student residences and lettings at low rents to friends and relatives.

- 120,000 (4%) regulated tenancies were contained within that total. The figure showed their continuing decline in the sector (from over 1 million in 1988);
- 304,000 (11%) tenancies were 'not available to the public' (a decline of tied accommodation rather than of lettings in student halls and blocks of flats).

Grouping together assured tenancies, resident landlord lettings and 'other' lettings (as Mullins and Murie (2006) had done before) produced a total of 2,345,000 lettings. This represented 85% of total lettings in the sector. It was clear that the unregulated part of the market (which is what Mullins and Murie called this grouping) had grown substantially in the 20 years since 1988. By contrast, and unsurprisingly, the regulated sector had declined, but it is important to recognise that regulated tenancies and fair rent registration were not automatically linked. Tenants had to apply to the Rent Officer Service (Valuation Office Agency) for a fair rent to be set. Many would not do this, either fearing the landlord's reaction or being ignorant of the possibility. So the growth of the unregulated sector is not simply due to removing 'rent control' or 'rent regulation'.

The most recent Household Report, for 2010/11, indicates that the private rented sector has continued to grow. It now contains a 'headline' figure of 3.62 million households, representing 17% of housing in England (CLG, 2012). The unregulated, assured tenancy part of the private rented sector is likely to be about half a million less than this, but still substantial, at about 3 million.

Mullins and Murie (2006, p 120) have commented that deregulation was a 'contested topic, before, during and after' the Conservative government's action to abolish new regulated tenancies and the fair rent regime. Were fair rents (represented by critics as restrictive 'regulation' or 'control') damaging growth? The Conservatives *presumed* that they were, even though it was unlikely that the majority of private regulated tenancies were let at 'fair rents'.

The unregulated market has grown steadily since 1988 but its most recent growth has to be regarded with some degree of caution. Firstly, financial deregulation resulted in the creation of the buy-to-let mortgage in 1996. This encouraged a surge of new individual amateur landlords whose predominant interest is in making money from renting out housing. They may not want to be a landlord for too long. Secondly, with the stalling of the owner-occupied sector, owners have turned temporarily to renting out their former homes (and becoming tenants themselves) while they wait for house prices to rise and mortgage lending to improve. So growth is not what it seems to be, and it may not last.

A focus on growth: landlords with buy-to-let mortgages and homeowners renting out their home because they cannot or will not sell

The current private rented sector provides a home for people who are looking for their first independent home, for people moving areas because of a new job and for people having to move quickly because of changed circumstances (for example, when couples split up). Relatively few of the people currently living in private rented housing see it as a long-term home: only 21% have lived in their current home for more than five years. Many long-term residents are older people. Tenancy turnover or 'churn' in the sector (with people moving in and out of tenancies) is very high: 35% of tenants have lived in their current tenancy less than 12 months, and 54% less than two years (DCLG, 2012b, pp 71–2).

Julie Rugg and David Rhodes (2008) identified a number of 'niches' or 'sub-markets'.

Box 7.5: Some sub-markets in the private rented sector

- Young professionals, whose presence in the private rented sector reflects a complex amalgam of choice and constraint.
- Students, whose needs are increasingly being met by larger, branded, institutional landlords.
- The housing benefit market, where landlord and tenant behaviour is largely framed by housing benefit administration.
- Slum rentals, at the very bottom of the private rented sector, where landlords accommodate often vulnerable households in extremely poor-quality property.
- Tied housing, which is a diminishing sub-sector nationally but still has an important role in some rural locations.
- High-income renters, often in corporate settings.
- Immigrants, whose most immediate option is private renting.
- Asylum seekers, housed though contractual arrangements with government agencies.
- Temporary accommodation, financed through specific subsidy from the DWP.
- Regulated tenancies, which are a dwindling portion of the market.

Source: Rugg and Rhodes (2008, p xiv)

Individual small-scale private landlordism seems to be an intrinsic part of the private rented sector, despite government attempts to tempt institutional investors to the sector. Ball has commented that this is not unusual internationally, given the nature of the investment (Ball, 2010, pp 26–30).

Box 7.6: Landlords Survey 2010: landlord characteristics

- In 2010, 89% of an estimated 1.2 million landlords in England were individuals or couples.
- 98% of those becoming a private landlord in 2007–10 were individuals.
- Only 5% were private companies.
- 78% owned one property.

> • Only 8% were full-time landlords. Most were unqualified and inexperienced landlords.
> • 43% used agents to manage their property.
> • 51% of properties that are used for private rental were bought after 2000.
> • A further 25% were bought between 1990 and 1999.
> • Only 50% of individual landlords expected to still be renting out property in 10 years' time. 24% of *new* landlords expected to leave the sector shortly (they had no plans to stay beyond about a year). 13% of *all* landlords expected to quit the sector within two years.
>
> *Source:* DCLG (2010, p 5)

The 'investment motive' has grown recently too. In 1993–94, 48% of private landlords in England were involved simply to make a profit. By 2010, 76% of individual private landlords regarded their property as primarily an investment or a future pension (DCLG, 2012a, p 29). This means that these landlords primarily regard their rented property as an appreciating capital asset, not someone's home. They charge market rents.

The strongest growth of the private rented sector has been in Northern Ireland and in the less-pressured markets of the North and the Midlands in England. Growth in Wales and Scotland has been relatively 'modest' (Pawson, 2012, p 14).

Two aspects of growth in the private rented sector will be considered here:

• the phenomenon of buy-to-let landlords, whose motives for landlordism are predominantly profit led;
• owner-occupiers who are 'reluctant' landlords: they want to sell their home but cannot find a buyer or will not drop their asking price.

Buy-to-let landlords

Buy-to-let mortgages were first introduced in 1996. They are financially advantageous to landlords, as they are closer to residential mortgages than business loans. The largest mortgage lenders in the market now have specialist buy-to-let teams and there are specialist providers such as Paragon. The main specialist provider, Bradford & Bingley, had to be bailed out by the taxpayer to avoid bankruptcy in 2007, and Paragon temporarily stopped trading at the same time because of lack of funds. Both were reliant on the wholesale market for funds, which dried up (see Chapter Nine). In 2000, 120,000 buy-to-let mortgages were agreed with landlords. By 2006, this had increased to 849,000 mortgages, worth just under £95 million (CML, quoted in Rugg and Rhodes, 2008, Table 2.3, p 129).

By the end of 2009, the CML reported that lenders had agreed a total of 1.2 million buy-to-let mortgages. Buy-to-let mortgages made up 65% of net lending in 2009. This is a very surprising figure when seen in the context of the mortgage famine for owner-occupiers (CML, 2012b). However, these numbers can be deceptive.

- In the peak year of 2006, 28% of the total private rented stock was being purchased on the basis of a buy-to-let mortgage, but buy-to-let borrowing was not all for additional property.
- Nearly one half (46%) of buy-to-let mortgages were taken out by existing landlords to refinance their existing borrowing on better terms (see Rugg and Rhodes, 2008, p 10, and Table 2.2, p 128).

The annual number of new buy-to-let mortgages has dropped dramatically since its peak in 2006–07, when about one third of rented property was being bought with a buy-to-let mortgage (Rugg and Rhodes, 2008, p 10). New lending is now one third of that figure (Pawson, 2012, p 16), although the specialist lending indicated in Table 4.1 above shows a much steeper decline than this: from a peak of 269,000 mortgage advances in 2007 to 24,000 in 2009.

The owner-occupier as 'reluctant' or 'accidental' landlord

The prolonged downturn of house prices and the difficulty in obtaining a mortgage since 2007 have led many owner-occupiers who need to move home to consider renting out their property. The incidence of this type of landlordism – where an owner who wants to sell decides to rent out for a short time instead – varies geographically, depending on the local market. The DCLG Landlords Survey 2010 found that among *new* landlords, 36% were now renting out their former home (it had not been bought for that purpose originally). More generally, considering *all* landlords, the Survey found that 22% of landlords had lived in their property before they put it on the rental market – either as owner-occupier of a self-contained home or as a resident landlord.

The extent of this type of landlordism is difficult to measure. Much is hidden.

- The sector has grown in areas where, historically, private renting has been weak or non-existent in recent times (the North-East,

North-West, East and West Midlands – see Pawson, 2012, p 15, using DCLG data). Council and/or housing association rented housing replaced poor-quality private housing that existed in these areas before, but turnover is now likely to be low and vacancies few.

- London has seen the growth of the private rented sector in absolute numbers but the market there is different, showing the extremes of luxury (with rents of £2,000 a week) and squalor (with packed bed and breakfast 'hotels'). At one point in 2009, in some parts of London and the South-East, there was a glut of homes available for private rent from 'reluctant' landlords as mortgages became impossible to obtain. Rent levels dropped as supply overran demand (Peachey, 2009) but this was a temporary, localised phenomenon, not a national trend.
- 'Reluctant' private landlords will be contributing property for rent that is likely to be better quality, in good repair and more recently built than has been common in private rented housing.

Selling up and moving on

Although these two types of small landlord have contributed to the sector's recent growth, this may not continue in the longer term. Just as in the Klondyke gold rush, many of these new, inexperienced and profit-hungry landlords may be here today and gone tomorrow. This is not unexpected. Scanlon and Whitehead (2005), researching when the market was buoyant, reported that buy-to-let landlords were happy to continue if house prices remained stable or increased and if they could get 'very good rental yields'. However, they suspected that the buy-to-let market was 'pro-cyclical rather than counter-cyclical' (p 3). As house prices declined and if private landlords had bought at the peak of the boom, they might now try to sell quickly so as to avoid negative equity. The most important point about the 'reluctant' or 'accidental' landlords is that they are renting out their former home *temporarily*, waiting for the market to change. In that sense, they are another wobbly prop supporting the growth of the sector.

Both buy-to-let and 'reluctant' landlords are amateurs in terms of housing management, many knowing next to nothing about the legal rights and responsibilities of landlord and tenant. The assured shorthold tenancy gives landlords power to end contracts quickly if they want to sell up, but some are not waiting for that and there has been a proliferation of illegal eviction and harassment in the sector (Cowan, 2011, pp 296–300; Reeve-Lewis, 2012), but relatively little criminal prosecution. This is not the place for a detailed account of the civil and criminal law on harassment and illegal eviction, but it is important to be aware that the context of such legal action has changed. Labour Housing Minister Richard Crossman introduced emergency legislation in 1964 to deal with any landlord's Rachman-like tendencies, but after 25 years of Conservative and New Labour neoliberalist policies, the history and reality of much of the private rented sector has been forgotten.

> The policy image of the landlord has turned almost 180 degrees so that [it] no longer refers to the social pariah status exemplified by Rachman(ism); rather ... housing policy is fixated by the 'good many landlords' in the sector (DETR/ DSS, 2000) whom we want to protect, and the concern that they might fall victim to the unscrupulous tenant ... Rather than benign (or malign) neglect, the sector is now favoured by government intervention to stimulate the market and protect landlords. (Cowan, 2011, p 309)

A much-complained-about compulsory registration system is in place in Scotland to improve standards. There are possibilities of the same in Wales and Northern Ireland (see Welsh Assembly, 2012, and Gray and McAnulty, 2011 in relation to Northern Ireland). Nevertheless, the prospect of a similar registration scheme in England has been dismissed by the Conservative Housing Minister in the Coalition government, a decision that is simply justified on the basis of 'no more red tape' (DCLG, 2012d)

Are private rented tenancies fit to live in and affordable? Do they provide a long-term home?

How different are the problems in the deregulated 'free' private rented sector from the past? Much is the same. One- or two-bedroomed property predominates. The majority of the sector is to be found in terraced housing, low-rise purpose-built flats and converted flats in large houses. In England, over one half (52%) of this housing was built before 1945. Over 40% was built before 1919 (DCLG, 2012a, p 8). New purpose-built buy-to-let flats make up only about 4% of the total (DCLG, 2010, p 27), although they are concentrated in particular cities and locations and so have had a disproportionate impact on the public's consciousness about the sector. Levels of disrepair are *still* significantly higher than in other tenures, despite an influx of newer property, because of 'reluctant' homeowner landlords. Over 37% of privately rented property in England failed the DHS in 2010/11, despite 25 years of landlords receiving unregulated rental income. More than this, the English Housing Survey found that:

> the likelihood of private renters living in dwellings in substantial disrepair also increased markedly the longer they had been resident in their current home (from 27% for those resident for less than one year to 54% of those resident 20 years or more). (DCLG, 2012b, p 5)

The average gross income of private renters in 2010 was £29,000, compared to £40,900 for owner-occupiers and £17,400 for social renters (DCLG, 2012b, p 18). In 2010, 60% of private tenants were in full-time work, with an average weekly wage/salary of nearly £600. Fifty-nine per cent said they planned to buy their own home in the future (DCLG, 2012b, p 18), confirming that the sector is still regarded as a staging-post to owner-occupation, and not as a permanent home. In 2010/11, average weekly rents in private rented housing were £160. This compares to average weekly rents in local authority/housing association housing of £79. Even average weekly mortgage costs of £143 (DCLG, 2012b, p 18) are less than the rents that private landlords are charging. Mortgage costs and private rents will vary across the country, but local authority and housing association rents have been subject to a New Labour policy (continued by the Coalition government) of rent restructuring (see Chapter Nine). This was designed to align the rents in these two sectors and increase them to sub-market rent levels. But, as can be seen, private sector rents are still much higher, especially in the South (London Assembly, 2011).

Turnover in the sector is very high, which is not surprising, given six-monthly assured shorthold tenancies. Thirty-five per cent of private tenants have lived in their home for less than one year and 54% for less than two years (DCLG, 2012b, pp 71–2). The poorest families and single people will be found in the worst housing. Many landlords will not accept tenants who rely on LHA in whole or in part to pay the rent. In addition, the LHA limits push these tenants into the cheapest third of the private rented market (see Chapter Ten). As was clear in the examples from the 1930s and 1950s, at the bottom end of the market landlords do not prioritise repairs when they are faced with excess demand for a vacancy. Rugg and Rhodes (2008, pp 69–70) comment that research has shown that landlords' gross rental yields have been higher on non-decent property than on equivalent well-maintained property. This means the landlords save money on management and maintenance, a strategy which could be employed successfully if there was a high turnover of tenants who might not see repairs as a 'pressing concern'.

Responding to a growing problem, New Labour introduced licensing of HMOs and selected licensing of the worst private sector landlords in the Housing Act 2004. This was its preferred way of improving standards: giving local authorities discretionary responsibility. There has been limited success with both these strategies, partly due to local authorities having insufficient resources to undertake this work and its low priority compared to other urgent issues (see Cowan, 2011, pp 66–71 for a detailed discussion).

Research in 2008 estimated 56,000 licensable HMOs in England, of which 23,000 had still not been licensed. The procedure is bureaucratic and costly: some landlords have tried to avoid registration by reducing the numbers of people and the numbers of storeys in their HMO(s) (BRE, 2010, points 5.1 and 7.1). Some have not bothered to apply. Apart from the complexity of the legislation, Cowan thought that it was possible that enforcement and prosecution were less likely to be pursued by a local authority if it relied on local HMOs to provide housing for people who would otherwise be homeless (Cowan, 2011, p 69).

The New Labour government introduced targets for local authorities that were using bed-and-breakfast hotels to provide temporary accommodation for homeless families. After April 2004, local authorities were financially penalised if any homeless family had to stay in bed-and-breakfast accommodation for more than six weeks. The target was successfully reached in 2004 and this use of bed-and-breakfast accommodation had been declining. Since 2010, this trend has reversed. In 2011/12, 3,960 statutory homeless households (8% of the total) were living long term in bed-and-breakfast hotels, placed there by local authorities. This number is nearly double (44%) that of 2010/11 (DCLG, 2012e).

Will conditions improve? The fate of the 'Rugg Review' of the sector (Rugg and Rhodes, 2008) is instructive. Commissioned by New Labour, the review made a number of decidedly conservative recommendations for improvements. After consulting widely, New Labour agreed to establish a new information service for tenants, to legislate to make written tenancy agreements a requirement, to establish a national register of landlords and to introduce legislation to improve lettings agency practice. The Coalition government has rejected all of these. Investment in rented housing for relatively low-income families and single people will probably remain dependent on individual landlords, with unplanned and uncontrolled growth and contraction following the wider vagaries of the economy. The cost of this approach for lower-income households will be explored in Chapter Ten.

REFLECTION 7.1

The prospects for private renting

What would make the private rented sector suitable as a sector providing permanent homes for single people and families with children?

Further reading

DCLG (2012f) *Review of the barriers to institutional investment in private rented homes*, http://www.communities.gov.uk/documents/housing/pdf/2204242.pdf.

London Assembly (2011) *Bleak houses: Improving London's private rented sector*. Available at: http://www.london.gov.uk/sites/default/files/Bleak-Houses-Final-Report.pdf.

Hal Pawson (2012) 'The changing scale and role of private renting in the UK housing market', in Hal Pawson and Steve Wilcox, *UK Housing Review 2011–2012*, Coventry: CIH, Heriot-Watt University and University of York, pp 14–23.

Julie Rugg and David Rhodes (2008) *The private rented sector: Its contribution and potential*, York: University of York.

Part Three

Issues with housing costs

EIGHT

'Marginal' owner-occupation

Introduction

Political discussion about owner-occupation has usually focused on the supposed positive attributes that ownership brings: a sense of independence, security and feeling of 'paying your own way'. Margaret Thatcher was fond also of asserting that citizens needed a stake in society, hence she promoted the right to buy with the idea of the 'property-owning democracy'. In turn, Tony Blair and Gordon Brown believed that extending homeownership would spread 'wealth'. There can be no denying that owner-occupation is popular in the UK, but the attributes claimed for it are not universal across the tenure. The positive view needs to be tempered with an awareness of the financial implications of extending owner-occupation down the income scale at a time when the 'safety net' for owner-occupiers who run into difficulties paying their mortgage is minimal.

Different aspects of owner-occupation at the margins will be considered in this chapter in order to demonstrate this darker view, as well as wider points. These are:

- moving into owner-occupation: first-time buyers and the implications of large deposits; shared ownership and equity sharing as a way into owner-occupation; council tenants and discounts under the 'right to buy';
- staying in owner-occupation: paying for repairs and maintenance;
- leaving owner-occupation: 'prime' owner-occupation, mortgage rescue and the likelihood of repossession; sub-prime owner-occupiers and the likelihood of repossession; 'spending the home' on long-term care.

Moving into owner-occupation

First-time buyers

First-time buyers have found it increasingly difficult to buy. In the early 2000s, the price of property increased by over 60%. However, before

2007 it was possible to obtain 100% mortgages or mortgages with a very high 'loan to value' ratio, generated from calculations of four, five or even six times the household income (see Box 2.2). This meant that people with no savings could obtain a mortgage for a substantial proportion or the full price of a property. They did not need a deposit.

Since the financial crisis of 2007/08, lenders have changed their approach to mortgage lending. Firstly, they are not keen to lend (see Table 4.1). Secondly, the multiples of household income used to calculate the mortgage have decreased and lenders require a much bigger deposit than before. This has led to a situation in which first-time buyers have become increasingly scarce in the mortgage market. In 2006, just before the financial crisis, 211,100 mortgages were agreed for first-time buyers, representing about 30% of the mortgage market. By 2009 this had fallen to 100,900 (Wilcox, 2011b, p 25), and numbers are still declining, so that first-time buyers are now of relatively minor importance to lenders.

Generally, if a bank or building society agrees to lend, the loan-to-value ratio used to decide how much to lend has decreased.

- At the beginning of 2008, 60% of the mortgage market was made up of mortgages covering 90% or more of the price of a house/flat. By 2009, this figure had declined to 10%. By 2010, it was 2% (Wilcox, 2011b, p 23).
- Unsurprisingly, within that figure, the 95% mortgage or 100% mortgage has dramatically declined, with numbers falling from 118,000 (2007), to 38,000 (2008) to 3,000 (2009), and it has now almost completely disappeared (Wilcox, 2011b, p 23).

The amount of money that first-time buyers are now expected to provide as a deposit is considerable. Table 8.1 shows the level of deposit required in 2010 by a first-time buyer if they obtained a mortgage covering 90% of the value of the property they wanted to buy. As 90% mortgages have disappeared since then, deposits have become even bigger.

First-time buyers may be able to save the amount required for the deposit from their wages/salaries, but many now get extra help to provide the deposit required. Table 8.2 shows the different sources of help that have been available to first-time buyers. Even before the global financial crisis of 2007–08, the relative contribution of savings to building up this sum was declining (down from 69% in the three years to 1995, to 60% in the three years to 2007). Over the same

Table 8.1: Deposits required with 90% mortgage advances in 2010

Region and country	90% loan-to-value ratio	First-time buyer prices
United Kingdom	£18,623	£186,228
North-East	£11,649	£116,489
North-West	£12,932	£129,324
Yorkshire and the Humber	£12,964	£129,644
East Midlands	£13,281	£132,809
West Midlands	£14,121	£141,210
East	£18,311	£183,112
London	£29,662	£296,617
South-East	£20,915	£209,148
South-West	£17,550	£175,504
England	£19,440	£194,402
Wales	£12,580	£125,795
Scotland	£12,934	£129,341
Northern Ireland	£12,345	£123,448

Source: Wilcox (2011b, p 24), using prices from Regulated Mortgage Survey, Q2 2010.

Table 8.2: Sources of contributions towards deposits for first-time buyers

Source	Percentages of first-time buyers who purchased in the three years up to:				
	1995	1998	2001	2004	2007
Savings	69	69	68	68	60
Gift/loan family/friends	22	22	24	22	29
Inheritance	6	6	6	8	6
Windfall	1	2	1	1	0
None	9	7	11	13	15

Source: Wilcox (2011b, p 24), using ONS *Survey of English Housing*.

Note: Multiple sources of contributions may be indicated in the survey.

period, money given or lent by family or friends grew in importance from 22% to 29%.

Eighty per cent of first-time buyers aged under 30 received money from parents (the 'Bank of Mum and Dad') to help with the deposit (Wilcox, 2011b, p 24, using CML information). Parents who contributed towards their adult offspring's deposit appeared to use savings for this, rather than borrowing against their own housing 'asset' to raise the money needed (as another form of asset-based welfare). First-time buyers who received gifts or loans to help them with the deposit ('assisted' borrowers) were able to buy their first home earlier, at an average age of 30 years. The CML has estimated that the number of householders under the age of 30 who have obtained a mortgage and paid a deposit *without* help from family and friends has declined from 120,900 in 2006 to 20,200 in 2009. This number is still falling.

Those who simply saved the deposit were older when they became first-time buyers, at an average age of 36 years. Unsurprisingly, they had higher incomes than those under 30 who were helped by family and friends, the average salary being £36,490 for 'unassisted' purchasers, as compared to £29,420 for those who received additional financial help (CML, 2008, quoted in Wilcox, 2011b, p 25). But, despite their higher income, they might nonetheless be further disadvantaged by lenders. Those who received extra money from parents and/or friends were likely to be able to put down a much bigger deposit than those who simply saved for their deposit.

> In the second quarter of 2008, assisted purchasers were, on average, able to provide a 25% deposit, compared to a 5% deposit for unassisted purchasers. (CML, 2008, quoted in Wilcox, 2011b, p 25)

This in turn led to 'assisted' purchasers receiving a better interest rate on their smaller bank or building society loan, thus reinforcing their financial advantage even though, generally, they had smaller incomes than older, 'unassisted' first-time buyers (Wilcox, 2011b, p 25).

Although house prices are declining (and are expected to continue to do so for some years yet) the number of first-time buyers will continue to fall. Average house prices relative to earnings and the amounts now required for deposits will make buying a house for the first time very difficult indeed (for a detailed discussion of mortgage availability see Wilcox, 2012c, pp 65-71). Young people may continue to buy if they have family or friends with substantial sums to give or lend to them for a deposit. Class divisions in the owner-occupied sector are evident, not just in relation to the quality, size and location of housing. Mortgage lending practices are making buying more difficult for working-class people who are less likely to have easy access to extra sources of funds for deposits.

Deregulation of the mortgage market produced a situation in which it seemed possible for many more people than before to obtain a mortgage. It has been calculated that it created a 30% expansion of the mortgage market for lenders, but what of borrowers? Lending practices encouraged people to think that they could afford to buy and maintain an owner-occupied property, when in fact they could not. The current Coalition government is still relying on owner-occupation to solve the country's housing problems, by extending a mortgage guarantee scheme. From 2014, the Help to Buy: Mortgage Guarantee scheme will enable lenders to use a government guarantee to support mortgages on new or old property. Mortgagors may have as little as 5% of the purchase price to offer as the deposit. The details have still to be worked out with lenders but for the government to provide guarantees for £130 billion of mortgage lending is reckless, given the recent history of the sector. Instead, urgent and difficult questions need to be answered about the tenure. Some years ago Chris Hamnett claimed that:

> Class and income strongly influence gains for comparable cohorts of buyers, but over the long term date of purchase is the most important determinant of absolute gains. (Hamnett, 1999, p 100)

With an increasingly volatile sector and severe housing shortages, the issue of date of purchase may not in the long run be important. The ability to pay initially and then tap into additional finance from family and friends over the short and longer term now seems crucial in achieving and sustaining owner-occupation. This has a class dimension, as better-off working-class households will be the first to be squeezed out of the sector. As secure long-term employment is becoming less common for middle-class professionals as well as for working-class families, it will become more difficult for most households to sustain the long-term financial commitment of mortgage repayments without extra financial help to deal with periods of unemployment or redundancy. Family and friends will have to provide the safety net that has been largely removed by successive governments. With relationships breaking up more regularly than in the past, asking for money will be a complicated transaction. As the sector becomes financially impossible for more people, what are the alternative options for owning your own home?

Shared ownership and equity sharing

Since the 1980s, governments have introduced a variety of schemes designed to enable low-income households to buy their homes. These were designed to reduce demand for council or housing association rented housing by encouraging those who had a job to consider a mortgage. Some schemes have formal income limits to ensure this. In introducing these schemes, there was an assumption that lenders would be willing to provide a mortgage if the mortgagor was liable for only part of the full cost of the property. Two such 'products' will be considered: shared ownership and shared equity.

Shared ownership schemes are the most well known (at least by the local authority and housing association staff who deal with them, if not the general public). Housing associations have built about 22,000 shared ownership properties a year in recent years. By 2009, associations had developed 135,000 homes categorised as 'intermediate homeownership' properties, about 85% of which were properties available for shared ownership. Since then, the numbers built have seriously declined and associations have had difficulty selling them (see Chapter Six). Lenders have started to view them as 'sub-prime' and are unwilling to give a mortgage for them.

A person buying into shared ownership is a long leaseholder of the association which develops the shared ownership property. They part-buy and part-rent the property. They can buy a minimum 25% 'share' of the property, and this can be increased in 10% steps until full purchase ('staircasing' up). A purchaser may be able to 'staircase' down, although this may prove difficult, especially if market conditions deteriorate (an association may not agree if it affects its profitability). The shared owner pays rent to the association for occupation of the property, but is liable for all internal repairs as soon as they have bought a 'share'.

Shared equity schemes involve a loan, taken out by the purchaser to buy a new property. Announced in the 2013 Budget, the Help to Buy scheme has been developed by the Coalition government to replace First Buy and other variants of this type of ownership developed by New Labour. An equity loan will be provided for a maximum of 20% of the price (guaranteed by the government) while the mortgagor pays a minimum 5% of the purchase price. No charge is levied on the equity loan for the first 5 years. It will be repaid when the house is sold, proportionate to the house value at that time. A minimum of 75% of the price is covered by a standard mortgage. The equity loan initially acts like a deposit, but it is not a deposit. The scheme has been extended to include anyone buying a newly built property worth up to £600,000. There are no income limits for potential purchasers in Help to Buy (a substantial change from First Buy where help was limited to those with a maximum total household income of £60,000 a year).

The potential profits from shared ownership enable associations to cross-subsidise the development of new rented social housing (see Chapter Six). It is not known how successful equity loans are, but the Coalition government has made it clear that it supports shared ownership and shared equity schemes.

> We will promote shared ownership schemes and help social
> tenants and others to own or part-own their home. (CLG,
> 2010c, para 12)

In both these arrangements, if the property is sold in the future, the value
of the 'owners'' equity is proportionate to their 'share' or the amount
that they have paid off the mortgage (minus the initial loan). A number
of concerns have been voiced about these schemes (see Mullins and
Murie, 2006, pp 102–7; Munroe, 2007). Shared ownership works in
London and the South-East and in other areas where prices are very
high and access to social rented housing is practically impossible. For
first-time buyers in other parts of the country, it is expensive relative
to owner-occupation.

Research on low-cost homeownership (where shared ownership
was the main scheme) found that residents were very pleased with
their property. Even in 2002, their profile was distinct from that of
most council or housing association tenants. They were better off and
had fewer children. Nearly one fifth (17%) had been owner-occupiers
before (in London, this was 3%). Half of the households were childless.
The majority (85%) were households in which at least one person
had a full-time job, with 71% in professional, intermediate clerical,
junior managerial or skilled manual jobs (Bramley et al, 2002). More
recently, research showed that the average income of shared ownership
households was £27,851 in England (£33,707 in London) in 2008/09
(CIH, 2010a).

Shared ownership is weighted in favour of the housing association
that develops it. 'Owners' are not owners, they are lessees. If they fail
to pay the rent (or periodic fee) they can be evicted (using mandatory
Ground 8 or discretionary grounds, as if they were tenants) and they
lose any value that they might have accumulated in the mortgaged part
of the property. The discussion on the case *Midland Heart v Richardson*
is salutary. Mandatory grounds were used by the housing association
for arrears of £1,941, depriving the owner of a property valued at over
£150,000. The arrears had built up while the owner was in a refuge
for her own safety. After a year, housing benefit could not be paid for
the shared ownership rental element and the refuge rent (see Cowan,
2011, pp 400–5).

Shared owners may find that they cannot afford any further shares
in their home because the rent payments take up too much of their
weekly income. If this is the case, they may find it impossible to move
to a larger home if their family grows. Neither are they able to transfer

as tenants, even though they are paying rent. As Mullins and Murie have pointed out:

> The usefulness of schemes to provide what the CML referred to as 'a foot on the home ownership ladder' is open to question if the next rung was an extremely long way up and there were few choices in the housing market. (Mullins and Murie, 2006, p 106)

There are questions that could be asked of low-cost homeownership schemes. Whose interests are they serving? Do these schemes benefit housing associations or house builders more than new homeowners? Who becomes a homeowner in this way? Might they have become owner-occupiers without the help provided by the scheme? These schemes run in different parts of the country, although the justification for them may not be apparent. Should they be restricted to particular high-pressure parts of the country (for example, London and the South-East)?

The right to buy and discounts

In the 1970s (and earlier in some local authorities) there were *discretionary* council house sales programmes, but the Conservative government elected in 1979 made *mandatory* council house sales and the 'right to buy' a flagship policy. Councils sold properties at substantial discounts, based on the type of council housing and a tenant's length of tenure. Under Conservative governments (1980–97) 1.3 million council houses were sold to sitting tenants. The peak year was 1989, when 139,722 council houses/flats were sold. Ray Forrest and Alan Murie (1988, p 88) estimated that the cost of discounts or 'receipts foregone' was an average of £1,000 million each year between 1980 and 1986.

Economists have argued over the cost of the sales and have devised formulae to work out the losses (see Wilcox, 2006). There are two difficulties with these technical approaches. There is no standard formula for the calculation, so the different assumptions used produce different costs. More importantly, decisions about the right to buy have been made on the basis of political ideology and/or pragmatism rather than economics. New Labour's Green Paper *Quality and Choice* (DETR/DSS, 2000, p 36) quoted a cost of £10,000 per house, calculated by using a discounting formula, which is not credible.

The New Labour government continued the right to buy, and by 2007 nearly 500,000 council homes had been sold under New Labour, an average of 50,000 a year (see Box 8.1 for the justifications for this policy provided by Conservative and New Labour governments). The number peaked at 85,000 in 2003, because tenants were trying to avoid reductions in discounts that were introduced by government regulation in 2002 in order to restrict sales in high-demand areas in the South-East and London (CLG, 2007, section 2.4). The Coalition government has promoted the right to buy too (see Box 8.3). It expects local authorities to use new receipts to contribute towards replacement Affordable Rent housing in their areas. If receipts cannot be used in this way, the government expects the money to be 'pooled' again (that is, returned to the HCA or GLA, both of which are expected to recycle pooled receipts into their wider housing programmes).

Box 8.1: Promoting the right to buy your council house

The Conservatives

Margaret Thatcher thought that council housing represented 'breeding grounds of socialism, dependency, vandalism and crime', whereas home ownership inculcated 'all the virtues of good citizenship.' (Campbell, 2003, p 234, quoted in Gregory, 2009, pp 30–1)

'In terms of housing policy, our priority of putting people first must mean more homeownership, greater freedom of choice, greater personal independence.' (Secretary of State for the Environment, 1979, quoted in Murie and Ferrari, 2003, p 7)

New Labour

In New Labour's first Green Paper on housing, produced in 2000, the government claimed that 'the dream of homeownership' was an 'aspiration' shared by '90%' of the population. 'Our policies will continue to help people to achieve their aspirations and we expect an increase over the coming years in the number of people who own their own home.' Prospective right-to-buy tenants and others were included in the comment that the government would provide 'further support' for those 'on the threshold of homeownership' and 'greater help for people on lower incomes to buy their own homes, promoting a culture of opportunity, choice and self-reliance and giving people more of a stake in their housing and neighbourhoods'. (DETR/DSS, 2000, p 30)

Up to 2003, sales were generally still increasing, reflective of a buoyant housing market where tenants could see the possibility of capital gains if they bought their home. The income levels of RTB-ers have always been lower than those of people using low-cost homeownership schemes, but this difference became more noticeable in what Mullins and Murie called the 'third wave' of sales from 1997 (Mullins and Murie, 2006, pp 93–102). Most middle-aged tenants with long tenancies and better incomes had already purchased. In the third wave, younger, more recent tenants jumped onto the bandwagon. Despite this surge, by 2004 sales were declining in all countries of the UK. In England, the lowest sales figure was 1,610 in 2009 (Pawson and Wilcox, 2012, p 125). There were a number of reasons for this:

- House prices had moved out of the reach of tenants, even with the benefit of discounts.
- Many local authorities did not have many properties that tenants wanted to buy. They might be living in flatted developments or homes built using non-traditional methods. Lenders have traditionally been reluctant to lend on these properties.
- Discounts had become lower relative to prices (Table 8.3). In response to concerns about abuse of the system, a number of measures were introduced in England in 2003, including a maximum discount cap of £16,000 for the high-pressure areas of London and the South-East. There was a flurry of sales as tenants determined to catch the higher discount while they could, but then sales declined again.
- The Housing Act 2004 extension of the qualifying period to five years in England and Wales also reduced sales.

Table 8.3: Maximum right-to-buy discounts in force up to 2011

County or region	Year introduced	Discount limit
Northern Ireland	2002	£24,000
Scotland (modernised right to buy only)	2002	£15,000
Wales	2003	£16,000
London, South-East	1999	£38,000
East	1999	£34,000
South West	1999	£30,000
North-West, West Midlands	1999	£26,000
East Midlands, Yorkshire and the Humber	1999	£24,000
North-East	1999	£22,000

Source: Wilcox (2012a, p 40), using respective government websites.

The right to buy is one policy area where the different countries of the UK can pursue different policies, and distinct approaches have emerged. Wilcox (2012d, p 41) has commented that the approaches now being followed in Scotland (which has abolished the scheme for new tenancies) and England (where discounts are increasing to £75,000) are the result of 'primarily political' decisions, rather than of economic ones. This policy has always been driven by different political ideologies. Under the Conservatives, it was associated with privatisation. Under New Labour it was neoliberalism in the guise of 'choice'. Now, with the Conservatives ascendant in the Coalition government, strategies to reduce the role of the state are resurgent.

Box 8.2: Scotland and the right to buy

In Scotland, there are different arrangements, depending on when a person became a council tenant.

- **Pre-2002:** there is no cap on maximum discounts.
- **Post-2002:** purchasers need to have been council tenants for five years in order to receive a 20% discount. They then receive an additional 1% discount for every additional year. The maximum discount is 35% (after 20 years as a tenant). There is a maximum cash limit of £15,000, whatever the valuation of the council house/flat.
- **Post-2002 high-pressure areas:** the Scottish government has suspended the scheme.
- **April 2011:** the scheme has been abolished for tenants of newly built social housing and new lettings generally.

More broadly than this, what have been the costs of this policy? Between 1980 and 2010, in England alone nearly 2 million council homes were sold to sitting tenants, many at substantially discounted prices. In Scotland, half a million council homes have been sold in the same period. Criticism of the costs incurred from this privatisation programme was considerable during the 'first phase' in the early 1980s, but it has become muted as discounts have decreased (see Davis and Wigfield, 2010, for one critique). It is notable that the Scottish Nationalists, who have had a long-standing critique of the right to buy, have now abolished it. Housing Minister Alex Neil remarked in 2010: 'The Scottish Government is investing a record £1.5 billion in affordable housing – including a new generation of council housing. These far reaching reforms will safeguard that investment for future generations' (Scottish Government, 2010).

There has never been a replacement programme of council housing to replace that sold off. So the tenure has shrunk, and it is no surprise that it is now practically impossible to obtain a council house. There are millions of people in the UK on council and housing association waiting lists. That is the long-term cost.

At an individual level, tenants who bought in the early 1980s may feel that they did the right thing for themselves and their families. Some will have moved on and bought a property elsewhere (in that sense, the policy gave them options that they might not have had before). Their former council properties will have been bought by owner–occupiers looking for slightly bigger homes. In that sense, the role of these early right-to-buy properties has changed. They are often now too expensive for first-time buyers.

Later right-to-buy sales on estates are proving more problematic, especially since 2007–08 and the global financial crisis. In less-pressured parts of the country, these ex-council homes are usually at the bottom of the pecking order of desirable homes. They may be difficult (or impossible) to sell. Empty or neglected property can make estate management difficult for local authorities. Private landlords may be the only people interested in buying, and their interest is profit, not maintenance.

There has been some abuse of the system especially in high-pressure areas, with relatives or companies pressuring older tenants to use their substantial discount to buy at a knock-down price. The property has then been sold, making a considerable amount of money. This led to scheme changes in 2003 and 2004 (but is likely to recur with the substantial increase in discount announced by the Coalition in 2012). Private landlords have bought up more difficult-to-sell property in high-pressure areas (like flats in tower blocks or maisonettes). In the London Borough of Barking and Dagenham, the British National Party sought to exploit tension between the long-established white community and migrants who rented ex-council housing from landlords (Harris, 2010).

The Survey of English Housing 2001–02, found that RTB-ers (at 12%) are more likely to be in mortgage arrears than other first-time buyers (at 10%), despite the discount that they received on the price. Against this background, the Coalition government has decided to increase discounts to £75,000 in England and has spent nearly £1 million on the scheme's promotion.

> **Box 8.3: Housing Minister Grant Shapps on the right to buy in England in 2012**
>
> 'For years, the Right to Buy for council tenants was undermined by punitive cuts to the discounts available, locking the door to home ownership for millions of hard-working people.

Now our revitalised Right to Buy scheme has trebled the discount in many areas ...

The Right to Buy gives something back to families who have worked hard and paid their rent, giving them more freedom to change their home to suit them and a sense of pride and ownership – not just in their home, but in their street and wider neighbourhood.'

Source: DCLG press release (2012)

The Coalition government wants to reduce the council house sector to the minimum and would prefer that it became a temporary tenure, used by people on the journey to permanent private renting or owner-occupation. It wants more council homes to be sold and would like to see any new tenancies let on 'flexible tenancies' with higher rents. This will put pressure on tenants to move, encouraging their 'social mobility' into owner-occupation or the private rented sector (CLG, 2010b). However, the Coalition's promise that there will be a programme of replacement council house building does not add up (see Box 8.4 and Chapter Five).

Box 8.4: What does the right-to-buy scheme mean for LSVT landlords?

Brian Simpson, Chief Executive of Wirral Partnership Homes, commented in 2012:

'as a large scale voluntary transfer organisation, we estimate that 7,400 of our 12,400 tenants still have the preserved right to buy so the changes will affect a large proportion of our tenants ...

... we recently received an application for the sale of a one bedroom flat valued at £50,000. After the tenant's maximum discount of £35,000 is applied the property will be offered for sale at £15,000. Previously the sale price for this home would have been 60% higher at £24,000.

To fund a 30% contribution towards the development of one new property, we estimate that we would need to sell three.'

(Simpson, 2012)

Note: The receipts from three sales would contribute only 30% of the cost of building a new home. The 70% of the outstanding cost would be borrowed.

Staying in owner-occupation

Paying for repairs and improvements

One of the major costs of owner-occupation is repairs and improvements, especially of older housing and more recently built flats (because of the quality of their construction). Between the 1960s and the 2010 CSR, some assistance was available to help owners to undertake this work in certain circumstances. The amount of money made available from central government to local government to pay for this, and the nature and extent of grants available, has waxed and waned, although it has now dried up entirely (see Chapter Three).

Interest in urban renewal replaced large-scale slum clearance programmes in the 1960s. Initially the focus was on grants to owners to install basic amenities such as bathrooms. This developed to include grants for improvements, for example dormer/Velux windows in roofs in order to open the roofspace up as an additional bedroom. This individual work was found wanting, as it often only had a piecemeal influence on an area's improvement. Gradually, improvement work evolved into enveloping or group repair work in many larger urban authorities, where the local authority took responsibility for coordinating the improvement of whole blocks of housing, for example, reroofing a terrace of houses and coordinating financial contributions from a range of different owners (see Leather and Mackintosh, 1994, p 17).

There were two 'boom' periods for grants from local authorities:

- 1972–74, when the Labour government increased the eligible costs for grant work in certain parts of the country;
- 1982–84, when the Conservative government agreed a blanket increase in repair grants to 90% of the eligible costs and their availability was extended to all pre-1919 housing.

The underlying presumption of the early grant regime was that this public investment (from government via local authorities) would encourage private investment. Leather and Mackintosh (1994, pp 11–25) have argued that this did not always happen. This was partly because of the design of grants and partly because of shortages of money in local authorities. This minimised the potential cumulative impact of improvements in an area.

In 1990 the system changed. Some grants were withdrawn, while others were targeted and means tested more tightly. The Conservative government's view was that repairs and improvements were the owner's responsibility. Resource constraints in local authorities in the 1980s and 1990s meant that in most urban areas of England less was spent at that time on dealing with disrepair and unfitness per property than in equivalent areas in Wales, Scotland and Northern Ireland (Leather and Mackintosh, 1994, p 17).

These arrangements continued for the private sector over the period of the New Labour government (1997–2010). Work to achieve the DHS was focused on the council and housing association sectors, with far less emphasis on the private sector. With a change of government and cuts in public expenditure, the remaining grant regime was targeted. Remaining grants for owner-occupiers have now been withdrawn (although there appears to be some discretion for urgent and serious work in Northern Ireland, funded via the NIHE).

Measuring disrepair and unfitness is difficult (and has been subject to definitional changes), but, given a lack of investment, the extent of serious disrepair and unfitness will be growing. Areas with the highest concentrations of substandard housing (including owner-occupied housing) include:

- in England – inner London, the rural South-West, the West Midlands and the North, especially the conurbations in these two areas;
- in Wales – South Wales valleys, Cardiff, Newport and the rural west of Wales;
- in Scotland – rural areas in the North and West and social rented housing in urban areas;
- in Northern Ireland – rural areas of the South and West and particular neighbourhoods, often in inner-city areas (Leather, 2000, p 14).

Table 8.4 suggests that there is a life cycle through which households may pass and their interest and ability to undertake this work (or to pay for someone else to do it) changes over this time. It also suggests some circumstances where investment is unlikely to be made (for example, major works are unlikely if there are young children in the house or if the householder(s) are retired and do not want the disruption). Apart from these individual personal circumstances, there are more general factors affecting whether repairs and improvements may be completed. These include:

- insufficient investment by government in grants and loans to individual marginal or poor owners to undertake major work, and

Table 8.4: Life cycle, length of occupancy and repair and improvement

Household life cycle	Length of stay/ occupancy path	Repair and improvement behaviour	Pressure points
Young household	Recent mover	Most active period. At minimum, will personalise and customise; at maximum, will undertake complete programme of refurbishment	Marginal owner. Foolhardy purchase/ investment choices. Underdeveloped contact networks
Household with children	Longer-established occupier, potential mover	Diminishing work requirements; tackle problems as they arise. Work to improve saleability	Competing spending priorities. Protecting children from disruption/ mess
'Empty nester' pre-retirement	Looking to the long term	Gets house 'finished'; works that will reduce future maintenance. Works to meet outstanding aspirations	Decision on whether to move or stay put
Older household	Long-term occupant	Ongoing diminution of amounts of works undertaken; very little aspirational work; even responsive repair work neglected	Cash poor, losing contact networks, diminishing DIY capacity, unwilling to face disruption
Household dissolution/death	Dwelling recycled to new generation, with degree of renovation depending on condition		

Source: Leather (2000, p 18). Reproduced by permission of the Joseph Rowntree Foundation

insufficient resources available to local authorities to undertake work like this on a neighbourhood basis (see Chapter Three);
- disproportionate growth in the numbers of older people who may not have the income to undertake major work and who also may not want the disruption;
- financial instability in households with difficult employment prospects, or the possibility of relationship breakdown, disrupting the model suggested in Table 8.4;
- increasing age of ex council tenants who bought their council house in the 1980s: they are likely now to be in their 70s and are more likely than other older people to have limited savings;
- ex council tenants who have bought flats on long leases: they will be in a similar situation, often faced with very large repair bills for

communal works that have to be undertaken by the local authority (see Chapter Five).

In the short term, the only way in which additional funds can be obtained to undertake necessary work is through equity withdrawal or second mortgages. Marginal owner-occupiers are less likely to be able to pay for repairs and improvements in this way. The problem of growing unfitness of property in the owner-occupied sector (especially in the inner cities) was foreseen in the 1970s and will not disappear without substantial government investment. With climate change and increasing energy costs, properties' poor thermal insulation and inadequate heating systems will lead to higher numbers of excess deaths brought on by cold and damp homes (the biggest hazard in the new housing health and safety rating system which Environmental Health Officers now use to assess the physical standards in a property, based on an assessment of any hazards to the occupants that may be present).

Leaving owner-occupation

'Prime' owner-occupation, mortgage rescue and repossession

David Cowan pointed out that the main reasons for repossession are relationship breakdown, unemployment and an inability to pay the agreed mortgage. The first two reasons can affect tenants as well as owner-occupiers. But owner-occupiers can become seriously financially over-committed:

> because of the previously (and perhaps current) poor regulation of lending practices, and the resultant over-extension of households not just when they purchase but also subsequently (second mortgages and equity-release arrangements. (Cowan, 2011, p 331)

Between 2005 and 2009 possession claims by lenders in the county courts rose from 107,993 (2005) to 133,001 (2008) and then fell to 87,248 (2009). In England and Wales they continue to fall (Wilcox, 2012a, p 29). About two-thirds resulted in a court order for possession (including suspended orders). By 2009, a different picture was emerging. Formal court action has been declining but mortgagors with 12 months arrears of mortgage are increasing dramatically (Wilcox, 2012a, p 29).

Multiple debts secured against the home are not uncommon now, given how many people literally 'spent the home' in the early years of the century. This marks a different and more serious situation for mortgagors, as compared to the 1990s, when this sort of problem was unusual (Ford et al, 2010). In these instances, court action and repossession are often inevitable. If the situation is more straightforward, with a 'prime' mortgage in arrears, the decline in court action from 2009 onwards may be explained by changes in the attitude of some lenders. They may decide that it is better to keep a mortgagor paying something rather than to go through an expensive procedure with little gain and some damage to their public image. This is more likely in the case of building societies and some major banks:

> Falling house prices, falling transactions, the costs of possession and the extent of exposure to risk, are central factors influencing how lenders respond to arrears. (Ford and Wallace, 2009, p 16)

Mortgagors in arrears may move before formal repossession is taken. They may:

- sell up and buy a cheaper home (although this is dependent on their having sufficient equity to provide a deposit and an income(s) to pay the next (reduced) mortgage);
- move to private rented housing or 'double up' with family or friends for a while and rent out their former home (so that the rental income pays the mortgage);
- hand in the keys to the lender and leave the lender to sell the property, with perhaps some hope of reducing additional arrears if it is sold quickly and professionally by an estate agent (which many lenders use). This strategy has been used more by mortgagors with multiple debts, including second mortgages and credit card debt secured against the home.

Repossession is now regarded as the option of last resort, when all else has failed. In November 2008 a pre-action protocol (PAP) was introduced for court proceedings that reinforced the 'last resort' nature of repossession for mortgage arrears. Lenders were 'virulently against the draft mortgage PAP during consultation' (Cowan, 2011, p 336), and so it is likely that the current protocol was something of a compromise between the New Labour government and the lenders. Lenders accepted it grudgingly, but they would not accept the need for sanctions if any lender did not comply with it. The protocol has led many lenders to review their procedures and change some practices, to the benefit of those in arrears; but the lack of sanctions means that different lenders still have different approaches, and differences can also emerge *within* the same lender. This will become clearer when we consider sub-prime lending.

The impact of the financial crisis in 2007/08 was such as to prompt the New Labour government to intervene in the market more proactively than it had been willing to do before. A number of safety-net initiatives were (re)introduced that have helped to dampen formal repossession figures. The numbers of mortgagors in arrears who are simply paying interest on their mortgage has increased.

Box 8.5: Support for mortgage interest (SMI)

New Labour action:
- For mortgagors who were claiming Jobseeker's Allowance or living on income support or disability living allowance, payment of mortgage interest within these benefits was started 13 weeks after arrears first appeared (rather than after 9 months, as previously).
- The mortgage limit up to which mortgage interest could be paid within these benefit payments was increased from £100,000 to £200,000.
- A fixed rate (above most mortgage interest rates) was introduced to calculate the interest payable in this way.

The government agreed with 'major lenders' that they would wait three months before taking possession action and that they would use that time to find alternatives to repossession. A number of schemes were introduced to reinforce the preference for 'rescuing' people in mortgage arrears. A mortgage rescue scheme was set up. If accepted for the scheme, an owner–occupier with serious mortgage arrears was legally transformed into an intermediate tenant or shared owner. This scheme continues. It is worth noting that the Coalition government has continued the mortgage rescue scheme but some measures have been reduced:

- The way in which mortgage interest is calculated for SMI has been changed to a lower, fixed amount.
- The Coalition government has formally consulted on whether to reintroduce the £100,000 mortgage limit and push the period of eligibility back to 39 weeks, as it was originally. (Wilcox, 2012a, pp 29–30; DWP, 2011)

The possibility of providing an adequate safety net for poorer owner-occupiers in financial difficulty seems to be even further away (see the discussion in Chapter Four).

Sub-prime mortgages

Discussions about housing 'wealth' have obscured the way in which a householder's economic position affects their position as an owner-occupier, and the difficulties that some may have in maintaining a mortgage. In the boom years of the early part of the 21st century many decided to buy a home even though their household income was insufficient and/or insecure. They were encouraged to do so. The mortgage industry advertised thousands of different mortgages, many of which were aimed at low-income households. Multiples of household income that were used to calculate a mortgage were high and 100% mortgages were possible.

Even more serious, 45% of mortgages in 2006/07 were 'self-certified', with some lenders making limited or no checks on income. It was clear that lenders' sole interest during this period was in extending their business, and some were reckless in doing so. Northern Rock was a good example, and Gordon Brown comments on this in his account of this period:

> The Financial Services Authority's report into the failure said that staff felt 'under pressure' to produce attractive arrears figures. As a result, the mortgage bank issued arrears figures that were half the industry average, and then, in their reports to investors, publicly congratulated themselves on their success. The true repossession figures were, in fact, 300 per cent higher than reported. (Brown, 2010, p 24)

The problem of sub-prime mortgages emerged before 2007 in the UK, but it was not acknowledged as such. It was the problem with no name. In 2005 Mark Stephens and Deborah Quilgars (2007) investigated arrears and repossessions in the UK involving 43 mortgage lenders. They found that there was no agreed definition of 'sub-prime' across mortgage lenders. The definition used by Stephens and Quilgars was that 'sub-prime' included mortgages given to people with a poor credit history, or given without income checks (where mortgagors either were self-employed or had an erratic household income). They found that:

- The banks and building societies involved in their research accounted for 76% and 22% of mortgages in the market, respectively, with specialist lenders lending just over 2% of mortgages out of the total.
- 10% of the mortgages issued by the 43 lenders were sub-prime. In their sample, sub-prime mortgages were most likely to be agreed by banks and specialist lenders, rather than by building societies.
- 11.3% of these sub-prime mortgages were in arrears, as compared to 2.9% of 'prime' mortgages.
- In 2005 there was an overall increase in mortgage repossessions of 58%, as compared to 2004. This was concentrated in the sub-prime sector. Repossessions in that sector rose by more than 150% between 2004 and 2005.

It was not possible to identify exactly how lenders dealt with arrears when sub-prime lending was involved (although this detail could be provided for prime mortgages). It was clear, however, that action was taken more quickly by lenders to recoup their money against sub-prime mortgagors in arrears, as compared to others (Stephens and Quilgars, 2007, p 12). The researchers calculated that there were 'considerable differences' in relation to the numbers of and speed with which properties were repossessed. They analysed CML data and showed that the rate of repossession was 10 times higher in the sub-prime sector than in the 'prime' sector in 2005 (p 14). Repossession may have declined for 'prime' mortgagors in arrears, but this seems to have been unlikely for sub-prime borrowers. These are more likely to be the families applying to local authorities for help because they are homeless. If they are accepted as 'statutory' homeless, they may be offered (in order of likelihood) an assured shorthold tenancy in the private rented sector, an assured tenancy with a housing association or (least likely) a secure tenancy with the council (if the authority still has council housing). For sub-prime borrowers, the risks of owner-occupation, including homelessness, far outweigh the benefits.

Paying for residential care by spending the home

The UK's population is gradually ageing with the proportion of older people expected to grow significantly. In addition, more people with disabilities are living longer. The need for social care services is growing rapidly. These services are currently provided by local authorities and the private sector, but the two sectors often do not coordinate what is available very well. Local authorities are legally obliged to assess individuals who may need adult social care services. If a person applies to their local authority for help, they will be considered for a range of services (some provided by the local authority, some by the private sector), but they will also be means tested to determine if they should pay for all or part of any service they receive.

Older owner-occupiers have become the first example of what 'asset-based welfare' is really about: the expectation that the individual, rather than the welfare state, will pay for particular services (in this case, social care). The issue has 'hit the headlines' consistently because of elderly owner-occupiers being obliged to sell their homes in order to pay for residential care. Each year, between 30,000 and 40,000 people have to sell their homes to pay for residential care. In response to continuing concern about this issue, and social care funding in general, there has been a welter of reports and White Papers over the years. The most recent was the Dilnot Commission on Funding of Care and Support, which was set up by the Coalition government and reported in July 2011 (Commission on Funding of Care and Support, 2011a). Its recommendations commanded widespread support (see Box 8.6 for the detail).

Box 8.6: 'Fairer Funding for All': The Dilnot Commission's recommendations, 2011

- 'Individuals' lifetime contributions towards their social care costs – which are currently potentially unlimited – should be capped. After the cap is reached, individuals would be eligible for full state support. This cap should be between £25,000 and £50,000. We consider that £35,000 is the most appropriate and fair figure.
- The means-tested threshold, above which people are liable for their full care costs, should be increased from £23,250 to £100,000.
- National eligibility criteria and portable assessments should be introduced to ensure greater consistency.
- All those who enter adulthood with a care and support need should be eligible for free state support immediately rather than being subjected to a means test'.

Source: Commission on Funding of Care and Support (2011a)

The justification for these recommendations was that:

- care costs can be high and unpredictable;
- the state currently steps in only when a person has exhausted all their assets, including selling their own home. Only £23,250 of a person's

assets can be exempted from a calculation of income that is made to determine entitlement to residential care paid for by the state;
• insurers will not cover such potential costs, as they are unpredictable.

The Dilnot Commission estimated that its proposals would cost £1.7 billion (at 2010/11 prices). One third of those eligible for residential care (and a quarter of those aged 65) would find that they had to pay no more than £35,000, whatever the actual costs of their care. The bulk of costs would become the collective responsibility of the welfare state, paid for largely through taxation. This estimate does not include the costs of improving care services. As Andrew Dilnot said:

> We should be celebrating the fact we are living longer and that younger people with disabilities are leading more independent lives than ever before. But instead we talk about the 'burden of ageing' and individuals are living in fear, worrying about meeting their care costs.
>
> The current system is confusing, unfair and unsustainable. People can't protect themselves against the risk of very high care costs and risk losing all their assets including their house. The problem will only get worse if left as it is, with the most vulnerable in our society being the ones to suffer. (Commission on Funding of Care and Support, 2011b)

New Labour's plan of a £20,000 cap to be paid from a person's estate once they had died was roundly criticised by the Conservatives during the 2010 general election, yet their own inquiry has produced more generous recommendations. In the event, the Coalition has responded in part with delaying tactics: their response to the Dilnot Commission took 18 months and the implementation of any of the main changes will not be until 2016.

The government has proposed that the cost of care in residential care homes should be capped at £72,000 from April 2016. Up to that point, the local authority will assess what a person needs by way of care and will provide a 'care account' to show them what they have paid to date that effectively contributes towards the £72,000 cap. They must have care needs that meet certain eligibility criteria (probably they will be similar to those that local authorities use now). People who have income (including the value of an owner-occupied home) of more than £118,000 will have to pay for their care up to the £72,000 cap. People with income between £17,500 and £118,000 will be means tested so will pay some of their care costs. Those who have income of less than £17,500 will not have to pay for their care costs in a residential care home: it will be paid for by the state. People who need residential care will still have to pay their hotel costs (accommodation and meals) estimated to cost about £10,000 a year at 2013 prices according to Age UK.

Many pensioners may find that they still need to sell their homes to go into residential care (because they have not reached the £72,000 cap, because of annual 'hotel' costs or because they have more complex care needs than can be provided through an evaluation of the cost of 'standard–care' alone).

These proposals are expected to cost about £1 billion up to 2020, to be paid for by freezing the level of inheritance tax between 2015 and 2018 and using money generated by proposed pension changes. The National Pensioners Convention was critical of these plans which, they said, 'simply tinker at the edges' of the wider social care system (National Pensioners Convention, 2013). Others have called the government's proposals 'timid'.

> Most ordinary families could still face losing their home to pay for care. When families realise what is being proposed, they will be in for a shock. The government is sneakily shifting the cost of care further and further on to older people and their families. (Burke, 2013)

REFLECTION 8.1

Are there limits to asset-based welfare?

Older people have been expected to sell their homes in order to pay for residential care. Is this fair, when they will have contributed to the welfare state since the Second World War? Are there other circumstances where homeowners should not be expected to borrow against their homes or sell them in order to pay for welfare needs of various kinds?

Further reading

Chartered Institute of Environmental Health (2013) *Memorandum to the Commons Select Committee on Communities and Local Government Inquiry into the Private Rented Housing Sector.* Available at: http://www.cieh.org/WorkArea/showcontent.aspx?id=45396.

Commission on Funding of Care and Support (2011) *Fairer care funding: The report of the Commission on Funding of Care and Support,* July, https://www.wp.dh.gov.uk/carecommission/files/2011/07/Fairer-Care-Funding-Report.pdf.

CLG (2011) Commons Select Committee – Regeneration, *Written evidence submitted by the Urban Renewal Officers' Group,* March 2011, http://www.publications.parliament.uk/pa/cm201012/cmselect/cmcomloc/1014/1014vw30.htm.

A starting-place for further reading on many aspects of homeownership is the Centre for Housing Policy at the University of York. See the range of reports and journal articles produced on homeownership: http://www.york.ac.uk/chp/expertise/homeownership/publications/.

NINE

A variety of rents

Introduction

Landlords see rents as income and, consequently, as a most important part of housing management. Tenants often have a more complicated view, especially if they are tenants of local authorities and housing associations. Yet in some past protests about expensive rents the interests of tenants have seemed very similar, whoever the landlord.

It is easy to see the issue of rents in a completely ahistorical way, devoid of political and economic context. In this chapter, the issue of rents will be examined more broadly than usual, identifying where conflicts over rents have led to change. Rent strikes and campaigning are largely 'hidden from history' in housing finance. This chapter is an attempt to begin to redress the balance. Arguably, this perspective will be most relevant in the years ahead.

This chapter moves from general points to looking at the different ways in which rents have been established in the private sector, local authorities and housing associations. It ends with consideration of 'rent convergence' between local authorities and housing associations and the likely prospects for more expensive 'affordable rents'. In this chapter the themes are:

- what is rent? – from the landlord's and tenant's perspective;
- the private rented sector – from controlled to market rents;
- local authority rents – from independence to rent restructuring;
- housing associations – cost rents, fair rents, assured rents, 'affordable rents'?
- rent convergence between local authorities and housing associations;
- changing principles for rents over time;
- the 'affordable rent' and its prospects.

What is rent?

'Rent' is a financial sum that is set by the landlord for a flat, a house or a room in a house. At its simplest, the rent is intended to be a payment by the tenant/licensee or occupier for the 'use and occupation' of that house or room. Most social landlords have separated service charges from the rent, but for a private tenant this may still be an inclusive figure.

It is sometimes assumed that the amount of rent represents some kind of settled agreement between the two parties of what a particular house, flat or room is 'worth'. This has been reflected in government policy and some academic writing. For example, this presumption that tenants could negotiate with landlords to reach a mutually satisfactory agreement about the rent to be charged was the basis of New Labour's introduction of the SLHA (now LHA) for private sector tenants.

The assumption that landlords and tenants are equal parties flies in the face of reality. The landlord, as the owner of the property, ultimately has the power to determine what happens to it. Ironically, this relationship of unequal power is really only clearly seen when someone is evicted from their home. The legal position of council and housing association tenants has become more secure since 1980, preventing their immediate eviction. Secure tenants of local authorities and, to a certain extent, association regulated and assured tenants are in a stronger position now than private tenants. However, these tenancy rights have diminished since the late 1990s with the introduction of 'starter' or 'shorthold' tenancies. The Coalition government's most recent plans for 'affordable rents' go hand-in-hand with reductions in security of tenure.

What might 'rent' represent to tenants?

Research on council housing finance and rents was commissioned by the New Labour government in 2009 when it was reviewing the HRA arrangements for local authorities (see Chapter Five). Council and housing association tenants were asked 'What should be included in the rent you pay?'. There were differing views about what should be provided:

> Whilst participants thought that 'housing' was strongly linked to property, they also felt it related to the community and wider environment ... As participants perceived housing-related services to include those related to their property and the community and wider environment, this led to some confusion as to who provided which services. (Taylor, 2009, p 7)

Unsurprisingly, given the complexities of 'rent restructuring', many tenants did not know how the rent was worked out and how it was spent by the landlord, except to provide housing management. There was no understanding of rent being used to pay the landlord's debt. Tenants all agreed that rents should be set 'fairly', but their understanding varied in what this meant in practice. It could mean:

- charging the same for similar properties;
- charging a rent related to the tenant's income.

These different perspectives will be seen in the historical parts of this chapter, as well as in more recent developments. They also apply to private tenancies. The link between rent and income has been important, and particularly so now, when housing benefit, designed to help those on the lowest incomes, is being withdrawn, taking us back to situations last seen before the Second World War.

How do landlords see 'rent'?

Rent means something different to the landlord. For the landlord, the rent represents *an income*. David Garnett and John Perry (Garnett and Perry, 2005, pp 46–9) explain that what a landlord is interested in is a 'total sufficiency rent'. This includes:

- the costs of repaying loans;
- an amount for future major repairs, management and maintenance costs;
- building insurance;
- an amount allowed for bad debts and voids;
- the cost of providing services.

Since this was written, the Coalition government has come to power and another factor should be emphasised for associations and local authorities, namely:

- the amount set aside towards building up surpluses to be used to cross-subsidise house building costs.

Consequently, if it is to build new homes, an association needs to obtain the maximum income possible through formula rent setting (under the rent restructuring regime). It needs the same approach to re-lets and new homes built within the framework of 'affordable rent', the Coalition's revenue-based model for building new homes. A local authority with council housing may plan more modest rent increases, depending on it business plan under the new 'self-financing' arrangements. A private landlord will act in the same way as a developing association, if it is planning to expand. In addition, a private landlord will add an amount to the rent for pure profit, charging a market rent.

The rest of this chapter is organised so that the different ways in which rent has been worked out in each tenure can be seen clearly. These are not historical accounts, although they draw on the past to identify the different and specific interests of landlords and tenants.

The private rented sector – from controlled to market rents

Controlled rents

Before the First World War (1914–18), most working-class people lived in the private rented sector. Conditions were often poor, but scarcity meant that rents were often very high relative to tenants' incomes, even for slum property. It took a world war and concerted protest action by tenants and factory workers in key industries before any government acted to change this (see Chapter One).

Peter Malpass and Alan Murie's explanation cannot be bettered (Box 9.1).

> ### Box 9.1: The Glasgow rent strike, 1915
>
> 'When the war began, housing production fell away from already low levels, thereby exacerbating the shortage, especially in areas of high demand resulting from concentrations of extra labour brought in to manufacture munitions. Some landlords exploited this situation by raising rents ... During 1915, working-class resentment of higher rents as an accompaniment to the slaughter in the trenches built up into a wave of rent strikes across the country. The centre of resistance was Glasgow, where a combination of existing bad housing conditions, a large influx of munitions workers and a well-organised labour movement led to a particularly solid and effective strike action. In the context of war, civil unrest of this sort, involving court cases, evictions, mass demonstrations and the use of force against the civilian population, obviously put considerable pressure on the government. The problem was resolved by emergency legislation at the end of 1915.'
>
> (Malpass and Murie, 1987, pp 46–7)

The significance of the rent strikes in Glasgow has been the subject of much debate (see Melling, 1983). For the first time, organised tenant resistance had

- led to government action to control rent increases that landlords would otherwise have been free to impose;
- provided more justification for state subsidies for local authority house building after the war.

Marion Bowley, one of the few academics who studied working-class incomes, rents and local authority subsidies for council house building in the 1920s and 1930s, dryly commented:

> Increases in rents staved off in deference to public opinion during the war could scarcely be regarded as an appropriate form of peace celebration. (Bowley, 1944, p 9)

Rent control had unexpected consequences. Following legislation in 1923, if the existing controlled tenant moved out, the tenancy became decontrolled and the landlord could charge whatever they wanted. But many tenants stayed put. With very low, erratic household incomes, they were protected from rent increases by the controlled rent. By the end of the 1930s, conditions in many of these properties were appalling, as landlords reduced or abandoned maintenance so as to ensure profits (see Chapter Seven). Spontaneous tenant protest about conditions and rents broke out in London, just before the outbreak of the Second World War.

Box 9.2: Tenant protest in Stepney, London, 1938–39

'Individual and collective action took off in Stepney in private rented tenement buildings and mansion blocks. Controlled and decontrolled tenants alike worked out demands: reductions in rent and lists of repairs to be completed. Some mansion blocks succeeded but others had to go on rent strike to achieve their aims. Landlords issued eviction notices. Tenants barricaded themselves in with barbed wire around the buildings and restricted access. Bailiffs and the police were actively engaged in breaking these down to evict tenants – all in the glare of publicity generated by the strikes which lasted for months.

The Communist Party decided that they would help with tenants' actions in dealing with the worst private landlords. They hoped to build support more generally among working class families to stave off the growth of working class fascism in London.

Protest and rent strikes against high rents and poor conditions grew and spread to other parts of London. Some tenements and mansion blocks secured successes:

> rents reduced, repairs done, arrears written off. These actions culminated in a national meeting in Birmingham of the newly-established National Tenants Federation (linking private and council tenants who had also been taking rent strike action against the level of council rents).
>
> A big rally in Hyde Park in July 1939 demanded a new Rent Act and better rights to repairs. It was addressed by tenants' leaders, the Labour MPs Aneurin Bevin and Ellen Wilkinson and Communist Party activists.'
>
> (Piratin, 1948, chapter 4)

The Second World War temporarily ended protests, but as soon as peace returned in 1945 the issue of expensive private sector and council rents and poor housing conditions in controlled and decontrolled property again came to the fore. This continuing pressure was one important reason for the massive council house building programme, initiated by Aneurin Bevin as Minister of Health in Clement Attlee's Labour government (see Chapter One, and Davis and Wigfield, 2010).

As far as Labour politicians were concerned, the decontrol of private rents was to be undertaken gradually, on an individual basis, not least because of housing shortages after the war. The Conservatives, elected in 1955 (with Antony Eden as Prime Minister, followed by Harold Macmillan from 1956), felt that action needed to be taken. The Housing Act 1957 lifted controls on private rents. The aim was to encourage the growth of a viable private rented sector where private landlords invested and made a profit (see Chapter Seven). However, lifting rent control quickly had consequences:

- Many private landlords substantially increased rents.
- Tenants were harassed and illegally evicted by slum landlords so that they could then sell with vacant possession. This process became known as Rachmanism (see Chapter Seven).
- Other landlords sold up as quickly as possible: an estimated 300,000 private rented properties were sold into owner occupation between 1958 and 1964.

More controlled tenancies were decontrolled in 1978, with the process being completed by the Housing Act 1980. This converted all remaining controlled tenancies into regulated ones. It ended what had become a significant protective measure for very poor tenants: most poor tenants could afford controlled rents, even though their housing might also be very poor because of lack of landlord investment.

Regulated 'fair rents'

The Labour Party, while out of government, had promised to introduce some degree of legal protection for thousands of tenants who had been 'decontrolled'. Once it was back in power in 1964, the work started to find a solution that would protect tenants and enable landlords to invest in their property. The 'fair rent' was the solution that was devised and legislated for in the Rent Act 1965 (see Chapter Seven).

Richard Crossman, the Housing Minister at the time, records in his famous diaries the meeting at which the idea of the 'fair rent' was created (Box 9.3).

Box 9.3: The birth of fair rents

'Wednesday 2 December 1964

Wednesday evening was the big evening for our rents policy meeting. I was pretty anxious when I went over to my room in the Ministry ... I got them all round a table and we set to work, discussing the Rent Bill on the basis of the paper provided by Arnold Goodman and Dennis Lloyd as a result of our meeting on the previous Monday. It was a paper in which the idea of the fair rent was sketched out for the first time. It really was an astonishing meeting because we managed to get something like agreement between these fourteen people, many of them lawyers, all of them knowing a great deal about the subject and with experience ranging from that of Arnold Goodman, a commercial lawyer in Fleet Street on the one hand and his friend Professor Dennis Lloyd, a pure academic, on the other. Then we had, at the other end of the scale, young Labour lawyers, and one property speculator. And finally, our own officials ... and myself. We started at 8.15 and at 11.45 we sat back because our job had been done.'

(Crossman, 1976, p 78)

The Bill containing the 'fair rent' clauses (and much else) then had to get through the parliamentary legislative process, including the committee stage. At the committee stage any Bill, including this one, is subject to clause-by-clause discussion. There was pressure from left-leaning backbench MPs. They were concerned that the rental difference between fair rents and controlled rents was likely to be too great for poorer tenants to pay. They wanted rents to be increased in stages as controlled tenancies were gradually decontrolled and taken into rent regulation (that is, the fair rent system). That aside, there was persistent, stubborn opposition from the Conservatives and Liberals on the committee. They did not want the 'fair rent' system at all. The

Bill survived the committee stage and the fair rent system became established in law with the Rent Act 1965.

'Fair rents' were initially set on formerly controlled tenancies. Housing association tenancies became eligible in the Housing Finance Act 1972. Furnished private tenancies without a resident landlord were included in the Rent Act 1974. A Rent Officer (now employed by the Valuation Office Agency) decides what a 'fair rent' should be. They have to consider a property's age, location, character and state of repair. They cannot consider the circumstances of the tenant or their income, or scarcity – that is, what the rent might be in the open market.

The fair rent system went hand in hand with Rent Act regulated tenancies introduced at the same time. The fair rent was designed to *modify* the market price, not to control it. There was an expectation that the system would protect tenants, while at the same time giving landlords sufficient incentives to continue to invest in the private rented sector. In practice, 'fair rents' were set at levels that seemed very high in some areas, and the appeal process did nothing to slow these increases. In that sense, critics were right.

It is clear that a fair rent is not a 'pure' market rent (set with regard to competition), and not a welfare-oriented rent either (set to ensure that a poor tenant can afford it). After much discussion, David Garnett and John Perry (2005, pp 42–4) decided that it is an 'administrative' rent – and one that *just* manages to survive in a decreasing number of long-established housing association and private tenancies (see Chapter Six).

Although fair rents still exist today, the Conservatives' Housing Act 1988 dismantled most of these arrangements. The Labour Party saw a positive role for rent regulation. The Conservatives believed that it inhibited investment by landlords. The 1988 Act took new housing association tenancies out of the fair rent system after January 1989. Fair rents can now be fixed only on pre-January 1989 housing association tenancies and some regulated private tenancies. The private rented sector continued to decline. This was the result of wider economic forces, not of rent control or rent regulation. In the 20th century, there were more profitable ways of making money than by providing rented housing.

Market rents

Private landlords now set market rents. These cover the costs of any mortgage(s) on the property they own, management and maintenance costs and an amount for their profit. There is more detailed discussion of the issue of rents in the sector and the how landlords might view the issue of 'rental yield' in Chapter Seven.

Local authority rents – from independence to rent restructuring

Setting their own rents

Marian Bowley commented that the different ways in which local authorities set rents up to the Second World War had been 'acquired as haphazardly as the British Empire [with] no sort of consistent principles, economic, social or moral' (Bowley, 1944, p 205). Different subsidy arrangements had been introduced by successive governments to encourage house building for 'general needs' or to provide for more targeted 'slum clearance'. Local authorities were able to set their own rents at that time, and there was a variety of ways of working out what to charge. Surprisingly, as Alison Ravetz has commented:

> The setting of rents was not a management function, but it was managers who collected them and applied any sanctions for non-payment. The ultimate penalty was eviction, which was routinely used before 1939, and what then faced the evicted was the old workhouse system [or its derivatives]. It is then curious that so much literature on estates … is silent on both rents and evictions. (Ravetz, 2001, p 125)

By 1927, the official expectation was that council rents would bring an economic return of two-thirds of the capital outlay, but many authorities set their rents below this. By this time, 'the succession of different acts, subsidies and dwelling types … brought about a huge and confusing variety of rent levels' (Ravetz, 2001, p 125). Even so, by the Second World War protest about the expense of council rents in some parts of the country had grown significantly.

Box 9.4: Council tenants' protest against rent rises, 1930s

[R]ent arrears grew alarmingly [in the 1930s], particularly on the former munitions estates. Disaffection extended even to the cream of tenants, and the protests of tenants associations became 'too numerous to chronicle'. Birmingham and Glasgow were big centres of protest, and a rent strike organised by the left wing

> National Union of Ex-Servicemen, though abortive, had some success in mobilizing tenants' wives.'
>
> (Ravetz, 2001, p 125)

Birmingham's council tenants, 49,000 strong, went on rent strike in 1939 led by local Labour councillors. Other cities followed. This was separate from the strike and protest of private tenants in London over rents and disrepair. Nevertheless, from a political point of view, this disparate public protest was an obvious sign of problems. There were also more serious issues than this public outrage.

The invisible private pressure of having to find money to pay more expensive rents bore down on individual families. Although the range of working-class people benefiting from council housing had extended by the Second World War, the rents were still high relative to the income of the poorest, who had often been rehoused from slums where they had paid very low controlled rents. Families were shocked by the expense of some council rents. For the same-sized property, council rents were 20–25% higher than controlled rents. Many new tenants struggled to pay the rent. Although housing standards were much better, moving into new council estates often led to other costs: longer journeys to work, isolation for women left in the house all day, no shops and no community facilities. A much-publicised and discussed 1936 study from Stockton-on-Tees found that a rise in mortality on new council estates was linked to malnutrition: families had to go without food in order to meet the rent and rates each week (Ravetz, 2001, p 126). Turnover was high on many new council estates, with 'moonlight flits' to avoid the rent collector and/or eviction being common.

Even though there was a confusing variety of ways to decide what rent to charge in council housing, Peter Malpass and Alan Murie identified four principles that linked all these arrangements, stretching from the 1930s to 1972 (Table 9.1).

These broad principles still allowed for different ideas about how to work out what to charge.

Differential rents

After 1935, differential rent schemes were established by a handful of local authorities. The idea was taken up more generally after the Second World War. This way of structuring rent charges was designed to enable rents to increase, sometimes quite dramatically. The poorest families caught in the change from low- to high-rent

Table 9.1: The four principles underlying rents and subsidies policy: mid-1930s to 1972

The inviolability of existing subsidies	Changes in subsidy levels affected only new houses built after specified dates; existing commitments under earlier Acts continued to be honoured. It was accepted that no government could interfere with payments pledged by its predecessors.
Subsidies not related to individual tenants' incomes	Housing subsidies were not related to the incomes of individual tenants. Subsidies were always expressed as so many pounds per house per year over a fixed period, irrespective of the needs of the tenants actually occupying … They were general subsidies, calculated in relation to construction costs and debt charges, rather than income-related subsidies.
Rent fixing a local authority responsibility	The principle of local autonomy in rent fixing was cherished by councillors and elaborately respected by ministers (whose speeches and circulars, however, also made it clear to local authorities what they were expected to do about rents).
A 'no profit' rule applied to HRAs	It was a basic tenet that council housing was not to be run for profit. Only small working balances were permitted to be carried forward in the HRA from one year to another, and any surplus could not be transferred to the general rate fund for the benefit of rate payers as a whole.

Source: Malpass and Murie (1987, pp 185–6).

schemes were supposed to be protected by a means-tested rebate scheme, provided by the local authority from surpluses generated by the higher rents.

Subsidies on council properties were pooled so that a standard scale of rents could be charged across the whole stock. Initially, differential rents devised in this manner were charged only on particular types of property. Rather than a minimum charge, usually there was a standard amount met by all tenants who might be eligible for a rebate. The household's income was used to calculate the rebate, leaving the outstanding amount to be paid in rent by the householder. This way of calculating rents was controversial:

- Poorer tenants feared the means test because of its strong association with the workhouse.
- Better-off tenants resented those poorer than themselves getting financial help to live in similar-quality properties.

The strength of feeling about these schemes was strong. 'Announcements of differential rents … provoked a lot of resistance and rent strikes. In Leeds, a Labour council was unseated by a strike in 1934' (Ravetz, 2001, p 126). Despite this, the idea did not disappear. After the Second World War, local authorities continued to set council rents locally. Some used differential schemes, while others did not, but the ideas associated with *pooling* subsidy and increasing rents to match *current* costs were beginning to take hold, and were particularly pushed forward in local authorities under Conservative control.

Box 9.5 illustrates this in the London Borough of St Pancras. There had been changes in political control over a relatively short period of time in the late 1950s, which exposed the differences in attitude towards rents between Labour and Conservative councillors.

Box 9.5: Tenant protest in St Pancras, London, 1956–62

In 1956 St Pancras was an authority under Labour control. Labour introduced a scheme with low levels of rent to be charged for each type of property.

The District Auditor confirmed that the scheme was reasonable but recommended a review using the yardstick provided by the 1957 Rent Act (setting rents at 2.33 x the rateable value of properties).

The District Auditor's recommendation was acted on by the Conservatives when they won control of St Pancras in 1959. They introduced maximum and minimum levels of rent based on 3 x the rateable value, plus a system of rebates. The new maximum level meant that many rents were now higher than the expensive rents charged to private tenants following the 1957 Rent Act. A new differential rent scheme for all the council stock was intended to bring actual payments down for poorer tenants.

Rents trebled on pre-1945 estates. They doubled on post-war estates. Fifty-two per cent of tenants had to pay the maximum rent level fixed, and many had no help through the rebate scheme. They had to pay the rent increases themselves, from their own resources.

During 1959–60 there were protest marches, a petition signed by 14,000 tenants, a rent strike, mass meetings, violent disorder and two highly publicised evictions.

The police were used to break up meetings and marches and, finally, to help bailiffs with evictions.

In 1962, the Labour Party was re-elected to a controlling position on the council, on the promise of a system of 'standard rents', but, once it was in office, the Conservatives' scheme was retained. The Labour council argued it would be illegal to scrap it. Rebates were improved and other arrangements were put in place for tenants who objected to 'means test forms'. The scheme was implemented from April 1963.

Source: Burn (1972)

At the height of the protest in St Pancras, over 2,000 council tenants were on partial rent strike, paying the original rent but not the increases. The action lasted 10 months. At the end of 1960 two tenants were forcibly evicted in a blaze of publicity. Many tenants were intimidated and gave up when faced with eviction. The council was left with £20,000 of rent arrears (£299,000 in today's prices).

Alison Ravetz (2001) has pointed out that there were two underlying features of rent strikes in the period up to the 1970s. These were:

- better-off tenants defending their privileged position – in actions such as in Birmingham and Leeds, where there was resentment at the prospect of differential rent schemes;
- unrest generated by the prospect and reality of unaffordable rents for people living on fixed or only slowly increasing incomes, as in St Pancras.

Some concessions were won and these were important to the tenants involved, but the impact of these protests remained local. The actions taken against the Housing Finance Act 1972 were of a different order and achieved national policy change, and will be considered later.

Rent pooling

Although rent pooling had been suggested by governments before as a way of setting rents, Malpass and Murie identify 1955 as the year in which this idea came of age. A Conservative government suggested it mainly in response to a growing problem with local authority subsidies for house building for rent.

One feature of subsidies identified in Table 9.1 was that they were honoured by successive governments. They were uprated through reference to the calculated gap between the average cost of a house and the annual rent that an average tenant might reasonably pay. Inflation made this equation difficult to maintain. Subsidies from the 1930s were still being received by local authorities and by now had covered all the original building costs. It might cost five times as much to build new council housing, so, together with the older subsidies, the Treasury was not happy at the prospective costs of council house building in the future, without some change to these arrangements.

The Conservative government's solution was to suggest rent pooling. This would enable subsidies from earlier times to effectively reduce current subsidy, and in the process would enable rents to be increased, especially on older council housing.

> [S]ubsidy could be reallocated to help keep down the rents on new houses and the rents of older houses could be allowed to rise towards levels commensurate with current wages ... Rent pooling was not just a local authority approach to rent fixing. It was a strategy adopted by central government which aimed to persuade authorities to raise rents. (Malpass and Murie, 1987, p 187)

The government could do this without breaching the principle of honouring subsidies already agreed (see Table 9.1). After 1955, it simply assumed that local authorities were pooling subsidies, and so new subsidy on new building was lower than it might have been.

Authorities were urged to establish means-tested rebate schemes for tenants who would otherwise find it difficult to pay the increased rents. By 1970, rent was more than 10% of average manual earnings and was increasing at a much faster rate than earnings. Rent rebate schemes were gradually introduced by local authorities, but even by 1969 only one third of authorities had a scheme (Ravetz, 2001, pp 126–7) Some Labour authorities, as a matter of principle, still preferred to make contributions to the HRA from the general rates rather than increase rents and introduce means testing for their tenants (see Chapter Five).

Current value rents

The Conservative government's Housing Finance Act 1972 represented the first attempt to establish a new system of subsidy payments and rent setting. Rents were to be set at current values as 'fair rents' (drawing on Labour's Rent Act 1965). Local authority subsidy entitlement would be worked out using current wages and prices as a starting-point. This was a reversal of the previous system in which subsidies accumulated and were paid by central government to local authorities, with rents being set separately by local authorities (independently of wages and prices). The Act was complicated and controversial. It established:

- 'fair rents' – council tenants were to be charged 'fair rents' (which were modified market rents). This would bring local authority rents in line with private sector fair rents. Rents would be calculated in the same way across the country. Housing associations were brought into the fair rent system at this point too;
- 'deficit subsidy' – if there was any revenue shortfall in the HRA after rents had been set, central government would pay the difference. This was known as a deficit subsidy. HRAs were allowed to generate a surplus for the first time;
- mandatory rent rebate schemes – these now had to be set up and paid for by every local authority, whether or not they wanted them. The scheme was to be funded out of the surpluses made on the more expensive fair rents.

Local authorities were unhappy with the impact of large rent increases that followed these changes. They also resented their loss of autonomy. Box 9.6 gives some flavour of what happened next, although a more detailed and comprehensive analysis is available in Leslie Sklair's 'The struggle against the Housing Finance Act' (1975).

Box 9.6: Action against the Housing Finance Act 1972

'Throughout the country eighty or more rent strikes took place, in some cases lasting for months and involving a large majority of tenants. A number of strikers were sent to prison and occasionally small reductions in the proposed rises were won.

The ALHE [Association of London Housing Estates] took a leading role in trying to persuade boroughs not to implement the Act, while its more militant rent committee called for strikes.

Overall the campaign was judged a failure as, with only a tiny handful of exceptions, authorities fell into line and began, however reluctantly, to put it into operation.

The protest campaign had been a complex one, with much factionalism and bitterness between tenant organisations, the Labour Party and the trade union movement, which never gave the hoped-for support.'

(Ravetz, 2001, p 152)

The Housing Finance Act 1972 was highly controversial. Not surprisingly, the Labour Party repealed it when it took office. In

February 1974 the newly elected Labour government of Harold Wilson immediately froze rents as part of that government's strategy for controlling inflation. A temporary system provided by the Housing Rents and Subsidies Act 1975 then simply reinstated the pre-1972 system. However, when the Conservatives came back into power in 1979 they returned to the ideas in the Housing Finance Act 1972 and built them into the Housing Act 1980. Under the Act:

- a system was established of calculating subsidy for council housing that was based on a 'notional' HRA;
- rent increases were *assumed* by the government when calculating local authority subsidies (whether or not rents had been increased);
- standard management and maintenance allowances (calculated and uprated by central government) were used to calculate the cost of local authorities' housing management services.

This represented considerable tightening of central government control, but there was still room for some local authority autonomy. Labour-controlled authorities were more likely to look for alternatives. Local authorities could still make additional contributions to the HRA if they wanted, using revenue from the local rates to keep their council rent increases below the level that central government wanted and expected. Alternatively, they could raise rents to a level above government assumptions, making surpluses in the HRA to pay for much-needed repairs and maintenance (see Davis and Wigfield, 2010). This was tolerated for a while by the Conservative government, but nine years later the legislation was tightened again with the Local Government and Housing Act 1989.

A New Labour government changed the subsidy system in the Local Government Act 2003 (see Chapter Five). A system of 'rent restructuring' for local authorities was introduced as part of these changes (to be considered later).

Housing associations – cost rents, fair rents, assured rents, 'affordable rents'?

Throughout most of the 20th century, housing associations have been a relatively small-scale phenomenon, as compared to the private rented sector and council housing. The history of housing associations' early beginnings and gradual growth can be found in Peter Malpass's *Housing associations and housing policy: A historical perspective* (2000). In this section, the focus will be on three kinds of rents relevant to associations: cost rents, fair rents and assured rents (up to 2002).

Cost rents

In the early 1960s the Conservative government was looking for ways in which the private rented sector might be revived. They had already decontrolled large numbers of private lettings; now they offered £25 million for associations to borrow in order to build rented housing with no subsidy. The first homes were completed by 1963. The 'cost rents' were substantially higher than those being charged by local councils at the time, and were too expensive for most manual workers. Using this borrowing capacity, 5,438 houses were built in England and Wales, now managed by 39 cost rent societies. Most were new, as existing housing associations were not keen on the initiative.

The government claimed success, but the experiment ended in 1972, when the Conservatives' Housing Finance Act converted cost rents to fair rents and made cost rent societies legally indistinguishable from traditional housing associations. Peter Malpass (2000) concluded that cost rent societies failed for two main reasons:

- They found it hard to raise money from building societies, which were wary about lending to these new, inexperienced organisations.
- The interest rates on loans were high, so the resultant cost rents were expensive and it was often cheaper to buy a home.

Fair rents

Fair rents were first introduced into housing associations by the Housing Finance Act 1972. They accompanied a new subsidy system that associations were expected to use. The Conservative government had indicated that change would be gradual for associations. In the event, they were given three and a half months to register all their properties as fair rents (Malpass, 2000, pp 148–9).

These 'moderated market rents' were later abandoned by local authorities, but were retained by associations until 1988. Chapter Six outlines the way in which fair rents were used to calculate housing association grant entitlement in association house building from 1974 to 1988.

Assured rents (and affordability)

The Conservative government's Housing Act 1988 enabled associations to set their own assured rents on newly built or re-let property from January 1989. Even before 1988, fair rents registered on association regulated tenancies were seen as expensive (especially when compared to local authority rents for similar property). Now there was a problem with the level of rents that associations themselves were setting on their new assured tenancies. Assured rents were charged on re-lets and newly built housing.

It was clear that associations were setting rents to help to pay for the private finance that they now used to develop new housing. But there was another problem, partly of their own making. In 1988/89, grant rates averaged 75%. By 1995/96, these had decreased to an average of 58%. Much of this reduction was due to over-ambitious and competitive development staff bidding *below* the published grant rates each year in order to be successful. Two-thirds (66%) of developing associations were actively driving down grant levels (Wilcox and Meen, 1995, p vi), with apparent disregard for the impact on rents.

The National Federation of Housing Associations (NFHA) (now the National Housing Federation) developed a series of definitions of 'affordability' that associations were supposed to consider in setting rents. One definition said that rents were affordable if a household was not obliged to pay more than 25% of net household income in rent. How effective were these NFHA definitions in restraining housing association rent increases? In a national survey of developing associations, Shaun Stevens (1995) found that:

- Eighteen per cent of rents on new properties were higher than the market equivalents determined by Rent Officers.
- Association rents had increased at twice the annual rate of inflation between 1990/91 and 1993/94.
- The numbers of associations that were rent pooling, where possible, so as to reduce rents (spreading increases across all their housing) had increased from 39% to 60% in the three years to 1994, but there were financial limits to this (not least the way in which fair rents were calculated).

By 1994, 84% of associations *considered* 'affordability' in their rent setting, but that did not mean that affordable rents were actually being charged. In 1995, the NFHA asked the government to change its policy and increase the fixed grant levels available for new building. This would mean that less expensive rents could be charged, and it would have reduced the housing benefit bill for the government (Stevens, 1995). At this point, the Conservative government 'was not for turning'. By the end of the 1990s, 70% of rents in the association sector breached the NFHA's own definition of affordability.

Rent convergence between local authorities and housing associations

The New Labour government elected in 1997 acknowledged that differences in local authority and housing association rents were the results of two different financial regimes. It decided to consult on changes to rent setting in the two sectors. In its Green Paper *Quality and Choice: a decent home for all* (DETR/DSS, 2000), the government discussed the issue in detail. It wanted a new rent setting system for local authorities and housing associations that would build on two principles: 'fairness' and 'choice'.

> ### Box 9.7: 'Fairness' and 'choice' in rent setting
>
> **Fairness**
> - The new rent setting system should produce the same rent for similar properties in the same location, whether they were owned by the local authority or by a housing association.
> - The same aspects should be valued in both sectors. This would produce 'consistency' across the two sectors. The quality of the house or flat, its location and the running costs were integral to this. This was what potential owners would consider, so tenants should too.
>
> **Choice**
> - Tenants should be able to choose what they wanted by considering price, not landlord. Rent, service charges and running costs were more important than whether the landlord was the council or an association.
> - New Labour thought that this would make tenants more 'responsible' in deciding where they lived and improve housing management.
> - Rent restructuring like this was intended to complement 'choice based lettings' and 'modernise' local authorities.
>
> *Source:* DETR/DSS (2000, chapter 10)

How did rent restructuring work?

The new system was introduced for the financial year 2002/03. Although a New Labour policy, the Coalition government has kept it. The original timetable was for rents to converge by 2012 but local authorities and housing associations will continue to establish the rents they will charge using this system up to 2015/16. At that point, their rents are expected to converge. Each year thereafter, both sectors will have the discretion to calculate increases or decreases in their rents on the basis of the Retail Price Index (RPI) + 0.5%.

It is a complicated system to administer. A 'formula rent' is calculated for each property type. The formula rent is the ideal or 'target rent' that the landlord is aiming for by the date of convergence. In the calculation of the formula rent, more weighting was given to earnings than to property values (so-called capital values). This was to try to dampen the influence of property values in areas that had particularly expensive property (for example London and the South East). There was a danger that unless the weighting for property value was limited to about 30%, the resultant rents would become completely unaffordable in these areas. A weighting for the number of bedrooms in a property was included to ensure that smaller properties had lower formula rents than larger ones. Table 9.2 provides the detail of the formula.

Table 9.2: Achieving 'rent convergence'

'Formula' or 'target' rents
Weekly rent is:

70% of the average rent for the sector $\times \dfrac{\text{average earnings in the area}}{\text{national average earnings}} \times$ bedroom weighting

plus

30% of the average rent for the sector $\times \dfrac{\text{capital value of the property}}{\text{national average property value}}$

This figure is then uprated by inflation plus 0.5% each year from 2001/02 values to the current year.

Actual rent and inflation – up or down?
This is limited each year to the Retail Price Index (RPI) figure of inflation..
A floor for reductions was introduced for 2010/11 for one year only if associations could show that reducing rent charges because of negative inflation put them in financial difficulty. The government reserves the right to do this again as necessary.

Actual rent increases/decreases - limits
These are limited to 0.5% +/– £2 a week on the actual rent.

Actual rent increases and caps
There are caps to actual rent increases based on the number of bedrooms in a property.

When council and housing association landlords review their social rents and how much they are going to charge for the following year, they follow these stages:

• take the actual rent for the last financial year and add an inflation figure (RPI) and the appropriate real terms increase (limited to 0.5% plus £2 a week);
• work out the difference between the formula or 'target' rent for that property type (worked out as described in Box 9.2) and the actual uprated rent;
• divide the difference between the two rents by ten and add that tenth to the actual uprated rent;
• check the rent caps for this property type in the formula rent – these caps are increased by 1% in real terms each year by the HCA and are absolute limits to the rent to be charged based on the number of bedrooms;
• check that the actual uprated rent figure is not exceeding RPI + 0.5% +/−£2. If it is, then the most that can be charged is RPI + 0.5% + £2 a week.

Inflation is considered using the RPI figure from September of the year before the financial year being considered (so RPI in September 2012 has been used for rents in 2013/14). The increases (or reductions) in the actual rent to be charged each year move the rent gradually in the direction of the 'target rent' or convergence figure. If a property becomes empty, the association can move to the formula rent or target rent immediately and increase it by 0.5% each year thereafter.

Originally, New Labour wanted rents in local authorities and housing associations to be similar for similar properties by 2012. Changes had to be made to the formula from 2006/07, bringing both sectors together with a shared approach in an attempt to ensure that the original date could be achieved. Suffice to say, it will take longer than this to ensure that rents converge in the way New Labour planned. The convergence date for social rented property has been pushed back to 2015/16 at the earliest.

Avoiding conflict over the new arrangements

The New Labour government recognised that there would be disagreement about this new way of setting rents. In general, local authority rents were expected to increase a great deal while associations' rents would increase more slowly or actually reduce in some areas. Its strategy was to ensure this process took time so change would take place gradually. In theory, local authorities had some possibility of setting rents that were not exactly as described above. Before 'self-financing' was introduced in 2012, they were issued guideline rent figures each financial year. The CLG used these when calculating the local authority's HRA subsidy position (see Chapter Five). Local authorities could vary rent increases around those guideline figures but in reality they had little leeway because of the link to government subsidy calculations. Similarly, housing associations are expected to follow the guidance on rents for social rented property issued by the HCA including rent guideline limits each year.

Nevertheless, the New Labour government had a degree of discretion about how the system worked. It changed the timetable for convergence when it became clear that this would not be possible by 2012. It also intervened when landlords complained vociferously about the level of rent increases being generated by the link to the RPI. They might be too high for comfort (as Newcastle protested in Box 9.8) or too low (prompting the NHF lobbying in Box 9.9). The source of recent disputes has been the RPI figure announced in September of each year; with rapidly increasing inflation or, alternatively, the possibility of negative inflation strongly influencing the rents to be charged in the next financial year, starting in April.

For example, in 2008, the September RPI was 5.5% but this had declined substantially by the following spring. Council and housing association tenants were faced with big rent increases at a time of falling employment and declining inflation. As the trade magazine *Inside Housing* commented, the situation was 'ludicrous' (Rogers, 2009).

Box 9.8: Margaret Beckett, Minister of Housing, halves the guideline rent figure for local authorities in 2009/10

In a House of Commons debate on 20 January 2009, Jim Cousins, MP for Newcastle upon Tyne, asked if the Minister could suspend or reduce the formula guideline rent increases for council tenants for 2009/10. *Hansard* records:

'… she knows, that council tenants throughout England face rent increases of between 5.5 and 7%. That is a heavy burden and councils place the responsibility for it at the door of the Government's formula rent guidelines. May we reconsider the matter? Nine thousand tenants in the city of Newcastle pay full rent and the burden on them is especially heavy. They do not want to be in the Cabinet; they want to get through the week. Is my Right Hon. Friend willing to meet council tenants from Newcastle and me so that we can explore ways through that genuine difficulty for so many decent people?'

(House of Commons Library, 2012a, p 6)

Margaret Beckett declined the meeting but the pressure on her department, the CLG, was intense. She finally announced a halving of the guideline rent increase. Associations were also advised via the TSA, that they too were not obliged to apply the full 5.5% guideline limit in 2009/10.

The following year, 2010/11, was more problematic for housing associations. In the TSA's draft guidance (a role now taken by the HCA) it was suggested that associations should reduce rents in the following year because the RPI was falling. A floor of −2% was proposed. Box 9.9 outlines the reaction of the NHF.

Box 9.9: The NHF reacts angrily, August 2009

'The NHF reacted angrily to [the TSA] draft direction on rents claiming that cutting rents by up to 2% in 2010/11 would cost the sector £260 million a year. It argued that this could reduce affordable housing development by 4000 homes a year from 2010.

Federation chief executive David Orr said: "We know that public spending is tight and you get a sense that in order to fund *Building Britain's Future* the Government shook every sofa in Whitehall to see what fell out. But then, having accumulated enough to make an impact, they undermine the capacity of the people they need to deliver it.

Reducing rents by 2% next year won't just leave a hole in capacity for one year, but forever. Not everyone will pull back from building – they will find cuts from elsewhere – but that hole in capacity translated into homes is 40,000 safe secure places for 40,000 families to thrive."'

(House of Commons Library, 2012a, p 10)

Note: The NHF is the trade body representing housing associations in England.

RPI did not fall to the extent expected and after lobbying from the National Federation, the CLG agreed changes. In the TSA's final published guidance, associations were required to reduce rents by 1% (unless target rents had not been reached, in which case the usual limit of 0.5% + £2 applied). What is interesting in this episode is that the voices of association tenants were barely heard even though they would have benefited from rent reductions.

Has this policy worked?

It is now expected that rent convergence will be achieved by 2015, with some exceptions. There have been unexpected consequences (Tang, 2008).

- The impact of using property/capital values has been to widen the differences in rents charged in different parts of the country especially between London/South-East and Yorkshire and the Humber.
- This rent-setting method has adversely affected associations in Yorkshire and the Humber: rents have fallen, reserves have had to be used to balance deficits, some associations have stopped building.
- Ten small 'minority ethnic' associations established in the 1980s merged with financially stronger associations because of financial viability problems derived in part from rent restructuring.

More local authorities moved into negative subsidy in their HRAs before 2012 because of increases in rents driven by rent restructuring (see Chapter Five), although the DCLG claimed that this was fed back to all authorities in increased management and maintenance allowances.

The Audit Commission's early estimate that rents would double in real terms, as compared to the 1980s (Garnett and Perry, 2005, p 289), proved to be an underestimate. The percentage increases in rents from 1988/89 compared to 2010/11 (the most recent figures available) indicate that the greatest increase in rents over that time has been experienced in the East region, at 283%. The least was 209%, in the North-East. Over a shorter period, in the 10 years from 2000 to 2011, the greatest increase in rents has been experienced by Yorkshire and the Humber, at 54% (entirely due to rent restructuring), while the lowest increase was in the North-West, at 38.5% (Pawson and Wilcox, 2012, Table 73).

Changing principles for rents over time

Earlier in this chapter, Table 9.1 listed the principles relating to rents and subsidy that had been used in the period 1930–72 for local authorities. Box 9.10 indicates the principles used for council housing since 1989.

The first four principles also provide a useful summary of the position of housing associations.

Box 9.10:The principles underlying rents policy in council housing from 1989

Rents should now:

- partly reflect the asset value and condition of the dwelling;
- be 'affordable' (though this has never been defined);
- partly reflect current incomes and prices;
- not be unduly distorted by the relative wealth of one authority compared to another;
- not contribute to or be subsidised by the General Fund;

Subsidy rather than rent should be treated as the 'residual'.

Source: Drawn from the discussion in Garnett and Perry (2005, pp 282–3)

As Garnett and Perry remark:

> We can see the development of policy on rents over the last 30 years or so as a shift from a 'welfare' approach where rents were set at levels just sufficient to cover costs (or even less than that if they were originally being subsidised by the General Fund) to one in which under the 1989 Act and more recently there has been an increasing emphasis on relating them to market values. (Garnett and Perry, 2005, p 282)

Although local authorities now have 'self-financing' HRAs, it is expected that they will continue with rent restructuring to establish their rents each year. The debt settlement was based on assumptions about rental income derived from this system, and their business plans up to 2015/16 may have been too. One major difficulty is the level of rent increases that the 'formula' generates based on the RPI. Tenants' wages and/or benefits are no longer being uprated by this inflation measure, so, cutbacks aside, tenants' incomes are losing their value compared to the rents that are being charged. Will this lead to more campaigning?

Rent levels – what values should be reflected in rent setting?

Many of the rent-setting methods used by 'social' landlords have used 'the market' as a benchmark for what may be charged. What other criteria might be used instead that better reflect the importance and significance of local authority and housing association rented housing?

The Affordable Rent programme

Private registered providers (associations, registered local authorities and private developers) have been offered a new way of developing housing that will affect the rents they charge. The Coalition's Affordable Rent programme for 2011–15, expects the 146 successful bidders to develop 'affordable housing' with little or no grant (see Chapter Six). Most are associations, but there are 15 private developers and 26 local authorities. They are expected to charge rents of up to 80% of market levels on the new property that they build and on a proportion of their re-lets. The tenancy to be offered will be 'flexible', possibly as short as two years. This may be convertible to a shared ownership property at the end of the initial term, but most tenancies will be reviewed then and either renewed or terminated.

The government's argument here is that these more expensive 'affordable rents' (set by looking at comparables in the private sector – RICS, 2011) will enable associations to build up surpluses and to increase private borrowing on the basis of increased rental income streams. Some associations have expressed disquiet at the expectation that they will be expected to borrow more from banks and building societies at a time when their income streams from rents are beginning to look less secure because of welfare benefit reductions and the end of direct payments (see Chapters Six and Ten). They may also be at the limit of what they can borrow. This model may not be replicated for these reasons. There are other possible difficulties:

- 'Affordable rents' may be acceptable to higher-income households not reliant on housing benefit, but what of others?
- A gap between current rents and 80% market rents is assumed, but what if there is no gap?
- How much additional re-let income has to be generated to fund this programme? The HCA estimates 3.5 social rent tenancies need to be

re-let at 'affordable rents' for every new property built but no one really knows. Several associations accepted for the Affordable Rent programme in 2011 have had to privately revise their calculations to include more re-lets in 2012.

Tenants are beginning to express disquiet at these proposals. Various pressure groups are also joining together to monitor the effects of the changes, including the CIH, NHF and Shelter, but this will not change government policy. Not all landlords have 'signed up' to the Coalition's programme. Of interest here is one local authority response, from LB Islington, relevant because of its circumstances outlined in Chapter Five. Is financial innovation like this the way forward on rents and new housing?

Box 9.11: 'The affordable rent programme does not work – but we have a solution', by Councillor James Murray, 2011

- '40% of Islington's council housing is bedsits or one bedroom flats. They need family housing.
- 3000 families on the waiting list are overcrowded.
- Social rents in Islington are 30–35% of market rents. Owner-occupation is out of reach and private renting is insecure and unaffordable.
- Islington's response is to reject the government's programme and ask associations to build family homes and charge social rents. The council is offering grant in the form of public land at discounted prices and capital from their New Homes Bonus allocation.
- They are expanding their council new build programme so will have 100 homes on site this year (2011–12). They are raising capital for this through selling one bedroom council flats on a shared ownership basis. The scheme is affordable to households on £24,000 a year, offering 40% shares. The council is prioritising applicants living in social housing, on the waiting list or with a local connection to the Borough.
- Initial figures suggest that selling these flats on this basis will raise £830,000: enough to fund 6 new family sized homes.'

(Murray, 2011)

Note: Councillor Murray is Executive member for Housing, Islington Council.

Further reading

The emphasis of this chapter has been partly to explain the ways in which rents have been set in the different tenures, but also the circumstances that led to protest by tenants and councillors (in some instances). To put this in a wider context see:

David Harvey (2005) *A brief history of neoliberalism*, reprinted 2011, Oxford: Oxford University Press, chapter 7, pp 198–206.

For more discussion on rents policy for council and housing association social rented property see: CIH with London and Quadrant Housing (2013) *We need to talk about rents – in the social and affordable housing sector*, Coventry: CIH.

The Red Brick blog, a site for progressive housing debate, may be useful: http://redbrickblog.wordpress.com/. This has posts commenting on current housing issues, with a great deal of information and connections to other sites.

TEN

Paying for housing with help from housing benefits

Introduction

The main way in which the welfare state provides help with housing costs has been through the housing benefit (HB) system. This is a system of benefit payments available to those who rent their homes who need financial help to meet the full cost of the rent. The scheme is available for those who live on low incomes or have no other income apart from benefit income (because they are unemployed, are long-term sick or disabled or have retired). The take-up rate for HB is about 85%, better than for other benefits. Higher take-up rates have been found in areas where the local authority encourages claims through take-up campaigns, accessible offices and helpful staff. Even so, each year anything up to £1,230 million remains unclaimed.

There is also help available for owner-occupiers if they have mortgage payments to meet and they become unemployed, long-term sick or disabled or are low-income pensioners. This financial help is related to mortgage interest, not payments of principal.

The HB scheme for housing association, council and privately renting tenants takes up most of this chapter. In addition, the impact of HB cutbacks on residents' ability to pay the rent in specialist voluntary or housing association homeless projects and private landlord temporary accommodation schemes will also be discussed. The bare bones of the HB system of help available and the cutbacks occurring are included here. More detailed information is available from Child Poverty Action Group, Shelter and Citizens Advice. The main themes in this chapter are:

- the background to the current HB scheme;
- changes to the HB scheme: the Coalition government's cutbacks;
- the LHA for private tenants;
- HB for council and housing association tenants;
- Support for Mortgage Interest for owner-occupiers;
- caps from 2013 and then Universal Credit;

- the Coalition government's arguments challenged: misleading, stigmatising and impoverishing for us all.

The background to the HB scheme

The original HB scheme was introduced in stages between 1982 and 1983. The scheme as established then still provides financial assistance to council and housing association tenants. The scheme for private tenants changed in 2008 to the SLHA (now the LHA). Both schemes will be considered in this chapter.

The calculation of a tenant's income is the same for HB and LHA. The difference between them is that while housing association and council tenants may receive help in relation to the full amount of rent that they pay, tenants of private landlords receive only a 'standard allowance', which may or may not match the full amount of rent that they have to pay their landlord.

The HB system was introduced in order to simplify housing payments to low-income households, replacing four separate schemes. It replaced:

- rent rebates and rent allowances, which were then available for tenants in low-paid work or receiving poor occupational pensions, to help with payments of rent;
- the system of paying housing costs as an integral part of what was then supplementary benefit (income support) for those of working age who were not in paid work, or supplementary pension (pensioner credits) for pensioners whose incomes were at or below the official poverty line.

A number of difficulties soon emerged. These have grown more problematic as the years have passed. These are scheme administration, increasing workloads and the incredible, rule-based complexity of the scheme.

> ### Box 10.1: Some problems with the HB scheme
>
> **Its complexity** – It was a 'unified' scheme, but difficult to understand.
>
> **The taper** – Some claimants in low-paid work find it difficult to earn enough to be better off financially in work because of the way the taper is used in relation to their earned income. It is too high, and they lose HB entitlement at low income levels.

> **Responding to changed circumstances** – HB administration lies with local authorities, even though it is a national scheme. Local administration and complex rules make it difficult to respond quickly to changed circumstances.
>
> **Service charges** – The interface with Supporting People has not been clear in some places. What counts as a housing cost and what counts as a support cost? Services in sheltered housing schemes are an example of this confusion.
>
> **Direct payments of HB** – This is common practice and helps landlords as well as tenants; but does direct payment of HB to the landlord take too much responsibility and control away from the tenant?

Partly because of these problems and partly because of the growing costs of administering the scheme, the New Labour government started to examine alternatives to HB. Since the mid-1990s, work on alternatives to the system involving 'shopping incentives' had been undertaken under the auspices of the Joseph Rowntree Foundation (JRF). The New Labour government's first housing Green Paper in 2000, *Quality and choice*, did not adopt any of these ideas. Instead, a chapter was devoted to discussing the problems of HB administration and exploring a wide range of alternatives.

Given growing HB expenditure, it was not long before work was under way to see if it was possible to introduce any of the JRF alternatives, while the government hoped at the same time to simplify the administration of the HB scheme. The government also wanted to make HB easier for claimants to understand, and to improve work incentives. A possible alternative was to be tried out first with claims from private tenants (Kemp, Wilcox and Rhodes, 2002). The government thought that it might be possible to consider it for council and housing association tenants but only after their rents had been integrated following rent restructuring (see Chapter Nine). So two different schemes now make up the HB system: HB and the LHA. Both will be considered in this chapter but first the cutbacks planned by the Coalition government for housing costs, announced in 2010, need to be outlined, as they are already affecting many tenants (see Wilcox, 2011a; House of Commons Library, 2012b).

Changes to the HB scheme: the Coalition government's cutbacks

The Coalition government's most controversial housing proposals relate to cutbacks to the HB scheme, announced by the Chancellor in 2010.

The government plans to 'save' £1,710 million from expenditure of £21.5 billion (2010/11 figures) by 2014/15, and in the process will introduce what Danny Dorling has called 'an era of engineered social polarisation' (Dorling, 2011, p 10).

Against these 'savings' it is notable that the government has introduced only two changes that represent financial gains: a fund for discretionary hardship payments and a new entitlement to a higher bedroom cap, to allow an extra room if a householder needs an additional bedroom for an overnight carer. These measures will cost £55 million.

Some changes have required primary legislation: the Welfare Reform Act 2012. Others have been introduced by regulation gradually, over several successive years. In this way, the government must be hoping that the political impact will be lessened. The impact on households reliant on HB or LHA will be severe and cumulative. The CIH, speaking for many, pointed out that

> the package as a whole takes little account of the primary policy objective for which housing benefit was created: to ensure that low income households have access to accommodation that reasonably meets their needs. (CIH, 2010b, p 5)

The Chancellor, George Osborne, claims that his Budget cuts are progressive (the richest households will be affected the most) and 'fair' (everyone should contribute to austerity savings). However, this view has been strongly challenged in England and the devolved administrations (where welfare benefits are reserved areas for the UK government). The IFS revealed that the worst-affected would be low-income households of working age, whether single people or two-parent/lone parent households caring for children (Browne and Levell, 2010). The leader of Glasgow council (where one third of households are out of work) called the cuts an act of 'social vandalism' (Social Policy Association, 2011, p 46).

LHA and the HB scheme in their entirety will be absorbed into the new Universal Credit, to be introduced from October 2013, but the regulations for the scheme will remain (House of Commons Library, 2013b).

Private sector tenants and the LHA will be considered first, as some cutbacks affected them from 2011.

The SLHA for private tenants

The New Labour government believed that the SLHA would make the HB system more straightforward and fairer for private tenants. It also wanted to protect work incentives and encourage initiative. A considerable amount of preparatory work was undertaken before the SLHA was introduced. An experimental local allowance scheme was piloted in nine pathfinder areas with 45,000 tenants for two years (from November 2003) in order to identify any possible problems. The Welfare Reform Act 2007 provided the legislation and the scheme 'went live' for new private tenants in 2008.

The main characteristics of the SLHA up to 2010

Amounts that claimants received were standardised, and paid over longer periods than HB for housing association and council tenants. This reduced administrative costs. There was a 'shopping incentive' of £15 included in the SLHA. If a tenant could find a rent below their SLHA, they could keep up to £15 a week of the difference.

> **Box 10.2: The main features of the standard local housing allowance scheme in 2008**
>
> • It was a standard amount (or allowance) towards the cost of rent, not usually the whole rent. The allowance varied, depending on the size and location of the private rented housing.
> • The median point of local rents for specific size of property in a specific area (based on rent information from the Valuation Office Agency) was used to decide the allowance, *not* the actual rent the tenant paid.*
> • The SLHA was calculated by reference to local rents, the tenant's income and the number of bedrooms they were expected to need.
> • The tenant's income was considered in the same way as in the HB calculation. SLHA was usually paid direct to the tenant, rather than to the landlord.
> • The SLHA was calculated on the assumption that the property had the appropriate number of bedrooms for the household.*
> • Anyone younger than 25 was entitled to SLHA only for the rent of a room with shared facilities (that is, a room in a shared house). This age distinction was carried through from the existing HB regulations.*
>
> *Note:* * Subsequently made more restrictive by the Coalition government.

Some tenants received less in SLHA than the rent they had to pay. Others received more because the SLHA was (and is) a broad-brush standard amount. (Local authorities had discretion as to whether to award an additional amount to anyone in serious financial difficulty.) No information is available about tenants who built up arrears because of this. Some will have been evicted; some will have moved before that happened. A few will have negotiated a lower rent figure with their landlord in exchange for direct payment of their SLHA to the landlord.

The point here is that the way in which New Labour's SLHA worked was already problematic for some private tenants. Paying private tenants less than what was needed to make up the full rent inevitably led to arrears and evictions. This problem has been compounded by the Coalition government.

Coalition cuts to the LHA from 2011

Six main features of the LHA have been changed, reducing the financial help given to private tenants. These changes have been introduced at different times, so the impact has been gradual but cumulative. Private tenants with new claims have been affected by the changes immediately (with a few transitional arrangements), but existing claimants have been drawn into these new arrangements when they have renewed their claims. The key changes to the existing SLHA are discussed here (see House of Commons Library, 2013a, for more detail).

The lowest third, not the median range of rents, for self-contained housing

HB staff now calculate LHA by reference to the lowest third of market rents in the locality (the 30th percentile), not the median rent (the 50th percentile). The DWP expects to save £425 million by 2014/15 through this measure.

The cheapest third of the private rented market is potentially available to a low-income private tenant. Private tenants reliant on LHA are being pushed more than before into the lower end of the private rented sector, where the worst conditions and security of tenure are to be found.

Even there, landlords may prefer tenants who do not claim LHA. The first report of a study commissioned by the DWP found in autumn 2011 that 62% of claimants in London and 47% living elsewhere in England, Scotland and Wales, found that landlords were 'generally unwilling to let their accommodation to tenants in receipt of HB' (Beatty et al, 2012, p 3).

The 'shopping incentive'

In the original SLHA scheme, claimants could keep up to £15 of their standard SLHA if they found a rent that was cheaper. This was called a 'shopping incentive' in the original scheme and was designed to encourage tenants to find cheaper housing. The Coalition government renamed the 'shopping incentive'. It became known as the 'excess' and was easily targeted for abolition.

Non-dependant deductions

From April 2011, increased non-dependant deductions have applied to private and social rented tenants (see later).

Single room rate up to age 35 years

From April 2012, single people aged under 35 are able to claim only for a room in a shared house. The estimated 'saving' here was £390 million. There are some transitional arrangements and exemptions, but the government's justification for this change was that if the average age for a first-time buyer is now in the mid-30s, why should anyone in receipt of LHA be any different?

Bedroom caps

A series of caps or upper limits were introduced from April 2011. These are based on the number of bedrooms considered appropriate for a tenant and their family (see later for how this is now calculated).

The bedroom caps act as limits to the amount of LHA that will be paid in any circumstances. The number of bedrooms and limits are: £250 for one bedroom; £290 for two bedrooms; £390 for three bedrooms and £400 for four or more bedrooms. The five or more bedroom cap has been abolished. The LHA figure is limited to the cap for four bedrooms. Children in larger families have to squeeze into less space and/or the family has to move.

CPI not RPI as the inflation measure

The Consumer Prices Index (CPI) replaced the Retail Prices Index (RPI) from April 2013 as the inflation measure used to uprate benefits. The CPI does not include housing costs in the calculation of price changes. It usually produces a lower inflation figure than the RPI. As rents increase faster than inflation, LHA will fall further behind actual rents. The government has now legislated to hold increases in benefits to 1% in 2014 and 2015, an enormously controversial measure because of its cumulative impact on the poorest.

A storm of political protest

The government has underestimated the impact of the cuts to the programme, both individually and cumulatively. The DWP claimed that about 14,000 tenants, mainly in London, would be affected, but independent analysis reveals a different picture.

The areas affected extend beyond London (where the most extreme circumstances will be found), to areas around London and as far away as Nottinghamshire and Scotland. The CIH immediately estimated that 500,000+ people would lose more than £10 a week as a result of three measures alone (LHA caps, the 30th percentile and the abolition of the £15 'excess'). This represented over half the 2010 SLHA caseload handled by local authorities (CIH, 2010b). The very heavy losses of over £15 a week will be experienced by over 68,000 people who live in one-, two- or three-bedroomed homes.

These cutbacks in the help given to low-income private tenants provoked a storm of protest across the political spectrum when they were announced. Conservative London Mayor Boris Johnson told the BBC in October 2010 that he would:

> emphatically resist any attempt to recreate a London where the rich and poor cannot live together … We will not see and we will not accept any kind of Kosovo–style social cleansing of London … On my watch, you are not going to see thousands of families evicted from the place where they have been living and have put down roots.

But steadily, that is what is happening. The most noticeable impact is in the London boroughs of Westminster, Hammersmith and Fulham, and Kensington and Chelsea. Westminster has no private rented housing with rent levels within the new bedroom caps for families. See Chapter Three for more detail of the boroughs affected.

LB Newham created a furore when it investigated the possibility of re-housing those made homeless by moving them to the North of England. More quietly, the DWP knows that mass movement will occur. It commissioned research in 19 case-study local authority areas, including three higher-rent London Boroughs (Westminster, Hackney and Brent) where an 'out-flow' of LHA recipients is expected in the future, and four other potential 'in-flow' areas in the South-East (Barking and Dagenham, Portsmouth, Tendring and Thanet) (Beatty et al, 2012, p 2).

Housing benefit for council and housing association tenants

Tenants of councils and housing associations are eligible for means-tested HB. The rules about non-dependant deductions, bedroom caps and uprating are shared across the scheme with LHA claimants. Key features of the HB scheme are:

- if the household income is at or below the 'needs allowance', the tenant will receive 100% of the 'eligible rent';
- for every £1 of income above the needs allowance, HB is reduced by 65p. This 'taper' is designed to reduce HB as earnings increase;
- the house/flat must not be 'unreasonably large';
- eligible service charges must be housing related and unavoidable;
- 'non-dependant' deductions are made from the eligible rent to take account of adult sons or daughters or other adults living in the property who are assumed to be making a contribution to the rent.

Coalition cuts to HB from 2011

The most significant cutbacks to HB for council and housing association tenants are taking place in 2013. Others have already been implemented. They are:

Non-dependant deductions

The majority of tenants affected by these changes have been council or housing association tenants (160,000 out of 213,000 households who are liable for these deductions). private tenants are less likely to have lived long term in that sector and have adult sons and daughters at home. In 2001 New Labour froze non-dependant deductions at £7.40 for 'non-dependants' without paid work. The Coalition government has calculated the value of this 10-year 'gap' and increased non-dependant deductions accordingly across the board in 2011.

For those over 18 years old not in paid work, the non-dependant deduction increased from £7.40 to £9.40 from April 2011. For those who are in paid work, the deductions were higher, depending on gross income. They now increase each year.

Property size – 'the bedroom tax'

The government has decided that HB will in future be calculated against the number of bedrooms that the household is considered to be entitled to rather, than the number that the household actually has in the house or flat. This is part of the Coalition's plan to reduce waiting lists – but this is simply a repeat of the 1950s 'Tory legends' that Richard Crossman uncovered (see Chapter Seven). The housing shortage will not be dealt with by what has been dubbed the 'bedroom tax.'

Reducing HB to match the number of bedrooms now deemed 'appropriate' is a crude device to try to improve the 'fit' between households and housing. The DWP has estimated that about 670,000 households will be affected and that the average loss of HB will be £13 a week (Arden, 2013).

As with LHA in the private sector, the new HB rules allow for one bedroom for each single adult or couple in a household. Children have to share unless they are aged over 16. If they are aged over 10, same-sex sharing is expected. If aged under 10, boys and girls are expected to share a room. Council and housing association allocation practice often has been different from this for good reasons. In some areas, more three-bedroomed family homes have been built than smaller properties so smaller families on the waiting list have been offered them. In the 1970s, flats at the top of tower blocks were found to be detrimental to the health of children. Landlords have preferred to rehouse single people or couples in them despite their having more than one bedroom. Some tenants on estates have seen their children grow and leave home. These are the families which provide stability to an estate. All of these households will probably have to leave their homes, not because they choose to, but because the HB that they receive towards the rent will not enable them to stay (see Gentleman, 2013, for a picture of the impact).

Each year, the turnover of most rented local authority or housing association homes is very low. Relatively few new properties are built too. (See the example of Leafy Glades in Chapter Six.) Most local authorities have not been able to build new council housing for some time and the bulk of the development programme for associations is in the South (see Chapter Six). While most new property for rent has been smaller one- or two-bedroom flats, especially in London, the numbers of families needing to downsize because of the bedroom tax, far outweighs the numbers actually available for letting (Arden, 2013).

These new rules, dubbed 'the bedroom tax', affect particular areas more than others. Generally, those areas worst affected are those where demand for three-bedroom family housing is lower: the North (one in five social rented tenants) and the Midlands (one in six). Many tenants are now faced with moving, even though they do not want to because they cannot make up the reduction in their HB/LHA. Table 10.1 shows the amounts that housing association tenants in the North have to pay for 'under-occupying' their home if they are claiming HB.

Table 10.1: The 'bedroom tax' in the North

Rent charged	£60–£70	£70–£80	£80–£90	£90–£100
One extra bedroom: you pay 14%	Pay £8.40 to £9.80	Pay £9.80 to £11.20	Pay £11.20 to £12.60	Pay £12.60 to £14
Two extra bedrooms: you pay 25%	Pay £15 to £17.50	Pay £17.50 to £20	Pay £20 to £22.50	Pay £22.50 to £25

Source: Leafy Glades HA tenants' newsletter, August 2012.

As with private tenants (who have lived with these new regulations for longer), these Coalition-inspired HB rules will destroy family stability and communities that have built up over the years. Two thirds of all those affected are disabled; many live in specially adapted housing (NHF, 2013, p 4). Pensioners are exempt, but only if everyone in the household has reached state pension age. From 2013 onwards it will be absolutely clear to the public that poor households are being forced to move from areas where they have probably lived for most of their lives. The financial and emotional costs of removal are high. Where will these households go?

The DWP has acknowledged that these plans are problematic and that social rented tenants may have to 'look further afield' than their existing landlord for somewhere to live of the 'right' size (see Pawson, 2011 for more detail). Some social landlords have run information campaigns, set up advice surgeries and arranged transfers where possible, but there are limits to what can be done. Some tenants will try to find the money from their household income but they are living at the poverty line already (they would not be entitled to HB otherwise). The level of rent arrears and evictions for arrears are expected to increase dramatically;

other households will leave before it gets to that stage. No one knows where people will go, but many local authorities are expecting a flood of homeless families and single householders.

The government expects most homeless families to be rehoused in the private rented sector. This is highly problematic. Those who are made homeless are in this situation because of avoidable benefit cutbacks. They will have had secure tenancies with full security of tenure. They will now be faced with finding housing in the private rented sector where lettings are made on six-monthly assured tenancies. Conditions are likely to be poor. Landlords may not be willing to accept anyone as a tenant who relies on benefit. With increased demand, private rents will increase. The bottom third of private tenancies in an area may still be more expensive than an association or council tenancy, even if only the allowance figure is paid (see Chapter Seven).

REFLECTION 10.1

What should a local authority do when the money runs out?

Housing benefit is a national scheme, implemented locally. What should a local authority do when the discretionary hardship fund runs out?

Caps from 2013 and then the Universal Credit

Finally, the Coalition government has made it clear that from 2013 there will be an additional set of caps in relation to benefit payments. These are being introduced first in London (initially in four selected boroughs from April 2013). They provide limits to the amount of income that a household living on welfare benefits can receive. Housing costs are to be drawn from within these limits (House of Commons Library, 2013b). They are:

- £350 for a single person
- £500 for a couple or lone parent with children.

The justification that the government has put forward for these household caps is 'equity'. It has argued that it cannot be 'fair' that someone in work can receive less in their pay packet than a household living on welfare benefits. These distinctions take no account of private sector rent levels and the real cost of living in some areas. They also make no allowance for the fact that some claimants who receive HB are homeless and likely to be paying high rents for temporary accommodation.

Specialist providers of refuges, and housing associations that run homeless schemes on behalf of local authorities in partnership with local authorities, have already flagged up problems. Some women currently receive HB for the refuge and the home they have left because of the violence. This will put residents' costs beyond the £500 cap in 2013. The impact of Universal Credit has also been identified as problematic and the Women's Aid Federation has been campaigning for change, as otherwise the prospect of refuges closing is very real (Women's Aid Federation England, 2012).

Many local authorities and housing associations provide temporary housing for homeless people by managing private lettings on behalf of private landlords. These schemes typically involve the private landlord leasing their property to the local authority or housing association. The private landlord receives a regular agreed rental income in exchange for the units that are being used by the local authority or housing association. Leases are generally for periods of between three and five years. In this way, local authorities have reduced their use of bed-and-breakfast hotels, but the level of rent charged may prove to be problematic for residents once the benefit cap of £500 is introduced in 2013. One housing association in London has made it clear that their temporary housing scheme will close because it will not be viable. This will create a very expensive problem for the local authority in finding alternative temporary housing for homeless residents.

These caps will be integrated within the Universal Credit system, now legislated for in the Welfare Reform Act 2012. It will be introduced over four years, from October 2013. Universal Credit is planned to replace Jobseeker's Allowance, Employment and Support Allowance, Income Support, Child Tax Credits, Working Tax Credits and Housing Benefit (HB and LHA). Much of the detail will be put into place during the lifetime of the next government, and by regulation rather than by legislation.

One of the aims of Universal Credit is to improve incentives to work and to help to create a 'dynamic' labour market. This seems unlikely, unless pushing desperate people into very poorly paid and insecure work is regarded in this light.

Support for Mortgage Interest

Any owner-occupier who loses their job or retires but still has a mortgage to pay may get help with the interest payment part of the mortgage. An owner-occupier has to be claiming income support, Jobseeker's Allowance, Employment and Support Allowance or Pension Credit. The waiting period of 39 weeks was reduced by the New Labour government to 13 weeks as a way of preventing a flood of mortgage repossessions in 2007/08. The mortgage interest for which support could be claimed was also extended from a mortgage limit of £100,000 to £200,000. Help is not time limited except for those claiming Jobseeker's Allowance, where the help with interest is time limited to two years only, whether or not the claimant has found another job.

Commentators have pointed out for years that the amount of help that low-income owner-occupiers receive from the welfare state is less than that received by other low-income claimants. This is unsatisfactory, but unlikely to change.

The Coalition government's arguments for cutbacks considered

The Coalition government's cutbacks to the HB scheme can be challenged in three main ways. They are:

- misleading – the public has been given inaccurate and misleading information;
- stigmatising – HB has increased because landlords have increased rents. Tenants do not 'shop around' for the most expensive housing if they are claiming LHA or HB. The government has stigmatised anyone reliant on benefits income by publicising stories about 'benefit scroungers' in order to justify cuts;
- impoverishing – for us all. Is this what we want from our welfare state?

Misleading

The former Housing Minister, Grant Shapps, commenting about the cuts to HB remarked:

> 'If you choose not to work it can't be right that you are better off than people who are working.

We believe that rents will come down as a result of the new cap, in the same way that rents have been driven up by the current system. Some people will face a shortfall in their rental payments but in many cases they will be able to make up the difference themselves.

People might not be able to live in the most expensive street in their area, but they will still be able to live in nearly one third of the properties in their neighbourhood. Some people will have to move within their area, but we all have to move according to our jobs, and that's life. There's no reason why you should be shielded from that everyday reality just because you're not working.' (Tayner, 2010)

Claiming benefit (including HB and LHA) is not a 'lifestyle choice', as was suggested. It is a necessity. HB has enabled poor households to pay for a roof over their heads. More than half the people claiming LHA are in paid work.

Tenants have virtually no control over the rent levels set by landlords. Rent restructuring in the council and housing association sectors was a New Labour policy, continued by the Coalition. It has led to significant increases in rents since 2003 (see Chapter Nine). Private landlords have increased rents further.

At the same time, more expensive rents and direct HB have become essential for association landlords in the production of new social rented housing. Secure rental streams (largely made up from direct payments of HB authorised by eligible tenants) now finance new building, not government grant (see Chapter Six).

Stigmatising

The *Daily Telegraph* reported in 2010 that the Chancellor, George Osborne:

> has been doing his best to whip up support for cutting the £21 billion housing benefit bill by pointing the finger at families who receive £104,000 per year to live in multi-million pound properties in the country's most desirable areas. (Tayner, 2010)

When the *Telegraph* investigated, it found that there were very few claimants renting at the higher end of the rental market. Far from LHA being for 'shameless spongers living in dream homes courtesy of the struggling taxpayer' (Tayner, 2010), the reporter found only three households in Westminster claiming £2,000 for weekly rent while only five councils had anyone claiming more than £1,000 a week in London. The points to be made are that this rent was income for the landlord, not the tenant, and the local authority had to agree that there was no cheaper alternative – points that seems to be lost in much discussion of this issue. The cap for four or more bedrooms is now £400 a week (see House of Commons Library, 2013, for more detail).

The actions of the Chancellor are instructive, nevertheless, as he was suggesting widespread abuse of the LHA system. Crisis, the homeless charity, has accused the government of 'peddling myths' in order to justify the cuts that it has implemented (Crisis, 2010).

This approach of emphasising 'scroungers', despite evidence to the contrary, has continued, despite much criticism. The disability charity Scope commissioned research just before the Paralympic Games in 2012. It revealed that almost half of disabled respondents (46%) reported that attitudes towards them had worsened over the previous year. Many had experienced aggression, hostility and name-calling from other people and many had been challenged by strangers in the street about the support they claim. Richard Hawkes, the Chief Executive of Scope, said:

> It is telling that these figures come as the Government continues to put the issue of weeding out illegitimate claimants at the heart of its welfare rhetoric ... we want the Government to mark the games with a new approach to welfare: tell the whole story ... (Scope, 31 July 2012)

Impoverishing for us all

Some time ago Zygmunt Bauman (2005, pp 55–6) discussed in detail the reasons why it is possible now for politicians in a wide range of countries to undermine, diminish and abolish the safety nets provided by the welfare state. He thought that neoliberalism, with its emphasis on the consumer society and so-called 'choice', was partly responsible. The welfare state is clearly focused on human needs and collective provision and does not chime well with individualist 'choice'.

Equally telling was his discussion of the impact of means testing. Universalism is more sustaining and inclusive for citizens, means testing much less so. It is easier to cut welfare benefits that are publicly devalued. The American cliché that 'programs for the poor are poor programs' sums up what the Coalition government is doing. Housing benefit (and any other benefit, for that matter) is becoming circumscribed and undermined. Voices of protest stoutly defending existing welfare state benefits and offering alternatives to the austerity programme have so far been drowned out (see Social Policy Association, 2011; JRF minimum income reports and blogs).

The changes to HB and LHA, and the prospect of caps under the Universal Credit, epitomise means testing at its extreme. It is crystal clear that the nature of the means testing is such that many HB claimants will find it impossible to cope. Those who claim HB and LHA do not have large amounts of savings and often do not have family and friends who are in a position to provide financial help. Social landlords will not be able to make properties with fewer bedrooms available for everyone who will need them. A low-wage economy makes it difficult for HB/LHA claimants to find jobs that will enable them gradually to improve their financial position and prospects.

Threading through previous chapters have been accounts of how people have challenged the status quo. In the past, tenants have campaigned against large rent increases and poor housing conditions. Sometimes they were successful, sometimes not. These campaigns involved petitions, demonstrations, letters to newspapers and rent strikes where rent increases or the full rent were withheld for months.

REFLECTION 10.2

Protecting homes and neighbourhoods

In the past, private and council tenants have campaigned to protect their homes and neighbourhoods. Will the same happen again in the face of the HB cutbacks, which are creating homelessness and extreme poverty for anyone reliant on this help?

Further reading

CIH (2012) 'Housing benefit cuts will put 800,000 homes out of reach', press release with connections to other sources, http://www.cih.org/news-article/display/vpathDCR/templatedata/cih/news-article/data/Housing_benefit_cuts_will_put_800000_homes_out_of_reach.

David Harvey (2005 and reprinted 2011) *A brief history of neoliberalism*, Oxford, Oxford University Press, chapter 7, pp 198–206.

National Audit Office (2012) *Managing the impact of housing benefit reform*, http://www.nao.org.uk/publications/1213/housing_benefit_reform. aspx.

Steve Wilcox (2013) 'Beginning to bite: the early impacts of the new local housing allowance regime' in H. Pawson, and S. Wilcox, *UK Housing Review 2013*, Coventry: CIH, Heriot-Watt University and the University of York.

A number of websites will be useful to update information:

Website for Shelter (in particular, its housing databank), http://england. shelter.org.uk/professional_resources/housing_databank

Website for Crisis (in particular, its sections on benefits and 'welfare reform'), http://www.crisis.org.uk/

Website for National Housing Federation (in particular its section on 'welfare reform'), http://www.housing.org.uk/policy/welfare_ reform.

Part Four

Discussion

ELEVEN

Is our housing system sustainable?

Introduction

At the centre of all the changes that have occurred in the UK's housing system is the debate about the extent to which the state can and should intervene to influence 'the market'. These arguments can be seen clearly as long ago as the First World War, when controlled rents were introduced to protect private tenants (and the war-time economy) from the self-interested profiteering of private landlords. One hundred years later, roles have switched so that 'the market' is now seen as the saviour from all that the state provides in relation to housing: in the eyes of critics, 'dependency' and a lack of 'social mobility'. How did we get to this point and how can we move beyond it?

This final chapter will look at this question in different ways. It has been written to provoke discussion and debate. The themes are:

- the market and the state – the 2007–08 financial crisis in retrospect;
- the re-emergence of class;
- changing times: owner-occupation and individualism – the end of a dream?
- changing times: the state reconsidered – another paradigm shift?

The market and the state – the 2007–08 global financial crisis in retrospect

The 2007–08 global financial crisis generated enormous problems for governments across the 'developed' world. New Labour under the Prime Minister Gordon Brown responded in a way that was reflective of Keynesian economics. What was of great significance was the central role of the state. Central government took action to protect the country from the imminent collapse of the banking system. Britain's best banks did not like it much, but, at the time, they had no alternative to nationalisation and recapitalisation. Ironically, Gordon Brown and

Alistair Darling did not care much for nationalisation, either, but it was nationalisation or economic chaos.

The current Coalition government sees its role differently. Turning a financial crisis and subsequent recession into political advantage, these Conservative and Liberal Democrat politicians now barely acknowledge the economic and financial catastrophe of 2007–08. They seek to blame the Labour Party (and Gordon Brown in particular) for their having to deal with the financial deficit that they took on when they formed the Coalition government in 2010. Since then, the Chancellor has pursued an austerity programme that he claims is fair and progressive, but is actually the opposite. The Chancellor would leave 'the wealth creators' in the private sector untouched, but is determined to substantially reduce government expenditure on the poorest. HB cuts are premised on Conservative ideas about class: if you are poor, 'know your place'. This political view, ruthlessly parodied by Charles Dickens in *The Chimes*, still has resonance more than 150 years later.

Another significant Conservative idea is the Chancellor's belief that the private sector will flourish once the public sector has gone. This idea – that public investment 'crowds out' private investment – is wrong. It was commonly heard when Margaret Thatcher was Prime Minister, but was proved conclusively to have no foundation (see the discussion in Walker and Walker, 2011, pp 54–5). A practical demonstration of the reliance of the private sector on public sector investment was provided by the Housing Market Renewal programme (scrapped by the Coalition). More generally, the construction industry has been slowly collapsing since house building and infrastructure programmes were substantially reduced or scrapped following the 2010 Budget and CSR and subsequent announcements.

Box 11.1: '... down we continue to go' – in 2012 and beyond?

'GDP is now lower than it was when George Osborne became Chancellor in 2010 ... Construction made the biggest negative contribution in the past two quarters ... driven by declines in the value of public housing and non-infrastructure public spending (−11 per cent and −17 per cent, respectively, quarter on quarter; and −18 per cent and −20 per cent, year on year). This looks like a collapse in construction, driven by the coalition's decision to kill off public investment.

The evidence is that public investment crowds in private investment, contrary to the coalition's bizarre claims that it crowds it out ...

> Large and medium-sized building contractors reported that output in the second quarter of 2012 was lower than during the first quarter of 2011, which in turn was lower than the fourth quarter of 2011. Public-sector investment continues to decline, and [there is] no sign of private-sector recovery to offset these cuts, leaving little optimism for recovery in the near future.'
>
> (Blanchflower, 2012, p 19)
>
> *Note:* David Blanchflower is Professor of Economics at Dartmouth College, New Hampshire, and Economics Editor of the *New Statesman*. He was a member of the Bank of England's Monetary Policy Committee from 2006 to 2009.

Council, housing association and private rented housing are all seriously affected by a range of changes instituted by the Coalition. Some of these resonate with New Labour approaches that pre-date the 2007–08 financial crisis. At their core, these changes are predicated on a belief that the state's role should be minimal. This is not dissimilar to the stance of the US Republican Party and it is clear that a US Republican-style social policy model informs Coalition thinking. Central is the belief that 'the market' should be given every opportunity to do what it apparently does best: create 'wealth'. The Chancellor has a singular belief in 'wealth makers' and 'the market', to the exclusion of the state and the public sector and he continues to talk of the 'bloated welfare system'. It is now barely acknowledged by Coalition politicians that 'wealth creators' in the banking industry used unchecked sub-prime mortgages, tied them up as 'asset-backed securities' with a triple A rating from credit ratings agencies and sold them on for profit, in the process creating the 'man-made economic assault' of the 2007–08 global financial crisis.

The re-emergence of class

Richard Hoggart wrote in his introduction to Orwell's *The Road to Wigan Pier* that:

> Class distinctions do not die; they merely learn new ways of expressing themselves ... Each decade we shiftily declare we have buried class; each decade the coffin stays empty. (Orwell, 1989, p. vii)

New Labour's approach to housing policy reinforced policies inherited from the Conservatives in 1997, for example the view that local authorities (the local state) by preference should be 'enablers' not direct service providers (see Chapters One and Three). In pursuing a neoliberal agenda, softened with elements of social democratic social policy, New Labour prepared some of the ground for the Coalition (Davis and Wigfield, 2012). Consequently, certain changes in the balance between the state and 'the market' have had 30 years in which to take root. In the second decade of the 21st century, three new ways in which class divisions have been emerging can be clearly seen. These are evident in:

- the poorest getting poorer, as a deliberate strategy;
- the restructuring of democratically controlled public services into the private domain;
- the growing extremes of wealth and poverty found in the UK, which are now concentrated in particular areas, pulling ideas of 'society' apart.

The implications of these changes will be outlined next and some questions will be raised about future alternatives.

The poorest getting poorer – the HB cuts

Changes to HB and the introduction of Universal Credit are accompanied by stronger 'conditionality' or work incentives. Benefit income will be withdrawn more quickly if conditions about attending a certain number of interviews or taking particular job offers (whatever the wage) are not complied with. The belief in punishing what many Conservatives regard as the 'underclass' (in previous years known more generally as the 'undeserving poor') runs deep (Mann, 1992; Levitas, 1998). Conservatives believe that their changes to HB and the introduction of Universal Credit will force a 'culture change' away from 'dependency' and towards 'social mobility' (Duncan-Smith, 2012). The Chancellor is also determined to reduce the overall cost of the HB scheme. 'Scrounger' rhetoric continues to dominate the Coalition's presentation of these reductions.

However, HB expenditure has increased for legitimate reasons, and not because tenants exploit the system to their own advantage. These are:

- the changing emphasis of government intervention in 'the market'. Successive governments have chosen to retreat from paying subsidies and grants to build new social housing. Instead, individual householders have become responsible, through rental payments, for the majority of the costs. So the switch has been from capital subsidy to personal subsidy, such that 80% of government spending on housing is now in the form of HB payments;

- rent restructuring in the social rented sector. Since 2002, housing associations and local authorities have been restructuring their rents, following government policy, aiming to converge in 2012 (now 2015/16). The effect of this exercise is that rents in both sectors are now much higher than they were in the 1990s relative to incomes. In some parts of the country they are very near market levels;

- more people in social housing are poorer. With demand high, new tenants are more likely to be poor and have few housing alternatives. They may be reliant on welfare benefits for all of their household income, or they may be in low-paid 'flexible' employment, receiving partial HB to help them pay the landlord's rent. Poverty has become more associated with this type of housing than in the past, but this does not represent 'dependency'. It is a current characteristic of the rationing process involved in becoming a tenant (people with few resources have even fewer alternatives). Part of the process shaping social housing has also been the right to buy, where successive governments have actively encouraged better-off council and housing associations tenants to become homeowners;

- increasing demand for private rented accommodation. As homeownership slips out of the reach of first-time buyers, many now have to consider renting privately, even though the cost and lack of security make it a poor, second-best option. Council or housing association tenancies are not available, due to long waiting lists. Many local authorities are also using the private rented sector to rehouse homeless people who have approached them as potentially statutory homeless. Private landlords can increase their rents to as much as the local market will stand because of the shortage of accommodation. As rents increase in the private sector, due to increased demand, so the costs of LHA will increase despite the limits to uprating it.

HB cuts do not address the real reasons for increases in HB expenditure. They simply hold tenants responsible for the high rents charged by landlords. Is this acceptable?

The restructuring of public assets and privatisation of services

New Labour's programme of council stock transfers has severely reduced public sector housing. Transferring council housing (public assets) to private housing associations (private organisations) has been accompanied by a loss of democratic control over these assets and a reduction in security of tenure for tenants who have transferred. Housing PFIs effectively do the same.

Large areas of the South-East, South and West of England no longer have any council housing and the same pattern exhibits itself in Wales and Scotland. Who now controls housing in these areas?

David Harvey (2005) has described the processes through which the private sector is now making substantial incursions into areas of life previously believed and intended to be publicly owned as 'accumulation through dispossession'.

Box 11.2: Definition: Accumulation through dispossession

Capitalist economic processes seek to make profit (surplus value derived from employees) in a seemingly never-ending cycle. Manufacturers, private service providers, banks or finance companies are constantly looking for opportunities in which to invest. Through this they hope to produce goods or services and make additional profit. This process is 'accumulation'.

Harvey has focused on recent developments where profits are now being sought by the private sector through buying public assets. This 'dispossesses' citizens of public assets and services that had been provided for them as citizens (not consumers) as a result of public policy, paid for by public investment (grants or borrowing) that was ultimately paid for by different forms of general taxation.

He has identified four main ways in which this is done: privatisation and commodification (for example, creating 'markets' out of welfare needs); financialisation (for example, the extension of marginal owner-occupation); the management and manipulation of crises, especially in relation to debt (think of austerity programmes); and finally, state redistribution (where the local or central state privatises public assets – think of council housing transfers).

Source: Harvey (2005, pp 160–5)

The individual right to buy scheme was a privatisation programme fuelled by large discounts, and taken up by 2.3 million council tenants in Great Britain. Mortgage lenders extended their business through the right to buy. This extension of the financial services industry into lower working-class families' lives was part of what has become known as the growing financialisation of the population. As Doreen Massey has remarked:

> Through the practices of privatisation, of health, pensions, housing, people became entangled with the finance sector in ways which the financiers could harvest for 'investment' in SIVs, derivatives and assets. By this means millions of people became both materially enrolled into the interests of finance in the short term (even if structurally in the long term their interests would be elsewhere) and ideologically acculturated into its ways of thinking. (Massey, 2010)

Many former council tenants are now marginal owner-occupiers. The parallels with sub-prime mortgage lending in the US are clear. For marginal and even middle-income households, buying a home is becoming a perilous activityJobs may now be far from secure for many. They may now be worrying about mortgage payments. If their home is repossessed because of non-payment of the mortgage, where is their obvious destination? Is it the local authority or a housing association? Little is available there. Is it the private rented sector, as the Coalition government prefers? Private landlords will benefit because of increased demand, but rent levels are rising too. Increased demand in the private rented sector will also affect public expenditure, as payments of LHA will increase, despite new restrictions.

Surely, introducing a form of rent control in the private rented sector and building more low-rent council housing would be a cheaper long-term solution?

Geographical concentrations of wealth and poverty

Poverty and wealth have physical as well as financial forms and there are some very worrying signs for the future in the way that urban space in the UK is owned and controlled. Geographically, many of the poorest in society are being forced to move into smaller homes in the social rented sector, and into poorer areas in the private rented sector.

Charles Dickens would have been familiar with this kind of poverty, forever pushing people downwards, constantly reinforcing 'place', in the social hierarchy as well as geographically. The changes to HB and Universal Credit are creating this household movement which affects single 'working age' people and families with children alike. Anyone reliant on welfare benefits is also becoming poorer because of reductions in the value of benefits year on year, whether or not they physically have to move. This is what the Coalition government means by 'social mobility': know your 'proper station' (Dickens, 1844, *The Chimes*).

At the other end of the class system, the richest continue to get richer. In 2007, the top 0.1% of British earners (that is, 30,000 people) had a combined income of £33 billion or about 4% of all personal earnings in the UK. These concentrations of extreme wealth started under Thatcherism, were not challenged by New Labour and are endorsed under the Coalition. The argument is that these people are necessary for the health of the economy. If they are taxed, the argument goes, they will move to another country and their 'wealth creating' abilities will go with them, but the High Pay Commission (2011) has produced compelling analysis which disproves this.

It is important to see the extent of the differences that have emerged since 1979. In 2010/11, the salary of the most senior executive in Barclays Bank was 75 times greater than that of the average worker there (in 1979 it had been 14.5 times greater). The Chief Officer's pay increased over that time from just over £87,000 in 1979 to over £4,300,000 in 2010/11. More generally, these differences are escalating. In 2010/11 a typical pay increase for a FTSE 100 company boss in the UK was 49%, while an average employee saw their salary increase by 2.7% (High Pay Commission, 2011, p 9). Income differentials like this are only more extreme in the US. Yet who actually creates the wealth in different private businesses, and the value in public services? We all do.

The geographical concentrations of very rich and very poor affect life chances. This has been pointed out by a wide range of commentators. Robert Peston concentrated on the problems attached to 'super-rich supercapitalists' in the banking community (Peston, 2008, pp 181–216). Susan Smith (2005) pointed out that the wealthiest areas in Britain are becoming wealthier at an extraordinary rate, leaving the worst and poorest areas far behind. This trend will continue:

> Between 1993–2003 the housing wealth of the 'best off' 10% of areas rose ten times more than the 'worst off' 10%, raising the possibility that because of the distribution of housing assets, the UK is becoming more divided by wealth now than it was in Victorian times. (Smith, 2005, p 4)

Bethan Thomas and Danny Dorling (2007) have extensively mapped these patterns of poverty and wealth in Britain. Alex Fenton (2010 and 2011) has looked in detail at how LHA changes will force private rented tenants into the poorer parts of London and surrounding poorer local authorities.

Should public policy be creating concentrations of the very poor? What should be done about the super-rich? What will the outcome of these divisions be for our society?

Changing times: owner-occupation and individualism – the end of a dream?

This book has demonstrated that politicians and people can change the direction in which services are provided and alter the balance between the public and the private ownership and control of assets. So, in the short term, what might need to be changed?

Owner-occupation, a tenure favoured by New Labour and the parties of the Coalition, may hold the key to unravelling some of the market extremes that are now evident. It may have reached its limit. This was not immediately obvious before the 2007–08 global financial crisis, but the link between owner-occupation and the economy that has been pointed out by Peter Malpass is important:

> In economic terms, owner occupation has come to play an important role in relation to both growth and management of the economy. The building, maintenance and improvement of owner occupied houses accounts for a significant proportion of the work of the construction industry while the business of buying and selling also generates large numbers of jobs. House prices, and people's expectations about whether they are going to rise or fall, influence consumer spending and therefore the rate of growth in the economy. When house prices are rising strongly, consumers feel better off and are ready to increase debt fuelled spending, underpinned by the appreciating asset represented by their houses. In short, the state of the housing market and the wider economy are intimately bound together. (Malpass, 2005, p 146)

It is not surprising that 'the home' in Britain is still equated with 'a castle'. Nineteen-thirties suburban 'keeping up with the Joneses' has been transformed into 21st-century, continuously upgrading consumer capitalism (see Chapter Four). Secured by CCTV from all intruders, today's owner-occupiers can improve and enhance their homes to suit themselves, sure in the knowledge that the department stores, building companies or DIY sector will provide for their every need: power showers with coloured lights, marble kitchen worktops, bedrooms with en-suites, roof gardens straight from the Chelsea Flower Show! If this is not what every owner currently has, it is what they are still being encouraged to want. Owner-occupiers all expect their home (or 'asset') to increase in value, enabling them to trade up or to engage in a spot of 'equity release' when they need a holiday, private education or private healthcare. Owner-occupiers certainly do not want government to interfere with *their* equity-derived borrowing, created from *their* own hard work.

Although owner-occupation has been one of the major drivers of consumer capitalism in the UK, this era of individualism may be drawing to a close, despite the Chancellor's rhetoric about an 'aspiration nation' still wanting only to buy. House prices are now tentatively rising in most parts of England and Wales, and continuing shortages will push them up further, but deposits and mortgages are increasingly unaffordable. Borrowing against equity has to be paid back. Jobs are becoming very insecure. At several points over the last century, academic commentators have pointed out that the limits of owner-occupation have been reached. This was a common view before the Second World War, in the late 1970s and again in the 1990s. They were all wrong, but it is clear that a great deal of the sector's recent growth has been due to the long-term demise of private landlordism or the right to buy council housing. The sub-prime debacle is surely as far as the sector can extend itself?

Politicians have been steadily dismantling welfare state protections, but owner-occupiers never had much of a safety net to start with for housing costs. Equity release may provide them with a cushion (even if they do not expect or want to use it in that way), but if they are unemployed for any length of time, they will need some form of benefits income in order to survive until they find another job. The Coalition's Universal Credit is being presented as an improvement. The old benefits system led to 'dependency'. The Coalition wants 'structural change' in the system, which in turn will lead to 'cultural change'. Universal Credit is based on much harsher conditions of entitlement that in practice will make people take any job rather than claim benefit. That is what 'conditionality' means.

A majority of the population seem to support these changes. Most will be owner-occupiers who have been encouraged to think that these changes will affect someone else, not them. Nevertheless, inevitably they will extend to the better-off working-class and middle-class professionals as cuts to the public sector continue beyond 2015.

Will the stigmatisation of anyone who may need help from the welfare state and the 'scrounger' stories used to justify cuts become far less acceptable as more and more citizens gradually come to realise what they have allowed the present government to remove: the *protections* of the welfare state, including the security of a home and protection from absolute poverty?

Changing times: the state reconsidered – another paradigm shift?

The present

In its *Housing Strategy*, the Coalition hands over responsibility for solutions to others, especially to 'the market':

> We need to get ... new house building moving again ... but we will not achieve this by attempting to control the market from Whitehall ... This government is doing things differently – freeing up local areas to provide the homes needed for their communities and enabling the market to work more efficiently and (DCLG, 2011c, p vii)

The Coalition's approach to housing is built on the premise that the private sector and private borrowing with minimal or no state support in the form of grant for social rented housing will produce sufficient housing, affordable or otherwise. It is unlikely to prove successful.

The Coalition government hoped to 'unblock' the market by ensuring the release of public land and helping developers with stalled schemes. Planning regulations have been changed so that private builders can renegotiate section 106 obligations so as to make more profit by reducing or avoiding a contribution of social housing, but only 105,000 new homes were built for private sale in 2010/11. Despite the New Homes Bonus, only 115,000 planning permissions were granted in 2011 (half the number that the building industry estimates it needs each year). The construction of new private homes looked decidedly shaky for 2012 and 2013. When will private house building take off?

The Affordable Rent programme also got off to a slow start, and even in 2012 housing associations were renegotiating agreements with the HCA: pulling out entirely, scaling down their building programmes or changing the mix (introducing more two-bedroomed houses to rehouse tenants moving because of the 'bedroom tax', in preference to the three-bedroomed houses originally agreed). What of local authorities? Hilary Benn, Shadow Communities Secretary, researched all local authorities in 2012 to find out the numbers of council homes being built. The figures were not surprising (Table 11.1).

Table 11.1: 'Labour councils building the most new social homes'

Local authorities	2012/13	2013/14	2014/15
Labour controlled	42 homes	28 homes	30 homes
Conservative controlled	9 homes	7 homes	4 homes
Liberal Democrat controlled	30 homes	n/a	n/a

Source: Inside Housing, 31 August 2012, p 4 (246 out of 324 authorities responding).

These are pointers for the future: the private sector struggling to build and the public sector unable to except at a very minimal level. Is this what we want?

The future

There is another way, but it will require the abandonment of ideas of the minimal state and a redirection of the austerity programme. It would take what has been called a 'paradigm shift' (see Hudson and Lowe, 2004, pp 47–52), a completely different way of understanding what is possible and what is needed. Practical politicians might call it a change in political direction, but, whatever it is called, it involves new ideas and a determination to see them through, despite objections and barriers. It must be about party–political consensus, and also a new kind of political leadership, emphasising different policies and different values (for example, low growth, less consumption, a focus on alleviating poverty and responding to climate change effectively).

Clement Attlee's Labour government after the Second World War is always referred back to as the epitome of government committed to social justice, especially in relation to its housing programme, devised by Aneurin Bevin. To surpass that achievement is a measure of the task awaiting a new government. How might its approaches differ from the present Coalition?

Some ideas that should be central are:

- a more interventionist role for the state, with more publicly owned services and renewed emphasis on public spending and public service. *Let's build the houses – quick!* (Davis and Wigfield, 2012) and *In place of austerity* (Whitfield, 2012) provide more detail on this sort of thinking;
- a different approach to dealing with the financial deficit. Walker and Walker (2011, p 54) have pointed out that the UK's debt relative to

GDP is not so different from France's or Germany's, yet the cuts in the 2010 Budget and CSR 'if achieved, presage the largest sustained and deepest retrenchment of public spending since the 1920s'. Instead, welfare benefits expenditure and local authority spending need to be protected and increased;

- increased income tax. This is a progressive strategy, although unpopular. The alternative – cuts, and increases in VAT – is regressive and hurts lower-income households far more than the better-off. Taxation for those who are better off should be increased. Other suggestions put forward include: a 50% tax rate on incomes over £100,000 would raise £4.7 billion; closing tax loopholes would raise £25 billion; a tax on vacant housing would raise £5 billion; a Tobin (Robin Hood) tax would raise £20 billion (Dolphin, 2010, cited in Walker and Walker, 2011);
- increased public expenditure on a council house building programme. Ironically, given that the party is in the Coalition, Liberal Democrat rank and file members at the party conference in 2012 discussed a paper suggesting a programme of 300,000 new social homes a year. A change of accounting rules to those used in Europe would enable local authorities to borrow against the value in their HRAs, potentially realising £50 billion in borrowing to build.

Ultimately, the electorate will decide which path is followed. In 1951, Clement Attlee, Prime Minister in the Labour government which established the welfare state after the Second World War, identified the profound differences in values between his Labour Party and the Conservatives of that time (Attlee, 1951/2012).

Box 11.3: The values are central

'We want a society of free men and women – free from poverty, free from fear, able to develop to the full their faculties in co-operation with their fellows ... everyone regarding his own private interest in the light of the interest of others, and of the community; ... a society free from gross inequalities and yet not regimented nor uniform.

Our opponents, on the other hand, regard the economic process primarily as giving an opportunity to the individual to advance his own interests; community interests, national interests, are regarded as a hypothetical by-product. Their motto is: "The world is my oyster; each one for himself."'

(Clement Attlee, 1951)

Politicians in 1945 had to deal with the enormous impact of six years of world war. Nevertheless, the values highlighted by Attlee were used to rebuild Britain then. A global financial crisis and recession, consumer culture and individualism create a completely different world now. But 'the spirit of '45' still resonates today.

Further reading

Duncan Bowie (2013) *Tackling squalor: the pivotal role of social housing*. Available at: http://classonline.org.uk/docs/2013_Policy_Paper_-_ Duncan_Bowie_(Social_State_-_Tackling_Squalor).pdf.

Cathy Davis and Alan Wigfield (2012) *Let's build the houses – quick!* Nottingham: Spokesman Books.

Tony Dolphin (2013) *New priorities for British economic policy*, London: Institute for Public Policy Research.

Stuart Hall, Doreen Massey and Michael Rustin (2013) *After neoliberalism: analysing the present*. Available at: http://www. lwbooks.co.uk/journals/soundings/pdfs/s53hallmasseyrustin. pdf?utm_source=emailhosts&utm_medium=email&utm_ campaign=2013-04-23_SG53. This is the first of a series of online chapters in a 'Soundings Manifesto' published in instalments in 2013. They include chapters on the economy, relational welfare and neoliberal common sense.

David Harvey (2005) *A brief history of neoliberalism*, Oxford: Oxford University Press.

Ken Loach (2013) 'The spirit of '45' – Loach's latest film is about the achievements of Attlee's Labour government in post-war Britain and the relevance of these ideas for today. For more information and links see: http://www.thespiritof45.com

My Fair London in association with The Equality Trust (2012) *Why inequality matters*, CLASS, http://classonline.org.uk/docs/Why_ Inequality_Matters.pdf.

Social Policy Association (2011) *In defence of welfare*, http://www.social-policy.org.uk/downloads/idow.pdf.

Dexter Whitfield (2012) *In place of austerity: Reconstructing the economy, state and public services*, Nottingham: Spokesman Books.

Richard Wilkinson and Kate Pickett (2010, revised edition) *The spirit level: Why equality is better for everyone*, London: Penguin.

References

Arden, C. (2013) 'Bedroom tax: shortage of small homes means many have nowhere to move', *The Guardian*, 8 March. Available at: http://www.guardian.co.uk/society/2013/mar/08/bedroom-tax-shortage-small-homes?INTCMP=SRCH.

Ashton, T. and Hempenstall, C. (2009) *Research into the financial benefits of the Supporting People programme 2009*, London: Capgemini for the CLG. Available at: www.communities.gov.uk/publications/housing/supportingpeoplefinance.

Attlee, C. (1951/2012) 'Towards a new Jerusalem – An extract from Attlee's speech to the 1951 Labour Conference in Scarborough', *New Statesman*, 13 August, p 27.

Audit Commission (2008) *Positively charged: Maximising the benefits of local government service charges*. Available at: www.audit-commission.gov.uk/SiteCollectionDocuments/AuditCommissionReports/NationalStudies/PositivelyChargedREPJan08.pdf.

Audit Commission (2009) *Building better lives: Getting the best from strategic housing*. Available at: www.audit-commission.gov.uk/nationalstudies/localgov/buildingbetterlives/Pages/buildingbetterlives.aspx.

Audit Commission (2011) *Tough times: Councils' responses to a challenging financial environment*. Available at: http://archive.audit-commission.gov.uk/auditcommission/subwebs/publications/studies/studyPDF/3697.pdf.

Bailey, R. (1977) *The homeless and the empty houses*, Harmondsworth: Penguin.

Ball, M. (1983) *Housing policy and economic power: The political economy of owner occupation*, London: Methuen and Co.

Ball, M. (2010) *The UK private rented sector as a source of affordable accommodation*, York: Joseph Rowntree Foundation.

Ball, M., Harloe, M. and Martens, M. (1988) *Housing and social change in Europe and the USA*, London: Routledge.

Bauman, Z. (2005) *Work, consumerism and the new poor*, Maidenhead: Open University Press.

BBC (1999) 'Building societies resist carpetbaggers', *BBC Business News*, 2 January. Available at: http://news.bbc.co.uk/1/hi/business/246673.stm.

BBC News (2009) *Timeline: Credit crunch to downturn*, 7 August. Available at: http://news.bbc.co.uk/1/hi/7521250.stm.

BBC News (2012) 'Birmingham Council announces cuts and job losses', 23 October. Available at: www.bbc.co.uk/news/uk-england-birmingham-20038979?print=true.

Beatty, C., Cole, I., Kemp, P., Marshall, B., Powell, R. and Wilson, I. (2012) *Monitoring the impact of changes to the Local Housing Allowance system of housing benefit: Summary of early findings*, London: DWP.

Blanchflower, D. (2012) 'Recession deniers should shut up as down we continue to go', *New Statesman*, 13 August, p 19.

Bowie, D. (2013) *Tackling squalor: the pivotal role of social housing*. Available at: http://classonline.org.uk/docs/2013_Policy_Paper_-_Duncan_Bowie_(Social_State_-_Tackling_Squalor).pdf.

Bowley, M. (1944) *Housing and the state*, London: Allen and Unwin.

Bramley, G., Morgan, J., Dunmore, K. and Cousins, L. (2002) *Evaluation of the low cost home ownership programme in England*, London: ODPM.

BRE (2010) *Evaluation of the impact of HMO licensing and selective licensing*, London: CLG.

Bromley, C. (2003) 'Has Britain become immune to inequality?', in A. Park, K. Curtice, K. Thomson, L. Jarvis, and C. Bromley (eds) *British social attitudes 20th report: Continuity and change over two decades*, London: Sage Publications, pp 71–92.

Brown, C. and Lloyd, T. (2011) 'Cuts fail to halt £2bn rise in housing benefit costs', *Inside Housing*, 26 April. Available at: www.insidehousing.co.uk/tenancies/cuts-fail-to-halt-%C2%A32bn-rise-in-housing-benefit-costs/6519345.article.

Brown, G. (2010) *Beyond the crash: Overcoming the first crisis of globalisation*, London: Simon & Schuster.

Browne, J. and Levell, P. (2010) *The distributional effect of tax and benefit reforms to be introduced between June 2010 and April 2014: A revised assessment*. IFS Briefing Note BN108, London: Institute for Fiscal Studies. Available at: www.ifs.org.uk/bns/bn108.pdf.

BSA (2012) *Mortgage market share statistics*. Available at: www.bsa.org.uk/docs/statisticspdfs/mortgages/mortgage_market_share_summary.pdf.

Burgess, G., Monk, S. and Whitehead, C. (2011) 'Delivering local infrastructure and affordable housing through the planning system: the future of planning obligations through Section 106', *People, Place and Policy Online*, vol 5, no 1. Available at: www.cchpr.landecon.cam.ac.uk/Downloads/local_infrastructure_affordable_housing_section106.pdf.

Burke, S. (2013) 'Three reasons to be fearful about a cap on social care costs', *The Guardian*, 12 February. Available at: http://www.guardian.co.uk/social-care-network/2013/feb/12/reasons-fearful-cap-social-care-costs.

Burn, D. (1972) *Rent strike St Pancras 1960*, London: Pluto Press.

Burnett, J. (1986) *A social history of housing 1815–1985* (2nd edn), London: Methuen.

Bury, R. (2012) 'Services cut for 46,000 vulnerable people', *Inside Housing*, 23 March. Available at: www.insidehousing.co.uk/care/services-cut-for-46000-vulnerable-people/6521072.article.

Chartered Institute of Environmental Health (2013) *Memorandum to the Commons Select Committee on Communities and Local Government Inquiry into the Private Rented Housing Sector.* Available at: http://www.cieh.org/WorkArea/showcontent.aspx?id=45396.

Chote, R., Crawford, R., Emmerson, C. and Tetlow, G. (2010) *Filling the hole: How do the three main UK parties plan to repair the public finances?* London: Institute for Fiscal Studies. Available at: www.ifs.org.uk/bns/bn99.pdf.

CIH (2010a) *Future directions in intermediate renting: A discussion paper*, Coventry: CIH.

CIH (2010b) *Briefing paper on the impact of changes to housing benefit and local housing allowance in the budget*, Coventry: CIH.

CIH (2011a) *CIH briefing on the Affordable Homes Programme Framework*, Coventry: CIH.

CIH (2011b) *UK Housing Review Briefing Paper*. Available at: http://housing.cih.co.uk/harrogate/live/documents/UKHR2011BriefingPaper.pdf.

CIH (2012) 'Housing benefit cuts will put 800,000 homes out of reach', Press Release with connections to other sources. Available at: www.cih.org/news-article/display/vpathDCR/templatedata/cih/news-article/data/Housing_benefit_cuts_will_put_800000_homes_out_of_reach.

CIH/Local Government Group (2010) *Supporting people: Supporting service change in a time of pressure: sharing lessons for service reconfiguration or decommissioning*, Coventry: CIH. Available at: www.cih.org/resources/PDF/Policy%20free%20download%20pdfs/Supporting%20people%20decommissioning.pdf.

CIH/London and Quadrant Housing (2013) *We need to talk about rents – in the social and affordable housing sector*, Coventry: CIH

CIH/Savills (2011) *Appreciating assets*, Coventry: CIH.

CLG (2007) *Homes for the future: More affordable, more sustainable*, Cm 7191, London: The Stationery Office. Available at: www.communities.gov.uk/documents/housing/pdf/439986.pdf.

CLG (2009a) *Reform of council housing finance*. Available at: www.communities.gov.uk/documents/housing/pdf/1290620.pdf.

CLG (2009b) *Statement from Communities and Local Government: Research into the financial benefits of the Supporting People programme: A report by Capgemini.* Available at: www.communities.gov.uk/documents/housing/pdf/capgeminireportstatement.pdf.

CLG (2010a) *Council housing: A real future, Prospectus.* Available at: www.communities.gov.uk/documents/housing/pdf/1512947.pdf.

CLG (2010b) *Local decisions: A fairer future for social housing.* Available at: www.communities.gov.uk/documents/housing/pdf/1775577.pdf.

CLG (2010c) *Support for Housing PFI projects – November 2010.* Available at: www.communities.gov.uk/documents/localgovernment/pdf/1775370.pdf.

CLG (2011) Commons Select Committee – Regeneration, *Written evidence submitted by the Urban Renewal Officers' Group*, March 2011. Available at: www.publications.parliament.uk/pa/cm201012/cmselect/cmcomloc/1014/1014vw30.htm.

CLG (2012) *The local government finance settlement in England: A guide to the basics.* Available at: www.local.communities.gov.uk/finance/1213/basicguid.pdf.

CLG Commons Select Committee (2009) *Thirteenth Report - The Supporting People Programme.* Available at: http://www.publications.parliament.uk/pa/cm200809/cmselect/cmcomloc/649/64902.htm.

CLG/HCA (2011) *2011–15 Affordable homes programme – framework.* Available at: www.homesandcommunities.co.uk/public/documents/Affordable-Homes-Framework.pdf.

CML (2012a) *Where do we go from here? How UK mortgage lenders see the UK market – past, present and future*, London: CML. Available at: http://www.cml.org.uk/cml/publications/research.

CML (2012b) *'Buy-to-let' policy paper*, last updated 3 November 2010. Available at: www.cml.org.uk/cml/policy/issues/5750.

Commission on Funding of Care and Support (2011a) *Fairer care funding: The report of the Commission on Funding of Care and Support*, July. Available at: https://www.wp.dh.gov.uk/carecommission/files/2011/07/Fairer-Care-Funding-Report.pdf.

Commission on Funding of Care and Support (2011b) *Our report - Fairer funding for all – the Commission's recommendations to government.* Available at: http://www.dilnotcommission.dh.gov.uk/our-report/.

Cowan, D. (2011) *Housing law and policy*, Cambridge: Cambridge University Press.

Craig, P. (1986) 'The house that Jerry built? Building societies, the state and the politics of owner-occupation', *Housing Studies*, vol 1, no 2, pp 87–108.

Crisis (2010) 'Government "peddling myths" to sell housing benefit cuts', press release archive. Available at: www.crisis.org.uk/pressreleases.php/419/government-lsquopeddling-myths-to-sell-housing-benefit-cuts.

Critchley, J. (1987) *Heseltine*, London: Andre Deutsch.

Crossman, R. (1976) *The Diaries of a Cabinet Minister, Volume One, Minister of Housing 1964–66*, London: Book Club Associates.

Daily Telegraph (2009) 'HBOS whistleblower Paul Moore: Evidence to the House of Commons "Banking crisis" hearing', 11 February. Available at: www.telegraph.co.uk/finance/newsbysector/banksandfinance/4590996/HBOS-whistleblower-Paul-Moore-Evidence-to-House-of-Commons-Banking-Crisis-hearing.html.

Darling, A. (2008) 'Maintaining stability in a global economy', the annual Mais Lecture at Cass Business School, London: City University London. Available at: http://webarchive.nationalarchives.gov.uk/+/www.hm-treasury.gov.uk/press_110_08.htm.

Darling, A. (2011) *Back from the brink: 1000 days at number 11*, London: Atlantic Books.

Davis, C. and Wigfield, A. (2010) *Did it have to be like this? A socialist critique of New Labour's performance*, Nottingham: Spokesman Books.

Davis, C. and Wigfield, A. (2012) *Let's build the houses – quick!* Nottingham: Spokesman Books.

DCLG (2010) *Private landlords survey*, London: DCLG. Available at: www.communities.gov.uk/documents/statistics/pdf/2010380.pdf.

DCLG (2011a) *Community infrastructure levy: An overview*. Available at: www.communities.gov.uk/documents/planningandbuilding/pdf/1897278.pdf.

DCLG (2011b) *Implementing self-financing for council housing*. Available at: www.communities.gov.uk/documents/housing/pdf/1831498.pdf.

DCLG (2011c) *Laying the foundations: A housing strategy for England*. Available at: www.communities.gov.uk/documents/housing/pdf/2033676.pdf.

DCLG (2012a) *English Housing Survey HOMES 2010*. Available at: www.communities.gov.uk/documents/statistics/pdf/2173483.pdf.

DCLG (2012b) *English Housing Survey HOUSEHOLDS 2010–11*. Available at: www.communities.gov.uk/documents/statistics/pdf/2173283.pdf.

DCLG (2012c) *Evidence review of the costs of homelessness*. Available at: www.communities.gov.uk/documents/housing/pdf/2200485.pdf.

DCLG (2012d) 'Shapps promise to landlords: no more red tape', press release, 10 June. Available at: www.communities.gov.uk/news/corporate/16111381.

DCLG (2012e) *Statutory homelessness: January to March 2012 and 2011/12, England, Housing Statistical Release*. Available at: www.communities.gov.uk/documents/statistics/pdf/2160776.pdf.

DCLG (2012f) *Review of the barriers to institutional investment in private rented homes*, http://www.communities.gov.uk/documents/housing/pdf/2204242.pdf.

DETR/DSS (2000) *Quality and choice: A decent home for all*, London: The Stationery Office.

Department of the Environment (1987) *Finance for housing associations: The government's proposals*, London: The Stationery Office.

Donnison, D. (1967) *The government of housing*, Harmondsworth: Penguin.

Dorling, D. (2011) 'Clearing the poor away', in Social Policy Association, *In defence of welfare*. Available at: www.social-policy.org.uk/downloads/idow.pdf.

Dowler, C. (2008) 'Model is broken say mega-associations', *Inside Housing*, 12 September. Available at: www.insidehousing.co.uk/model-is-broken-say-mega-associations/6501077.article.

Duncan-Smith, I. (2012) Leonard Steinberg Memorial Lecture, Policy Exchange Westminster, London, 5 May. Available at: www.dwp.gov.uk/newsroom/ministers-speeches/2012/09-05-12.shtml.

Dunning, J. (2011) 'Expert guide to personalisation', *Community Care*, 19 August. Available at: www.communitycare.co.uk/Articles/19/08/2011/109083/personalisation.htm.

DWP (2011) *Support for mortgage interest. Informal call for evidence*, London: Department for Work and Pensions. Available at: www.dwp.gov.uk/docs/support-for-mortgage-interest-call-for-evidence.pdf.

Fenton, A. (2010) *How will changes to Local Housing Allowance affect low-income tenants in private rented housing?* Cambridge Centre for Housing and Planning Research. Available at: www.cchpr.landecon.cam.ac.uk/Downloads/lha_reform_effects_prs-fenton-Sep2010.pdf.

Fenton, A. (2011) *Housing Benefit reform and the spatial segregation of low-income households in London*, Cambridge: Cambridge Centre for Housing and Planning Research. Available at: www.cchpr.landecon.cam.ac.uk/Downloads/hb_reform_london_spatial_implications-cchpr2011.pdf.

Foot, M. (1997) *Aneurin Bevan 1945–1960*, London: Gollanz.

Ford, J. and Wallace, A. (2009) *Uncharged territory? Managing mortgage arrears and possessions*, London: Shelter.

Ford, J., Burrows, R. and Nettleton, S. (2001) *Home ownership in a risk society*, Bristol: The Policy Press.

Ford, J., Bretherton, J., Jones, A. and Rhodes, D. (2010) *Giving up home ownership: A qualitative study of voluntary possession and selling because of financial difficulties*, London: CLG.

Forrest, R. and Murie, A. (1988) *Selling the welfare state: The privatisation of public housing*, London: Routledge.

Fryer, P. (1984) *Staying power: The history of black people in Britain*, London: Pluto Press.

Garnett, D. and Perry, J. (2005) *Housing finance*, Coventry: CIH.

Gentleman, A. (2013) 'The human cost of the bedroom tax', *The Guardian*, 8 March. Available at: www.guardian.co.uk/society/2013/mar/08/human-cost-of-bedroom-tax.

Gibb, K. and Monro, M. (1991) *Housing finance in the UK*, Basingstoke: Macmillan.

Gibson, M. and Langstaff, M. (1982) *An introduction to urban renewal*, London: Hutchinson and Co.

Gray, P. and McAnulty, U. (2011) *The private rented sector in Northern Ireland*, Belfast: NIHE.

Greater London Authority (2012a) 'The Mayor's role'. Available at: www.london.gov.uk/priorities/housing/working-partnership/role-mayor-london.

Greater London Authority (2012b) 'The Mayor's housing covenant', Available at: www.london.gov.uk/housingcovenant.

Gregory, J. (2009) *In the mix: Narrowing the gap between public and private housing*, Fabian Policy Report 62, London: Fabian Society.

Hall, S. (2003) 'New Labour's double-shuffle', *Soundings: A Journal of Politics and Culture*, issue 24, 'A market state?' (summer).

Hall, S., Massey, D. and Rustin, M. (2013) *After neoliberalism: analysing the present.* Available at: http://www.lwbooks.co.uk/journals/soundings/pdfs/s53hallmasseyrustin.pdf?utm_source=emailhosts&utm_medium=email&utm_campaign=2013-04-23_SG53.

Hamnett, C. (1999) *Winners and losers: Home ownership in modern Britain*, London: UCL Press.

Hardman, I. (2011) 'New homes bonus will "penalise" deprived areas', *Inside Housing*, 14 April. Available at: www.insidehousing.co.uk//6514507.article.

Harloe, M. (1995) *The people's home? Social rented housing in Europe and America*, Oxford: Blackwell.

Harris, J. (2010) 'Griffin vs Hodge: the battle for Barking', *The Guardian*, 13 March. Available at: www.guardian.co.uk/politics/2010/mar/13/nick-griffin-margaret-hodge-barking-dagenham.

Harvey, D. (2000) *Spaces of hope*, Edinburgh: Edinburgh University Press.

Harvey, D. (2005) *A brief history of neoliberalism*, Oxford: Oxford University Press.

HCA (2011) 'Councils set to receive decent homes funding for the first time as HCA confirms £2.1 billion allocation', press release, 17 February. Available at: www.homesandcommunities.co.uk/news/councils-set-receive-decent-homes-funding-first-time-hca-confirms-%C2%A321bn-allocation.

HCA (2012) *Quarterly survey of private registered providers*, 2012-13 Quarter 3. Available at: www.homesandcommunities.co.uk/ourwork/publications.

HCA/TSA (2011) *New affordable homes: What for whom and where have registered providers been building between 1989–2009*, London: HCA. Available at: www.homesandcommunities.co.uk/new-affordable-homes.

Heffernan, R. (2011) 'Labour's New Labour legacy: politics after Blair and Brown', *Political Studies*, vol 9, pp 163–77.

Hennessy, P. (2000) *The Prime Minister: the office and its holders since 1945*, London: Allen Lane, The Penguin Press.

Hetherington, P. (2013) 'England's cities are being sold short, and councils' patience has snapped'. Available at: www.guardian.co.uk/society/2013/feb/19/cities-england-sold-short-services?INTCMP=SRCH.

High Pay Commission (2011) *Cheques with balances: Why tackling high pay is in the national interest, Final report of the High Pay Commission*, London: Compass. Available at: http://highpaycommission.co.uk/wp-content/uploads/2011/11/HPC_final_report_WEB.pdf.

Hills, J. (1991) *Unravelling housing finance: Subsidies, benefits and taxation*, Oxford: Clarendon Press.

Hills, J. (2004) *Inequality and the state*, Oxford: Oxford University Press.

Hills, J. and Stewart, K. (2005) *A more equal society? New Labour, poverty, inequality and exclusion*, Bristol: Policy Press.

HM Government (2009) *Building Britain's future*, Cm 7654, London: The Stationery Office. Available at: www.official-documents.gov.uk/document/cm76/7654/7654.pdf.

HM Treasury (2007) *Pre-Budget Report and Comprehensive Spending Review*, Cm 7227, London: The Stationery Office. Available at: http://webarchive.nationalarchives.gov.uk/+/http:/www.hm-treasury.gov.uk/pbr_csr/pbr_csr07_index.cfm.

HM Treasury (2009) *Budget 2009: Building Britain's future*, HC 407, London: The Stationery Office, chapter 4, pp 45–70. Available at: http://webarchive.nationalarchives.gov.uk/+/www.hm-treasury.gov.uk/d/Budget2009/bud09_chapter3_222.pdf.

HM Treasury (2010) *The Spending Review*, Cm 7942, London: The Stationery Office. Available at: http://cdn.hm-treasury.gov.uk/sr2010_completereport.pdf.

Holliday, I. (2000) 'Is the British state hollowing out?' *Political Quarterly*, vol 71, no 2, pp 167–76.

House of Commons (1965) Debate on the Milner Holland Report, 22 March 1965. *House of Commons Debates*, vol 709, cc52–181. Available at: http://hansard.millbanksystems.com/commons/1965/mar/22/housing-milner-holland-report.

House of Commons Council Housing Group (2010) *Council housing: Time to invest: fair funding, investment and building council housing. Our report to the Government's Review of Council Housing Finance.* Available at: www.support4councilhousing.org.uk/report/resources/HOCCHG_TimeToInvest.pdf.

House of Commons Library (2011) Standard Note: Affordable rent model, SN/SP/5933, Available at: http://www.parliament.uk/briefing-papers/SN05933.

House of Commons Library (2012a) Standard Note: Rent setting for social housing tenancies, SN/SP/1090. Available at: www.parliament.uk/briefing-papers/SN01090.

House of Commons Library (2012b) Standard Note: Measures to reduce housing benefit expenditure – an overview, SN/SP/5638, Available at http://www.parliament.uk/briefing-papers/SN/SP/5638.

House of Commons Library (2013) Standard Note: The reform of housing benefit (local housing allowance) for tenants in private rented housing, SN04957. Available at: http://www.parliament.uk/briefing-papers/SN04957

House of Commons Library (2013b) Standard Note: The draft Universal Credit regulations, SN06548. Available at: http://www.parliament.uk/briefing-papers/SN06548.

Hudson, J. and Lowe, S. (2004) *Understanding the policy process*, Bristol: The Policy Press.

Islington LBC *Service and Financial Plan 2006/07–2008/09*, now integrated into *Annual Statement of Accounts* for relevant years.

Islington LBC (2011a) *Draft Statement of Accounts 2011/12.* Available at: www.islington.gov.uk/publicrecords/library/Finance/Information/Advice-and-information/2012-2013/(2012-06-29)-Islington-Council-Draft-Statement-of-Accounts.pdf.

Islington LBC (2011b) 'Islington housing comes home', press release, 17 November. Available at: www.islington.gov.uk/islington/news-events/news-releases/2011/11/Pages/PR4553.aspx.

Judge, L. (2012) *Ending child poverty by 2020, progress made and lessons learned*. Available at: http://www.cpag.org.uk/sites/default/files/CPAG-ECPby2020-1212.pdf.

Karn, V., Kemeny, J. and Williams, P. (1985) *Home ownership in the inner city: Salvation or despair?* Aldershot: Gower.

Kemp, P., Wilcox, S. and Rhodes, D. (2002) *Reforming Housing Benefit for private tenants and tax credit recipients*, York: Joseph Rowntree Foundation. Available at: www.jrf.org.uk/publications/reforming-housing-benefit-private-tenants-and-tax-credit-recipients.

Kisby, B. (2010) 'The Big Society: power to the people?' *Political Quarterly*, vol 81, no 4, October–December.

Labour Party (1997) *New Labour because Britain deserves better*. Available at: www.labour-party.org.uk/manifestos/1997/1997-labour-manifesto.shtml.

Leather, P. (2000) *Crumbling castles: Helping owners to repair and maintain their homes*, York: Joseph Rowntree Foundation.

Leather, P. and Mackintosh, S. (1994) *The future of housing renewal policy*, York: Joseph Rowntree Foundation.

Leng, G. and Davies, A. (2011) *The local authority role in housing markets*, Coventry: CIH.

Levitas, R. (1998) *The inclusive society? Social exclusion and New Labour*, Basingstoke: Macmillan.

Local Government Association (2013) *LGA response to finance settlement 2013–14 and 2014–15*. Available at: www.local.gov.uk/web/guest/finance/-/journal_content/56/10171/3843900/ARTICLE-TEMPLATE.

London Assembly (2011) *Bleak houses: Improving London's private rented sector*, London: GLA. Available at: www.london.gov.uk/sites/default/files/Bleak-Houses-Final-Report.pdf

London Stock Exchange (2010) *Bonds – trading bonds on the London Stock Exchange. A guide for private investors*. Available at: www.londonstockexchange.com/traders-and-brokers/security-types/retail-bonds/brochure.pdf.

Lowe, S. (2011) *The housing debate*, Bristol: The Policy Press.

Malpass, P. (2000) *Housing associations and housing policy, a historical perspective*, Basingstoke: Macmillan.

Malpass, P. (2005) *Housing and the welfare state: The development of housing policy in Britain*, Basingstoke: Palgrave Macmillan.

Malpass, P. and Mullins, D. (2002) 'Local authority housing stock transfer in the UK, from local initiative to national policy', *Housing Studies*, vol 17, no 4, pp 673–86.

Malpass, P. and Murie, A. (1987) *Housing policy and practice* (2nd edn), Basingstoke: Macmillan.

Malpass, P. and Murie, A. (1990) *Housing policy and practice* (3rd edn), Basingstoke: Macmillan.

Malpass, P. and Murie, A. (1999) *Housing policy and practice* (5th edn), Basingstoke: Macmillan.

Malpass, P. and Victory, C. (2010) 'The modernisation of social housing in England', *International Journal of Housing Policy*, vol 10, no 1, pp 3–18.

Mann, K. (1992) *The making of an English 'underclass'? The social divisions of welfare and labour*, Milton Keynes: Open University Press.

Marshall, T. (2008) 'The hidden truth', *Roof*, May/June.

Massey, D. (2010) 'The political struggle ahead', in *Lawrence and Wishart Reading Room*. Available at: www.lwbooks.co.uk/ReadingRoom/public/massey.html.

Melling, J. (1983) *Rent strikes: People's struggle for housing in West Scotland 1890–1916*, Edinburgh: Polygon Books.

Mullins, D. and Murie, A. (2006) *Housing policy in the UK*, Basingstoke: Palgrave Macmillan.

Munroe, M. (2007) 'Evaluating policy towards increasing owner occupation', *Housing Studies*, vol 22, no 2, pp 243–60.

Murie, A. and Ferrari, E. (2003) *Reforming the right to buy in England*, Birmingham: Centre for Urban and Regional Studies, University of Birmingham.

Murray, J. (2011) 'The affordable rent programme does not work – but we have a solution', *Guardian Professional,* 9 August.

My Fair London in association with The Equality Trust (2012) *Why inequality matters,* CLASS. Available at: http://classonline.org.uk/docs/Why_Inequality_Matters.pdf.

Nasiripour, S. (2012) 'Regulator spurred in push for swaps rules', *Financial Times*, 21 May. Available at: www.ft.com/cms/s/0/b3fc468e-a371-11e1-988e-00144feabdc0.html#axzz1vXiTxHb8.

National Audit Office (2009) *Maintaining financial stability across the United Kingdom's banking system*, London: The Stationery Office. Available at: http://media.nao.org.uk/uploads/2009/12/091091.pdf

National Audit Office (2010) *PFI in housing*, Report by the Comptroller and Auditor General, HC 71, Session 2010–2011, London: The Stationery Office.

National Audit Office (2011) *Maintaining the financial stability of UK banks*, London: The Stationery Office. Available at: http://media.nao.org.uk/uploads/2010/12/1011676.pdf

National Audit Office (2012) *Managing the impact of housing benefit reform*. Available at: www.nao.org.uk/publications/1213/housing_benefit_reform.aspx.

National Housing Federation (2011) *Radical reform: Real flexibility*, London: NHF.

National Housing Federation (2013) *The bedroom tax – some home truths*. Available at: http://www.housing.org.uk/pdf/Bedroom%20tax%20home%20truths.pdf.

National Pensioners Convention (2013) *Social care funding briefing paper*. Available at: http://npcuk.org/1200.

Orwell, G. (1989) *The road to Wigan Pier*, Harmondsworth: Penguin (originally published London:Victor Gollancz Ltd, 1937).

Oxford Economics (2011) *Housing market analysis*, National Housing Federation, July.

Pawson, H. (2011) *Welfare reform and social housing*, York: Housing Quality Network.

Pawson, H. and Wilcox, S. (2013) *UK Housing Review 2013*, Coventry: CIH, Heriot-Watt University and University of York.

Pawson, H. (2012) 'The changing scale and role of private renting in the UK housing market', in H. Pawson and S. Wilcox (eds) *UK Housing Review 2011/12*, Coventry: CIH, Heriot-Watt University and University of York, pp 14–23.

Pawson, H. and Mullins, D. (2010) *After council housing: Britain's new social landlords*, Basingstoke: Palgrave Macmillan.

Pawson, H. and Wilcox, S. (2011) *UK Housing Review 2010/11*, Coventry: CIH.

Pawson, H. and Wilcox, S. (2012) *UK Housing Review 2011/12*, Coventry: CIH.

Pawson, H., Sosenko, F., Cowan, D., Croft, J., Cole, M. and Hunter, C. (2010) *Rent arrears management practices in the housing association sector*, London: Housing Corporation. Available from: www.tenantservicesauthority.org/upload/pdf/Rent_arrears_management_practices.pdf.

Peachey, K. (2009) 'Changing times for the UK rental market', *BBC News channel*. Available at: http://news.bbc.co.uk/1/hi/business/8036534.stm.

Perry, J. (2012) *Let's get building: The case for local authority investment in rented homes to help drive economic growth*, Scarborough: National Federation of ALMOs with ARCH, CIH, LGA and in association with CWAG.

Peston, R. (2008) *Who runs Britain?* London: Hodder and Stoughton.

Piratin, P. (1948) *Our flag stays red* (reissued 2006), London: Lawrence and Wishart.

Puzzanghera, J. and Scott Reckard, E. (2010) 'Washington Mutual created "mortgage time bomb" Senate panel say', *Los Angeles Times*, 13 April.

Ramesh, R. (2012) 'Available rented housing cuts in your area: download the data', *Guardian,* 23 January. Available at: www.guardian.co.uk/news/datablog/2012/jan/01/available-rented-housing-map.

Ravetz, A. (2001) *Council housing and culture*, London: Routledge.

Reeve-Lewis, B. (2012) 'Why councils should take civil action against rogue private landlords', *Guardian Housing Network Blog.* Available at: www.guardian.co.uk/housing-network/2012/jul/06/rogue-private-landlords-civil-criminal/print.

Rhodes, R.A.W. (1994) 'The hollowing out of the state', *Political Quarterly*, vol 65, pp 138–51.

RICS (2011) *Market rent: A user guide for providers of affordable rented housing.* Available at: www.rics.org/site/download_feed.aspx?fileID =11034&fileExtension=PDF.

Rogers, E. (2009) 'This is a ludicrous situation', *Inside Housing*, 23 January. Available at: www.insidehousing.co.uk/analysis/in-depth/'this-is-a-ludicrous-situation'/6502698.article.

Rugg, J. and Rhodes, D. (2008) *The private rented sector: Its contribution and potential,* York: University of York.

Scanlon, K. and Whitehead, C. (2005) *The profile and intentions of buy-to-let investors*, London: London School of Economics (available on the CML website).

Scope (2012) 'Disabled people point to issue of "benefit scroungers" as discrimination increases', press release, 31 July. Available at: www.scope.org.uk/news/discrimination.

Sefton, T. and Sutherland, H. (2005) 'Inequality and poverty under New Labour', in J. Hills and K. Stewart (eds) *A more equal society: New Labour, poverty, inequality and exclusion*, Bristol: The Policy Press, pp 231-50.

Sheffield City Council (2012) *Working for you*, Sheffield: Sheffield City Council.

Short, R. (1963) 'Labour must have the courage to say that not only has private landlordism failed the people, but that the next Labour Government intends to get rid of it altogether ...', *Tribune*, 6 September.

Simpson, B. (2012) 'What does the right to buy scheme mean for LSVT landlords?' *Guardian Professional,* 16 April. Available at: www.guardian.co.uk/housing-network/2012/apr/16/right-to-buy-lsvt-landlords.

Sklair, L. (1975) 'The struggle against the Housing Finance Act', *Socialist Register*, vol 12, pp 250–92.

Smith, S. (2005) 'Risky business? The challenge of residential mortgage markets', *Housing Finance International*, June, p 7.

Smith, S. (2007) *Banking on housing: Spending the home: full research report. ESRC End of Award Report,* RES-154-25-0012. Swindon: ESRC.

Smith, S., Cook, N. and Searle, B.A. (2007) *From canny consumer to care-full citizen: Towards a nation of home stewardship?* An ESRC/AHRC Cultures of Consumption Programme Working Paper, No 35. Available at: www.consume.bbk.ac.uk/working_papers/SmithBohWkgPapNov07.pdf.

Social Policy Association (2011) *In defence of welfare.* Available at: www.social-policy.org.uk/downloads/idow.pdf.

Social Security Advisory Committee (2010) *Report of the Social Security Advisory Committee under Section 174(1) of the Social Security Administration Act 1992 and the statement by the Secretary of State for Work and Pensions in accordance with Section 174(2) of that Act,* London: The Stationery Office. Available at: www.official-documents.gov.uk/document/other/9780108509551/9780108509551.pdf.

Stephens, M. (2007) 'Mortgage market deregulation and its consequences', *Housing Studies*, vol 22, no 2, pp 201–20.

Stephens, M. (2011) *Tackling housing market volatility in the UK*, York: Joseph Rowntree Foundation. Available at: www.jrf.org.uk/sites/files/jrf/housing-markets-volatility-full.pdf.

Stephens, M. and Quilgars, D. (2007) 'Managing mortgage arrears and possessions in the UK', *Housing Finance International,* September, pp 9–15.

Stephens, M. and Williams, P. (2012) *Tackling housing market volatility in the UK: A progress report.* Available at: http://www.jrf.org.uk/publications/housing-market-volatility-progress.

Stevens, S. (1995) *Housing associations and market rents. Association rents and their rent policies 1991–1994,* London: NFHA.

Stratton, A. and Seager, A. (2008) 'Darling invokes Keynes as he eases spending rules to fight recession', *The Guardian*, 20 October. Available at: www.guardian.co.uk/politics/2008/oct/20/economy-recession-treasury-energy-housing?INTCMP=SRCH.

Tang, C. (2008) 'Between "market" and "welfare": Rent restructuring policy and the housing association sector', *Housing Studies*, vol 23, no 5, pp 737–59.

Taylor, N. (2009) *Tenants' attitudes towards council housing finance and rents policy: To inform the review of council housing finance*, London: CLG. Available at: www.communities.gov.uk/documents/housing/pdf/1290156.pdf.

Taylor-Gooby, P. (2011) 'The UK welfare state going west', in Social Policy Association, *In defence of welfare: The impacts of the spending review*, pp 12–15.

Tayner, G. (2010) 'Housing benefit reform: a toxic battleground', *Daily Telegraph*, 30 October. Available at: www.telegraph.co.uk/news/politics/8097684/Housing-benefit-reform-A-toxic-battleground.html.

Thomas, B. and Dorling, D. (2007) *Identity in Britain: A cradle to grave atlas*, Bristol: The Policy Press.

Towers, J. and Walby, S. (2012) *Measuring the impact of cuts in public expenditure on the provision of services to prevent violence against women and girls*, Report for Northern Rock Foundation and Trust for London. Available at: www.trustforlondon.org.uk/VAWG%20Full%20report.pdf.

Waite, A. (2009) *Arms length managemenet organisations: freedoms, flexibilities and the future*, Appleby in Westmorland: AWICS.

Walker, A. and Walker, C. (2011) 'From the politics and policy of the cuts to an outline of an oppositional strategy', in Social Policy Association, *In defence of welfare*, pp 55–7.

Welsh Assembly (2012) 'Chance for landlords and lettings agents to have their say', *Welsh Assembly News*, 6 July. Available at: http://wales.gov.uk/newsroom/housingandcommunity/2012/120706landlords/?lang=en.

Whitehead, C. and Williams, P. (2011) 'Causes and consequences? Exploring the shape and direction of the housing system in the UK post the financial crisis', *Housing Studies*, vol 26, no 7-8, pp 1157-69.

Whitfield, D. (2012) *In place of austerity: Reconstructing the economy, state and public services*, Nottingham: Spokesman.

Wilcox, S. (2006) 'A financial evaluation of the right to buy', *UK Housing Review, 2006/07*, Coventry: CIH/Building Societies Association.

Wilcox, S. (2008) *UK Housing Review, 2008/09*, Coventry: CIH and the Building Societies Association.

Wilcox, S. (2009) 'Devolution and housing', *UK Housing Review, 2009/10*, Coventry: CIH/Building Societies Association.

Wilcox, S. (2011a) 'Constraining choices: the housing benefit reforms', *UK Housing Review, 2010/11*, Coventry: CIH, University of York and Heriot Watt University, pp 31–40.

Wilcox, S. (2011b) 'The deposit barrier to home ownership', *UK Housing Review, 2010/11,* Coventry: CIH, University of York and Heriot Watt University, pp 21–30.

Wilcox, S. (2011c) 'Housing expenditure trends and plans', *UK Housing Review 2010/11,* Coventry: CIH, University of York and Heriot Watt University, pp 67–71.

Wilcox, S. (2012a) 'Homeowners alone', in H. Pawson and S. Wilcox, *UK Housing Review 2011/12,* Coventry: CIH, Heriot-Watt University and University of York, pp 25–32.

Wilcox, S. (2012b) 'Housing expenditure trends and plans', in H. Pawson and S. Wilcox, *UK Housing Review 2011/12,* Coventry: CIH, Heriot-Watt University and University of York, pp 67–76.

Wilcox, S. (2012c) 'Private housing' in H. Pawson and S. Wilcox, *UK Housing Review 2011/12,* Coventry: CIH, Heriot-Watt University and University of York, pp 65–71.

Wilcox, S. (2012d) 'The quickening pace of devolution', in H. Pawson and S. Wilcox, *UK Housing Review 2011/12,* Coventry: CIH, Heriot-Watt University and University of York, pp 33–42.

Wilcox, S. and Fitzpatrick, S. with Stephens, M., Pleace, N., Wallace, A. and Rhodes, D. (2010) *The impact of devolution: Housing and homelessness,* York: Joseph Rowntree Foundation. Available at: www.jrf.org.uk/sites/files/jrf/impact-of-devolution-long-term-care-housing.pdf.

Wilcox, S. and Pawson, H. (2010) *UK Housing Review Briefing Paper,* Coventry: CIH.

Wilcox, S. and Meen, G. (1995) *The cost of higher rents,* London: NFHA.

Wilcox, S. and Williams, P. (2009) 'The emerging New Order', *UK Housing Review, 2009/2010,* Coventry: CIH and the Building Societies Association, pp 41–50.

Wilkes, R. (2001) 'Can pay, won't pay. So it was for Elsy Borders, the housewife who became a folk hero when she organised a mortgage strike', *Daily Telegraph*, 25 July. Available at: www.telegraph.co.uk/property/3291336/Inside-story-insanity.html.

Women's Aid Federation England (2012) 'Women's Aid letter featured in The Times: 27 July 2012'. Available at: www.womensaid.org.uk/page.asp?section=0001000100150008&sectionTitle=What%27s+New&dm_i=674,WPQR,KIRD0,2PLF7,1.

Index